Violence, Gender and Justice

Violence, Gender
and Justice

Maggie Wykes and Kirsty Welsh

Los Angeles • London • New Delhi • Singapore • Washington DC

SAGE Publications Ltd
1 Oliver's Yard
55 City Road
London EC1Y 1SP

SAGE Publications Inc.
2455 Teller Road
Thousand Oaks, California 91320

SAGE Publications India Pvt Ltd
B 1/I 1 Mohan Cooperative Industrial Area
Mathura Road
New Delhi 110 044

SAGE Publications Asia-Pacific Pte Ltd
33 Pekin Street #02-01
Far East Square
Singapore 048763

Library of Congress Control Number: 2008935472

British Library Cataloguing in Publication data

A catalogue record for this book is available from the
British Library

ISBN 978-1-4129-2336-1
ISBN 978-1-4129-2337-8 (pbk)

Typeset by C&M Digitals (P) Ltd, Chennai, India
Printed in Great Britain by TJ International Ltd, Padstow, Cornwall
Printed on paper from sustainable resources

Mixed Sources
Product group from well-managed
forests and other controlled sources
www.fsc.org Cert no. SGS-COC-2482
FSC   © 1996 Forest Stewardship Council

Violence, Gender and Justice is for

Jessica (born 21.02.2005)
Thomas William (born 11.01.2007)
Annie Grace (born 04.10.2007)

with love and hope

CONTENTS

1

INTRODUCING *VIOLENCE, GENDER AND JUSTICE*

Most of the time when we read about, hear about and talk about 'crime' and 'criminals', we are actually reading, hearing and talking about men and men's behaviour.

> Men commit more crimes than women. In 2002 male offenders in England and Wales outnumbered female offenders by more than four to one ... Men outnumber women in all major crime categories. Between 85 and 95 per cent of offenders found guilty of burglary, robbery, drug offences, criminal damage or violence against the person are male. Although the number of offenders are relatively small, 98 per cent of people found guilty of, or cautioned for, sexual offences are male. (National Statistics UK 2006)

Yet despite that overwhelming domination of crime by men, it is very rare that masculinity is the focus of blame or explanation, rather reporting of violence between men often alludes to alcohol as causal and street violence between youths considers religion, race, gangs and failing families. In these kinds of crime men feature systematically as both offenders and victims, very often strangers to one another, with women rarely involved except occasionally as sufferers of collateral damage. However, when it comes to violence between males and females there is a very different pattern, where those involved often know each other or are related, where men are nearly always perpetrators and women and girls are nearly always victims. Yet in such cases too, the masculinity of offending is almost never addressed whilst the femininity of the victims comes under close scrutiny and is often attributed with blame for the crime against them.

Evidence and Violence

Research shows that violence and abuse in a domestic setting are clearly a gender issue. Overwhelmingly, women and children experience violence and abuse from men. Women do not perpetrate violence or abuse against men or children to any-where near the same extent. A BBC *Panorama* programme, 'Hitting Home', (2003) gathered statistics highlighting that 'almost 50,000 women and children a year shelter in refuges from violence'. In the city of Sheffield (pop. approx. 500,000) in England, where the authors are based: '12% of women are likely to be living in households where there is domestic abuse, with around 15,000 children between them. In a class of 30 school children, 2–4 children on average are likely to be living with domestic abuse', and 'Domestic Abuse Projects in Sheffield supported 320 women and 500 children in safe accommodation, and a further 1,200 women with telephone outreach support' (Sheffield City Council 2003). Nationally, although domestic violence is chronically under-reported, research still estimates that it:

- accounts for 16% of all violent crime
- has more repeat victims than any other crime (on average there will have been 35 assaults before a victim calls the police)
- costs in excess of £23bn a year
- claims the lives of two women each week and 30 men per year
- is the largest cause of morbidity worldwide in women aged 19–44, greater than war, cancer or motor vehicle accidents. (Crime in England and Wales 04/05 report)

Rape is also a deeply gendered crime. Although there are male on male rapes these are comparatively rare (Gregory and Lees 1999) whilst the figures for rape of women by men remain horrifying and the figures for conviction for rape even more so. The British Crime Survey recorded 12,630 rapes of women in England and Wales in 2006/7 and 1,150 of men (Nicholas et al. 2007). In 2000 the BCS identified 45% of rape as partner rapes; 47% of assailants were known to the victim and just 8% were strangers (Myhill and Allen 2002). As with domestic violence, rape is often a crime perpetrated by men on women with whom they have/have had an intimate relationship. Despite significant changes in the law with the introduction of the Sexual Offences Act 2003, more sensitive policing of sexual crime and higher levels of reporting than ever, successful prosecutions are rare. Journalist Katherine Viner summed up the situation in 2004:

> Few like to look at them, but the statistics on rape convictions are unbearably bleak: reported rape has trebled in the past decade; less than 6% of reported rapes result in a conviction; less than 20% of rapes are reported to the police. There is more rape, and it is easier to get away with. The law itself is not to blame. MP Vera Baird was the driver behind the Sexual Offences Act, which came into force in May. A man may no longer claim that he believed a woman was consenting to sex; a jury must instead be convinced that his belief was 'reasonable' … But the act must be closely monitored if it is to have any effect at all, because it is in the hands of judges, lawyers and juries … How did Judge Michael Roach let off trainee croupier Michael Barrett with a conditional discharge for having sex with a 12-year-old girl

with the comment, 'I trust you to behave yourself now'? ... As for the police, we need sexual assault referral centres (Sarcs) in each of the 43 police forces – where victims have access to women doctors, counsellors and specialist non-uniformed officers. And finally, the public. It is jurors who acquit presentable young men who look just like their sons; it is jurors who assume that women in short skirts are asking for it. So what is needed is a high-profile, hard-hitting public information campaign debunking the myths about rape ... The overwhelming majority of rapists are friends, boyfriends, husbands, ex-lovers, men in bars. (Viner 2004)

Myths, miscarriage of justice and mismanagement are clearly implicated in the statistics for conviction but little critique is offered of the men who rape the women they know. Similarly, when it comes to abuse of children it is overwhelmingly men who perpetrate and almost entirely men when the abuse is sexual. The NSPCC chronicles the evidence that home and family can be a dangerous and damaging place for children:

- Every week in England and Wales one to two children will die following cruelty.
- One per cent of children experienced sexual abuse by a parent or carer and another three per cent by another relative during childhood. Eleven per cent of children experience sexual abuse by people known but unrelated to them.
- There are on average 80 child homicides recorded in England and Wales each year.
- On average one child is killed by their parent or carer every week in England and Wales.
- More than a quarter of all rapes recorded by the police are committed against children under 16 years of age.
- The National Commission of Inquiry into the Prevention of Child Abuse estimates that the cost of child abuse to statutory and voluntary agencies is £1 billion per year in the UK. (NSPCC 2007)

Even the term child sexual abuse disguises the fact that this is rape of often very young children by adult men and is often incest by fathers, father figures and other close male relatives. Yet Britain's popular shock-horror tabloid newspapers never feature the headline 'DAD RAPES BABY DAUGHTER', preferring to focus on the dangerous stranger or, in the case of systematic incestuous abuse in Cleveland in the 1980s, blaming over-zealous diagnosis by doctors and/or colluding mothers (Campbell 1988). As with rape and domestic violence, the men who do offend against children most – fathers, step-fathers, uncles, family friends – do not feature in the accounts. In the Soham case the *Sun* (18 December 2003) offered a 24-page pullout and a front page labelling Huntley 'The Serial Paedophile' with the main story headed 'Sick Lust', but very little is said about his status in the school and community where he was known and trusted by the little girls he killed. Men only feature in such accounts when they can be labelled outside the dominant ideal of heterosexual, paternal masculinity as paedophiles, mad, evil or beasts.

Also, similar problems exist with convictions for child sex abuse as they do with rape, although there is much less readily available data on child sex abuse. The Home Office consultations prior to the new Sexual Offences Act 2003 included a response from Christian groups in the UK:

> Right across the board, convictions for sexual offences against children have been falling year after year. *The report shows that from 1985 to 1995 convictions for the six most serious sexual offences against children fell by 31%.* Professor Grubin points out that *reports* of gross indecency with children 14 and under (girls and boys) *more than doubled* from 633 to 1,287 over the ten year period to 1995, yet *convictions declined.* There is clearly a serious problem with enforcement of laws against child sex offences. (Christian Institute 2001)

Although all these profoundly gender-differentiated crimes are nearly always committed by men, men *per se* are rarely featured in explanations, either in news about such crime or within policy documents. Offending men are also significantly absent from much criminological work unless qualified by some other variable such as race, youth, religion or class or described in an ungendered way, as in beast, evil or mad. They are often missing too in feminist criminology, which has always tended to prefer the experience of women in relation to crime, with the partial consequence at least that despite its intense focus on gender and crime since the mid-1970s, Frances Heidensohn could argue in 2002 that 'a long journey hasn't taken us very far' (2002: 524) in terms of preventing the victimisation of women.

The existence of such news accounts and data alongside Heidensohn's comment explains this book's focus on the representation, experiences and treatment of men and women as victims and criminals. The book examines whether and how offending patterns differ according to gender and explores the connections between gender, offending and victimisation. It also explores the treatment and experiences of men and women within the criminal justice system and argues that in order best to understand crime and criminal justice, criminologists must understand both as gendered. The focus is interpersonal gendered violence – sexual violence, 'domestic' violence, 'domestic' murder, rape, prostitution and child abuse – because these crimes are those most clearly involving gender differentiation between offender and victim and it is that profound difference in men's and women's place in crime that is both continuing to damage women and defy change. The book explores how sexual and 'domestic' violence have been and are represented in popular discourse, in the law, in criminal justice processes and in service provision, and it traces developments in these areas, using case-studies and international comparisons.

Our broad aims are to examine theoretical issues around violence, gender, culture and representation and to explore the reality of violent crime, and responses to it, in relation to gender. The book integrates rationally the two broad areas of theory and evidence. It presents an introduction to different theories centred on the connections between gender, sexuality and violence and encourages readers to begin to see the strengths and weaknesses in each theory in explaining these connections. The book also introduces readers to gendered violent crime and examines the law, policy and practice in relation to gender and violence. Information is presented about issues such as domestic abuse, murder, male on male violence, rape, prostitution and child abuse. Connections between these issues are drawn out and responses to them are discussed. Here, the Sexual Offences Act 2003 and the Domestic Violence Crime Victims Act 2004 are examined, as are recent Government initiatives, such as the Home Office's Violence Against Women initiative, the 2003 *Safety and Justice* paper on domestic violence and the July 2004 *Paying the Price* consultation paper on prostitution.

The book focuses closely on how frequently intimacy or familiarity of some kind provides the context for the most gendered crimes and how, often, women and children are the victims of male violence, but also acknowledges male on male, and stranger violence, as well as women who kill or sexually assault. Because the issues raised here appear in different disciplines – law, criminology, socio-legal studies, criminal justice, sociological studies, social policy, cultural studies, gender studies, media studies, and so on, a broad approach is used to bring together the material, to learn from diversity and to critically explore a range of theory.

Gender as a key criminological variable is the main focus of the book and so we concentrate on those areas of the most extremely gender-differentiated offending and victimisation; violence and particularly sexualised violence. So we concentrate on interpersonal *violence* in relation to gender rather than on gender and crime *per se*. The logic to this is that violence is the area both where gender roles are most clearly differentiated and where the most danger and damage occur. Violence is of course also present in other contexts. Male on male violence between individuals and groups is common and concerning but offers little comparative basis for a consideration of gender. Violence also occurs in war and terror, with male perpetrators the norm and women and children often 'collateral damage', but in these cases the violence may not actually be labelled as criminal or criminally intended nor may victims even be identified as gendered by perpetrators. The exception is rape in war which deserves and requires attention in its own right beyond the scope of this book.

Crimes that are violent and overwhelmingly clearly gendered are rape, domestic violence and child abuse. Each of these occurs most commonly within the intimate relationships of family and sexual partnership, despite the media hyperbole about dangerous strangers and internet paedophiles, and it is this intimacy that the book explores in depth, although it also considers prostitution as a normally gendered crime that is sometimes physically violent and, arguably in the case of enforcement by pimps and traffickers, amounts to rape. The empirical evidence about violence and gender is unpicked and assessed in terms of where the knowledge comes from, how it is generated, how useful it is, how it is used, whether theory is properly informed and whether that theory in turn illuminates the relationship between violence and gender in any way that might enable a change in the situation. The implications for justice of the way that gendered crime is so often violent are explored as is the relationship more broadly between gender and justice.

Organisation of the Book

Chapter 2, 'Cold-blooded Lies', examines what we know about violence, gender and justice, which comes mostly from the news media, as few of us actually ever really experience violence in our lives. The chapter begins by considering the role of journalism in violence, gender and justice and uses media sources to focus on some of the most dramatic cases of the late twentieth and early twenty-first centuries (for example the West case; Sarah Payne; Sarah Thornton; O.J. Simpson; Jill Dando; Peter Sutcliffe; William Kennedy Smith). It continues with the 'Soham case' in Cambridgeshire, UK, in 2002. Soham as a narrative offers a wide range of crime motifs that raise theoretical questions about the empirical data which appear to illustrate a relationship between violence, gender and sexuality. Through such cases it identifies a range of violent crimes that are arguably gender dependent and closely related to sexual and gendered identity. The reasons behind the high profile of these cases are discussed, alongside an assessment of the role of the mass media in setting an agenda for criminology, politics and the law. The implications of such representations are evaluated in relation to gender and to justice (Heidensohn 1985; Carter and Weaver 2003; Wykes 1998, 2001; Gunter et al. 2003).

Chapter 3, 'Intimacy, Secrets and Statistics', reviews the actual data on violent and sexual crime. It looks in detail at the statistical evidence, extricating details about both victims and offenders and problematising the relationship between victim and offender in violent, sexual crimes. It draws on local and national crime/victimisation surveys (Painter 1991; Dominy and Radford 1996; Painter and Farrington 1998; Stanko et al. 1998; Mooney 1999; Mirlees-Black 1999; Myhill and Allen 2002; Walby and Allen 2004) and compares the UK data with that available internationally in order to establish the predominant patterns for crimes of violence and sexual offending. More than anything it seeks to reveal the nature of the relationship between victim and offender that is so often characterised by intimacy in such crime but most frequently publicised as anything other than intimate.

Chapter 4, 'Gendering Criminology?', considers the roles of criminology and feminist politics in theorising such crime. It critically assesses the contribution of feminist thinking to criminology, in particular the focus on women which led to a welcome and significant concentration on the victim (Smart 1976, 1995; Heidensohn 1985; Allen 1987; Carlen and Worrall 1987; Walklate 2001). It stresses the consequent lack of attention to offending and hence to the masculinities implicated in offending. It assesses the extent to which this lack, with a few exceptions (Newburn and Stanko 1994; Collier 1998), has not only impoverished theory but also supported a diversion of resources away from the real sites of violence towards the rare and extreme cases that comply with news values, political interests and public prurience.

Chapter 5, 'Confronting Violence: People, Policies and Places', looks at the many agencies and organisations that become involved and policies that become applicable when violence has occurred. This chapter looks at the tools available for confronting violence and the inhibitions on any kind of resolution. Why for example are convictions for rape at an all-time low (Harris and Grace 1999; Gregory and Lees 1999; Kelly et al. 2005)? Why is domestic violence often dealt with by volunteers funded by lottery money? Why are trafficked women only offered assistance if they co-operate in the prosecution of their traffickers (UN 2008)? The chapter argues that reluctance to fully acknowledge the context of violence as not only highly gendered but also frequently intimate and familial has disabled the means of addressing it. It suggests that recent government initiatives, although giving the impression of change, rather amplify these processes.

Chapter 6, 'The Family of Man', turns towards the spaces and relationships that are actually most likely to support violence and sexual abuse: the family and close community (Grubin 1998; McIntosh 1988; Saraga 2001). It reviews the history of the family and considers how familial norms not only actively construct gendered subjectivity but also provide the context for much sexual and violent offending. It deconstructs the myth of the dangerous stranger and in its place focuses closely on the extent to which offending between men and women and between adults and children is overwhelmingly found to involve offenders and victims who know each other well and/or live close to or with one another.

Chapter 7, 'The Law, the Courts and Conviction', focuses on violence and the law and examines how the law has contextualised those settings in which violence takes place. The focus is rape which raises some of the most complex and divisive questions about violence, gender and justice. Why, for example, was it only in 1991 that the 'anachronistic and offensive' ((1991) 2 All E.R. 257 *per* Lord Lane) common law provision that gave husbands a right to rape their wives was removed? The chapter also considers the deeply gendered assumptions about female sexuality that have characterised the law's approach. Why has it taken until the Sexual Offences Act 2003 to gender-neutralise the offences of loitering or soliciting and kerb-crawling? Why can women still not 'rape'? Why, in rape trials, is a previous sexual relationship between the complainant and the accused 'so relevant to the issue of consent that to exclude it would endanger the fairness of the trial ((2002) 1 A.C. para. 46)? This chapter argues that most initiatives to interrupt the long history of the relationship between sex and violence have in fact often left the dangerous body free to act again. It considers why this has happened, the need to refocus on the offender, to address the dangerousness of close relationships and place the ordinary intimacy of most crimes against the body in the spotlight.

Chapter 8, 'Embodying Violence: Masculinity, Culture and Crime', returns to theory to re-evaluate the relationship between gender and crime in the light of the actual evidence and the initiatives that act on violent and sexual crime. It looks at how men are missing from criminological, policy and media discourses of male crime and the implications for understanding either crime or masculinity. It considers the role of the body, both in the acting out of crime and the acquiring of gendered subjectivity (Motz 2001; Shilling 2003) and looks at theories of gendered subjectivity (Butler 1990, 1993; Connell 1987; Collier 1998). It considers how and if theory can explain the affinity between male bodies, masculinity and crime.

Chapter 9, 'The Cost of Gendered Crime', offers a summation. This last chapter considers the real cost in terms of harm as well as money of the constant focusing of resources and policies on the rare and extreme cases of predatory strangers, evil terrorists and mad rapists, and assesses the broad implications for justice and human rights of gendered crime. To conclude, the chapter assesses the implications of current failures inherent in current publicity, practice and policy; failures that to some extent at least are the responsibility of theorists.

Case-study markers within the chapters indicate significant criminal cases, research or legal issues that merit further reflection and/or research.

Notes: Issues for Reflection are included at the close of each chapter. These are intended to develop points made in the text and also make suggestions for developing and exploring the readings, data, law, theory and cases referred to in each chapter.

A *Complementary Readings* section concludes each chapter with suggestions for other readings relevant to the chapter. Some are early classic and seminal references. Readers can benefit from looking both at the suggested text, but also at other publications from the authors cited in our bibliography. There are also suggestions of more recent work that complements this book either by offering different contexts and perspectives or by developing areas or events mentioned here in more detail.

Last, this book makes depressing reading not from intent but because of the reality of the cost in every sense of gendered violence, not least to justice but most of all in female lives, sometimes literally.

2

'COLD-BLOODED LIES'*

Mediating Sex 'n Violence

Chapter 2 uses media sources to discuss some of the most dramatic criminal cases of the later twentieth and early twenty-first centuries, including: the West case, O.J. Simpson and the McCann case. It begins by considering the salience of the media for criminology, for gender and for justice. The reasons behind the high profile of some cases are discussed, alongside an assessment of the role of the mass media in setting an agenda for criminology, politics and the law. The implications of such representations are evaluated, not least because the way they are represented demonstrates how powerfully influential Lombrosian and Freudian theories of crime and deviance remain within popular culture and beyond, despite many decades of criminological theoretical development in Britain and the US. The discussion of violent gendered crime continues with a close analysis of the case in 2002 that raised, directly and indirectly, so many of the questions about gender, violence and justice that this book addresses and to some extent inspired the book itself, the Soham murders in Cambridgeshire. The chapter concludes by assessing the impact of such cases of gendered violence both within criminal justice and beyond. Constituents or motifs such as sexuality; violence; abuse; male offending; female victimisation; complicity; age of consent; heterosexuality; hegemonic masculinity; home; family; policing; community; media; justice; and agencies, feature not only in many other dramatic cases but also in the everyday violences against women and children that rarely reach the news and arguably act constitutively on a continuum to reproduce gendered inequality, roles and values through institutional discourse, ordinary interactions and identity.

Crime News

Crime has a particular salience for the media, whether fictional in film or soap opera (Osborne and Kidd-Hewitt 1996; Gunter et al. 2003) or factual as in the news (Chibnall 1977; Wykes 2001; Jewkes 2004). It allows for the narrative playing out of familiar cultural myths of good versus evil with resolutions normally

---

*Daily Mail, 6 September 2003

including the victory of the hero and the vanquishing of the villain (Propp 1968). Represented crime thrills because it threatens – but only symbolically. By inducing imagined fear, it reassures the vast majority of any mass audience (who will never be the victim of serious crime and especially not of violence) of the rectitude and legitimacy of their safe and secure reality. 'Crime is news because its treatment evokes threats to but also re-affirms the consensual morality of the society' (Hall et al. 1978: 66).

Crime is also news because those constituents of fear and reassurance ensure that news media featuring crime will attract large audiences and the mass media, whether factual or fictional, are first and foremost businesses. Moreover, in Britain, media businesses, and particularly journalism businesses, enjoy something of a symbiotic relationship with government (Tunstall 1996). So for criminologists news about crime may provide insights into the public understanding of crime, and into the relationship between power and the construction of sensibilities about crime. How such crime is reported matters because for most people, most of the time, news is our only experience of, and means of constructing an opinion about, crime. In terms of public understanding, the news may not tell us literally what to think but it offers views of the many aspects of the world few of us really experience. These are chosen for us from life's rich tapestry and represented to us according to the blend of powerful ideologies that characterise journalism – capitalism and political affiliation are just two – and much is necessarily excluded or 'symbolically annihilated' (Tuchman 1978). News values and journalistic ideology provide a very particular way of seeing (Berger 1973) that because of repetition, authority and lack of competition can appear to be the truth about the world. Lukes (1986) argued that in that process, because of the close affiliations between media, state and capital, journalism acts on behalf of the powerful. The representation and selection of news events substitutes symbolic control for real force by offering foci and understanding commensurate with the interests of power. Furthermore, it does this repeatedly and to mass audiences. Media institutions arguably play a major role in orchestrating our social relations and cultural values simply because the 'daily reading of a newspaper is an accepted part of the daily ritual of millions' (Young 1990: viii). It remains so even though some of us may access that newspaper on the internet.

Yet that partiality of representation, in the guise of journalistic objectivity and truth, may too easily legitimate many forms of action and intervention, from vigilantist to legislative, whilst other real and more pervasive issues of crime and deviance may remain unaddressed if they lie outside the ideological and commercial remit of the news media. Criminologists should be interested in news because it is embedded in power yet supplies audiences with everyday commentaries about crime. So criminologists should use news warily as a source for their own profession but also analyse the potential connection between the press, public understanding of crime, policy and political action.

Alongside capital and government, journalism is arguably characterised by a further ideological trajectory, patriarchy. Most journalists of influence remain men, or occasionally women who need to emulate men in order to hack it (Christmas 1996); most newspaper content remains male-centred in an unacknowledged way that renders issues of family, sexuality, relationships and health as suitable for the women's pages or features supplements, as if such issues are not relevant to male lives (Van Zoonen 1998).

So journalists are characterised both by class interests (Tunstall 1996) and gender values but they also operate according to a further set of values very specific to their profession – values that suggest which events should be reported. Sex and violence crimes are particularly newsworthy – especially if the sex is in some way illicit and can be described as immoral, deviant, aggressive, homosexual or paedophiliac. The combination of extreme crime with the titillation of sex – still so much a taboo area for public, or probably any, discourse in the UK, fit the value criteria identified by Galtung and Ruge (1965) as underpinning a good story: especially the criteria of negativity, drama, personifiability and cultural resonance. Better still, such violence is still relatively rare, despite all the press hyperbole about the 'violent society'. Rarity is another news value criterion.

During the last 20 years in England and Wales, the British Crime Survey has recorded self-reported victimisation rates for assault. In 2002 these were stated to be 676 per 10,000 adults, about 6.5%. However, much lower numbers are both reported to and recorded by the police. Convictions are fewer than 150 per 100,000 of the population in England and Wales, circa 1.5% (ESRC Violence Research Programme 2002: 40). Moreover, 'over two-thirds of violent crimes were minor wounding ... homicides and more serious offences of violence accounted for 0.5% of all recorded crime' (Home Office 1999: 4). Even the 2006 BCS data which collates reported crime rather than recorded and includes common assault, wounding, robbery and snatch theft but does not include homicide (as the victims cannot be surveyed) and other types of violent crime, like firearms offences, shows a continuing reduction and relative scarcity of serious violence. Violent crime has fallen by around 43% since its peak in 1995 and has remained relatively stable between 2004/05 and 2005/06. In 2005/06, 3.4% of people experienced a violent incident. In just under half (49%) of all such incidents there was no injury (BCS 2005/06). The attractiveness for journalism of the rare story of extreme violence involving a stranger is even clearer when the BCS reveals that of 2,420,000 violent offences in England and Wales in 2005/06 not only did half result in no injury but half were committed by known assailants, reducing the number of available stranger/danger stories.

So gender often only becomes 'hard' news when it is linked to crime, particularly to violent crime and preferably to unusual violent crime which often gets so much coverage that it makes the rare event of something like stranger rape appear frequent, normal and therefore 'ordinary' (Carter 1998), whilst real 'ordinary' gendered violence such as domestic abuse or sexual harassment barely feature as news (Stanko 1990). When the violent perpetrator is unknown yet another criterion is satisfied because the story gains continuity – it may run for days or even weeks, providing acres of titillating copy and the kind of serial 'running story' that brings in mass audiences, and of course the accompanying revenue, on a daily basis. The dangerous stranger attacking the preferably innocent, young, blonde, virginal, famous (eliteness is a further news value) or maternal woman is the scoop to die for in hack-land.

Murder, gender and media

For journalists the murders of young mother, Rachel Nickell, in 1992 and engaged TV presenter, Jill Dando, in 1999 were ideal 'crime news' because these were respectable women (and also blonde and attractive), apparently attacked by 'evil beasts' and 'dangerous strangers' and grieved over by a loving husband, fiancé and fathers. No one is serving a sentence for the murder of Rachel Nickell on Wimbledon Common, London. The attack was witnessed by her toddler son. Colin Stagg was convicted for murdering Nickell but acquitted on appeal due to police entrapment. Stagg complained bitterly about the media:

> Colin Stagg, the man acquitted of the murder of the young mother Rachel Nickell, is to take part in a TV industry debate on the rise in crime-based programmes on television ... It is thought that Mr Stagg will attack the media circus that followed his trial, and describe how he has been hounded since his acquittal. (*Guardian* 15 July 2002)

An added bonus for the news in Dando's case was her elite, celebrity status. She was described as the Golden Girl and ironically was most well known for presenting *Crimewatch*, a popular primetime programme that invited viewers to help solve real crimes. Her star status was perhaps rather exaggerated as in:

> The newsflashes reporting the murder of Jill Dando stopped Britain in its tracks. It was one of those rare moments when almost everybody remembers where they were. In the days and weeks which followed the shooting on April 26th 1999, a sense of shock, mourning and finally puzzlement gripped Britain. Time and again the question was posed in newspapers, on television and in pubs and homes across the country – why her? A lack of obvious motive was one of the most difficult aspects of the investigation. (*Guardian* 15 July 2002)

The man sentenced for killing TV presenter Dando appealed but had his first appeal rejected. George was the community 'loony' and his lawyers claimed forensic evidence, which was the main source of incrimination, was probably contaminated. The press constructed a narrative of him as a stalking obsessive, even hinting that he had tracked Dando online. He was both bad and mad:

> He was a convicted sex offender and had a history of psychological problems. When he was 22 he was convicted of attempting to rape a language student. And he was once arrested in combat gear outside the London home of the Princess of Wales. (BBC News 29 July 2002)

In June 2007 he was given further leave to appeal when a successful challenge was brought to the reliability of forensic evidence, a single speck of residue from the gun used to kill Miss Dando that he always claimed police had 'planted'. He was cleared in July 2008 having served eight years in prison.

Such murders allow journalists to generate the sexual innuendo and romantic drama for audiences with which they can 'fascinate, titillate, and then reassure by condemning' (Young 1974 in Chibnall 1977: 31). They satisfy both professional news values, and, by generating big sales, profit motives. Ironically, in neither case did the dangerous stranger they vilified appear to have actually conducted the killing. Neither of these cases offered much of a negative or blaming account of the women victims, who were after all respectable, young and attractive. The one exception was perhaps the *Daily Star* (26 May 2000) which published an image of Dando in black leather with the headline 'Dando suspect: was he driven mad by sexy pose?' Carter and Weaver saw this as an attempt to query Dando's respectable image and thus explain her murder by making the story fit the usual template of blaming the victim for their own death because they 'failed to contain their sexuality within patriarchal limits' (2003: 40). Several other cases from the 1990s illustrate that description of a normal template well.

Rachel McLean disappeared in 1991. The press reports in April 1991 immediately assumed the killer was a 'dangerous stranger' and the *Sunday Telegraph* highlighted 'The danger beneath the dreaming spires' (28 April 1991). The police also succumbed to this theory because it took them over a week to find Rachel's body beneath the floor of her own bedroom. In December 1991, her boyfriend, John Tanner, was sentenced to life for murdering her. The press made much of Tanner and McLean's passionate love affair with headlines such as 'Fatal Obsession'[1] and persistent references to *crime passionel* and Rachel's infidelity (entirely a lie to support Tanner's plea of provocation). Rachel was depicted as glamorous, worldly, secretive and dark. The *Sun* (4 December 1991) offered a photo of Tanner clutching a teddy bear next to one of Rachel in a low-cut dress looking every inch the glamorous vamp, even a *femme fatale*. Less was written on Tanner's ability to sleep next to her body, write to the woman he had killed, take part in a reconstruction of the crime to try and cover his tracks or his previous history of 'stalking'. Instead he was a 'classics student'. There was much detail about his childhood, family and the fact he was 'one of New Zealand's most gifted boys' (*Sun* 4 December 1991). He had a 'brilliant mind' and had been left shattered and lonely by his crime. His defence counsel described the affair with Rachel as 'No run of the mill, humdrum tale. This we have heard, was a love story ... a passionate relationship' (*Daily Express* 6 December 1991). So special that it seems impossible for journalists to question how a middle-class, educated, heterosexual, white man, with all the associated privileges, might not only kill but be arrogant enough to blame his victim.

In the same year in the trial of John Perry, the press informed us that the victim, his wife Arminda, was promiscuous and had worked as a prostitute in the Philippines prior to their marriage. Perry blamed his act on the discovery of his wife's affair with a neighbour and told the court 'she was slashing at me with a knife and I hit her somewhere on the face with my fist. Then it all went rather blank' (*Daily Telegraph* 23 November 1991). Yet his composure returned sufficiently for him to dismember her in 'an extremely orderly way' (*Independent* 21 November 1991), cook her and feed her to their cat. The cat featured very prominently in the tabloid photographs – much more prominently than Arminda – and all we learnt about John Perry was his age and occupation. John

Perry had in fact decided to save the cost of alimony, £72.67 per week, for which he would be liable after the divorce she sought, by killing his wife. Although Perry was sentenced to life, two jurors were prepared to accept the plea of provocation on the grounds of her promiscuity and the press focused on her foreignness and sexual history as if they were symptoms of her eventual murder.

Not only are women very often depicted as responsible for of their own demise but when they have killed they are doubly damned both as women and for breaking the law. Malcolm Thornton, an ex-policeman, had been a heavy drinker who had agreed to go to a clinic but then had resumed drinking after marrying Sara Thornton (see Chapter 4 case-study). There was an inference in these accounts that somehow Sara drove him to drink and maybe to violence. The judge at her trial commented of Sara that there were 'other alternatives available such as walking out or going upstairs' (*Guardian* 30 July 1991). Despite his beatings of her and the lack of police action (he was an ex-policeman), there is no critique of white, employed, heterosexual, marital masculinity – let alone policing as 'hegemonic masculinity' (Fielding 1994). However, the newspaper reports listed Sara's abortions, drug-use, previous marriage, suicide attempts, history of mental illness, career, trips to conferences and dislike of underwear. Sara Thornton was, herself, acutely aware of being tried not only as a criminal but as a woman who was too liberal, too independent, too feminist.

Celebrity crime

In the US, celebrity (eliteness is another news value making a crime attractive to journalists) featured in several high-profile media cases that demonstrated issues of gender and justice. Celebrity crime seems to have a growing appeal to the media as the global electronic context raises the value of internationally known stars (Wykes 2007). In 1991 a young member of the famous American Kennedy family was tried and acquitted of rape, despite three other women coming forward to say they too had been similarly assaulted:

> William Kennedy Smith met a woman at a bar, invited her back home late at night and apparently had sex with her on the lawn. She says it was rape, and the police believed her story enough to charge him with the crime. Perhaps it was the bruises on her leg; or the instincts of the investigators who found her, panicked and shaking, curled up in the foetal position on a couch; or the lie-detector tests she passed. (Gibbs 1991)

The case was one of so-called 'date rape' a phrase that in itself diminishes the act to something casual, maybe even just consensual sex regretted the morning after. Millions tuned in to daytime television to watch the courtroom in Palm Beach. American feminist Naomi Wolf noted that the press generated massive publicity and made money out of William Kennedy Smith and then were 'suddenly on the alert about whether Smith would get a fair trial' (Gibbs 1991). More recently, in 2004, Kennedy was again acquitted of sexual offending, this time of harassment.

However, the celebrity case that was most entirely public was that of black US football star, O.J. Simpson, known as The Juice.

Case-study: O.J. Simpson

The attraction of the case was perhaps race, maybe that it happened in the La La land of celebrity obsessed Los Angeles, or perhaps it was the filmed chase at its outset that brought the reality into viewers' homes. This present camera was also seen as relevant to the public fascination with the Bulger[2] case in Liverpool in 1992 when CCTV footage of two little boys and the abducted toddler they eventually killed made people feel like witnesses (Young 1996). Mediatisation began with a chase of OJ's car, as he fled arrest, filmed from a helicopter. It then moved to the televised courtroom drama and spread to internet blogs and chatrooms. People queued for hours for space in the courtroom, where the ordinary crime of domestic murder was given the twist of celebrity and race to lift it from everyday gendered violence. O.J.'s wife Nicole was a white woman and her friend, also murdered, was a white man. Her head was nearly severed in the frenzied attack. O.J. had been very famous but was long retired in 1994 when the murder happened, yet such was the draw of the case that: 'On CNN, Larry King told his viewers, 'If we had God booked and O.J. was available, we'd move God' (Graham 2004).

After eleven months Simpson was acquitted, leaving for many a bitter aftertaste of injustice and infotainment rather than information. There was 'Simpson himself, all insouciance and arrogance, blaming his dead ex-wife's fast ways for her brutal demise' (Graham 2004) and indeed, as in other cases of intimate killing, it was Nicole's sexuality that was foregrounded in the media and in court to explain her death rather than O.J.'s history of domestic violence, which ran to 62 incidents and a conviction for spousal battery against her in 1993.

Even now the racial tension allied to the case makes it difficult to question the verdict despite his conviction in October 2008 for kidnapping and armed robbery. Another diversion was that the racial element of the case obfuscated the masculinity behind it (see Chapter 8 for further accounts of diversions) and raised already high feelings in a divided city around whether a black man might get justice given all the publicity. These diversions from the intimacy and brutality of this gendered violence were often covert in the mainstream media but the cyber trial was free of all constraints. It was, as Featherstone (1995) claimed, trial by disembodied, global, virtual voice. Brown notes the viciousness of the cyber postings that claimed: 'A black man who has already been tried and convicted in the eyes of white (Jew) controlled media is going to fry' (2003: 57). The same poster notes that 'a bitch is behind' any sort of trouble a man is in (Brown 2003: 57). So succinct, the media and *femmes fatales* are framed again rather than a famous man.

Sex 'n Violence

Female sexuality of a rather different kind featured in a British case when police began to excavate bodies of young women from a house in Gloucester.

Case-study: the West case[3]

The family who lived in that house were the Wests: the children went to school; neighbours came for tea; lodgers moved in and out; family members visited and babies were born. In late 1994 Fred and Rose were arrested and charged with the multiple murders of 12 young women. Fred hanged himself in prison in the New Year and that, alongside his status as husband/father/handyman, seems to have made it difficult for journalists to apply the usual non-human/non-male/abnormal terms of 'beast', 'animal' (Clark 1992), 'evil' or 'mad'.[3] Instead the inference was that:

> For Rose, Fred had been a good husband, a reliable provider who allowed her to have the large family she craved. He had also encouraged and condoned her passion for violent lesbian sex and been willing in crude terms to clear up afterwards. (Sounes 1996: 23)

The facts that Fred had already killed at least twice before they met; collected homemade pornography; had a prison sentence; had been a pimp and picked up Rose when she was 15 and he 28, could only be teased out by reading 'between the lines' of the news. Neither the tabloid/conservative nor the broadsheet/liberal press offered a radical account, which might have questioned the social relations that enabled such atrocities. Nor did either address masculinity as a problem: the conservative press minimally interrogated Fred as a damaged phenomenon but not as a man/husband/father, whilst the liberal agenda was to divert the debate from a failure of family to a failure of institutional services.[4]

Damaged men exemplify a pathologisation of sexual and violent crime evident in news accounts of male violence. Like Fred West, Peter Sutcliffe 'The Yorkshire Ripper' had suffered a head injury and the press routinely reported this in both cases as causal. Although why a knock to the head might result in sexually violent misogyny is never explained. Instead a mixture of biological theory to explain violence and Freudian explanations for sexual perversion remain high on the agenda of popular media accounts. Sutcliffe was nicknamed the street-cleaner by the press because of his murder of prostitutes amongst his 13 victims during the later 1970s. He was eventually diagnosed as a paranoid psychophrenic. A biography by Gordon Burn (1985) claimed Sutcliffe was weak, bullied and timid and had an extremely close relationship with his mother, Kathleen. Even the title of Burn's account: *Somebody's Husband; Somebody's*

Son suggested female collusion. More recently, the fascination with the Ripper remains, as do Freudian explanations, for example here blaming his wife rather than his mother: 'She was sexually cold, devoid of love for him and totally self centred and domineering. In many ways she was responsible for disturbing this man's mind' (Ripper website).

The popular currency of such accounts represents the ongoing authority of both biological and Freudian theory despite consistent challenges to both, particularly from feminism (see Chapter 4).

Paedophile panic

Crimes against children are nearly always gendered (adult male offender/female child victim) and, like crimes against women, most often committed by men known or related to the child, often within a family context. Yet these normal offences again rarely make news, just as ordinary domestic murders do not (Carter 1998). Such stories appear only to assume shock-horror value when the abuse is virtual or a child is abducted, which in both cases removes the story from the reality of sexual violence against children, creating something of an illusion and even perhaps false consciousness about violence, gender and family.

Again celebrity adds to the frisson and news value of such stories. In 1999 the newspapers covered the case of one time pop-star Gary Glitter. Glitter was cleared of under-age sex charges but convicted of downloading child pornography from the internet. He received a sentence of four months. Despite his acquittal of the sex charges, the press still found ways of labelling him as a paedophile with headlines like 'Beast raped me aged 8' (*News of the World* 14 November 1999) and 'Glitter put me through hell at 14' (*Sun* 10 November 1999) whilst subtly implying a certain seductiveness on the part of the young female complainant, 'Pervert's Princess ... in white hot pants and skimpy top' (*Mirror* 13 November 1999). As a famous person Glitter added a further criterion to the newsworthiness of the 'sex 'n violence' story – eliteness. He was a 'Monster masquerading under the mask of glam rock' (*Daily Mail* 18 November 1999) and consistently labelled as other than a man – sicko; pervert; depraved; evil; and, damningly, the 'illegitimate son of a cleaning lady' (*The Times* 13 November 1999), again hinting at some link between mothering and perverted male sexuality. These terms move discussions of child sex outside of any framework linked to adult male familial heterosexuality (Kitzinger 1996) despite these men being the most likely to abuse.

Scotland Yard admits most child abusers are well educated 'white males aged between 36 and 45. The majority are in a long term relationship, married or have children' (*Observer Magazine* 2007: 25), as exemplified by another celebrity case. Successful actor Chris Langham: '58-year-old father of five was recently found guilty of possessing grade 5 images, the category reserved for the worst portraits of sadism and bestiality' (*Observer Magazine* 2007: 25). Langham had used the internet and claimed he was doing research, and it is the internet and the distribution of child pornography that seems to be the main focus of much police and press concern rather than the criminality of a father and husband. The use of the internet for accessing child pornography has developed over a decade into a contemporary set of cultural anxieties about the new medium and enabled some powerful headlines such as 'Twisted secrets of the web' (*Sun* 13 November 1999) and 'Who is policing the internet?' (*Mirror* 13 November 1999). There is a failure to address the men who produce net-porn (often abusing their own children to do so) in favour of demonising the worldwide web, reminiscent of the earlier panics about emergent media such as video and even comics. Since the Glitter trial the 'paedophile' has become the bogeyman of British childhood with his playground, the worldwide web, deeply implicated.

In the summer of 2000 the media furore over 'dangerous strangers' and 'evil beasts' assaulting our children fuelled the reconstructive process away from the family or familiar to the paedophile, with reports of the murder of a little girl in Sussex. Pre-empting the arrest of a known sex-offender, the *News of the World* offered 'names and photographs of child sex offenders living near you' (24 July 2000) and other papers joined in with 'Police must warn parents of monsters' (*Mirror* 25 July 2000) and 'Crackdown on perverts long overdue' (*Mirror* 27 July 2000). Anxiety was focused on the streets and parks, on sex offenders released into the community and the failure of the law, not on the reality of child sex offenders living with children behind the closed doors of their own homes. Anxiety also focused on represented rather than real abuse. The television series *The Hunt for Britain's Paedophiles* (BBC2 June 2002) focused on the work of Scotland Yard's specialist paedophile unit but seemed more concerned about represented rather than real child sexual abuse. The programmes were detailed and very descriptive accounts that broadcast thinly disguised examples of child pornography in the name of documentary and justice. The problem male for the programme makers, and the police they depicted, was represented as the anonymous 'paed-porn-voyeurs' who buy and watch such material, not the father featured in a clip buggering his baby daughter.

This resistance to confronting the reality of most crime against children involving 'familiar men' was epitomised in the summer of 2007 when a British family on holiday in Portugal became the focus of the global media obsession with child abduction, paedophiles and the internet.

Case-study: Madeleine McCann

When Madeleine McCann was first reported missing from the family's rented villa in May all the focus was on finding the dangerous pervert, with a local man's computer being seized and hints about child net pornography, child trafficking and paedophiles filling the media. Within four days: 'Portuguese newspaper Correio de Manha said Madeleine may have been kidnapped by a paedophile ring' (Timeline 2007). The *Sun* was more outspoken, blaming

Portugal and calling for tougher anti-paedophile laws and claiming that for police the fear is that:

> Maddie, three, was stolen to order by an international gang of perverts. ... Unlike here, Portugal has NO sex offenders register – and its relaxed policing has made it a magnet for sun-seeking paedophiles from Britain and the rest of Europe. (Sullivan 2007)

The *Daily Express* added some titillation about internet pornography and a suspect's relationship to his mother, when Robert Murat was questioned and his computer was seized:

> It has been reported that several links to paedophile websites, encrypted emails and messages were found on three computers removed from Murat's home during a dramatic police raid on Monday. It was also claimed that video tapes showing depraved sexual acts and bestiality were also found at the Villa Liliana, where Murat lives with his elderly mother Jennifer. (Drake and Pilditch 2007)

Murat was a respected member of the community and even helped with the search. He was released without any charge and successfully sued the press for damages.

The internet became a massive source of publicity in the search for Madeleine, her father set up a blog and it was also a site for donations to help the search. Her doctor parents appeared daily, going to the Catholic church, meeting the Pope, clutching their young twins and cuddling missing Madeleine's soft toy. Even footballer David Beckham made a television appeal; the same footballer whose team shirt the little girls murdered at Soham had been wearing. For four months the world looked at trafficking, pornography, kidnap, the internet, murder and failed policing, then quite suddenly the investigation turned to the family and on the weekend of 7 September 2007 both parents became suspects.

At the time of writing, the case is unsolved and the child still missing but it took a very long time for suspicion to turn from dirty men in real or cyber Mackintoshes to the family, despite that being the place where most children are hurt and therefore perhaps the most sensible place to try to eliminate first. This lapse and diversion may well have been partly because of the preferred focuses of crime news on rare events and strangers and partly because, as Chapter 6 discusses, the family is so central to our values and sense of self that we take for granted that it is a good place, particularly when it is white, middle class, attractive, reproductive, religious and respectable as in the McCann's case.

On the same weekend a four-page-long article on the online child pornographer the 'Son of God' offered two sentences to explain why there had been no outcry about the 31 children featured in Cox's live webcam sites: 'The truth is they were never missing. The babies and children ritually abused via webcam were rescued from their own homes'. All the remainder of the article was concerned with why Cox viewed this material rather than an outraged discussion of the 'clips of fathers abusing their own children' (*Observer* 9 September 2007: 25).

Many high-profile crimes are about violence, often sexual, against women and girls who are usually known or related to the men who attack them. They are crimes that seem often poorly policed and obfuscatingly reported, even unjustly reported, in the press. They are crimes where media accounts prefer to tell stories about strangers/paeds/beasts and mad men online, in secret and in the dark rather than fathers, husbands, boyfriends, colleagues, teachers or priests in homes, schools and communities. These are crimes where, whatever the context, women themselves, whether victims, perpetrators or associates, are systematically blamed for the violences of men, as also happened in Soham in 2002.

Soham

On 4 August 2002 in England, two 10-year-old school-girls, Holly Wells and Jessica Chapman, disappeared from the Cambridgeshire town of Soham. The *Sun*'s headline on 6 August was: 'DID FIEND LURE THEM: Chatroom pervert fear' (Troup 2002). Soham is ordinary. It is a small town of about 8,500 inhabitants. It is situated on the fens. It has an annual pumpkin fair, a majorette troupe, a brass band and a carnival. In that close community early on a summer's evening, the two 10-year-old girls dressed in Manchester United football shirts left the family home of one, Holly, where a barbecue was going on, to walk through the town. They hadn't got permission and weren't missed for two hours. It was assumed they had been abducted. Their bodies were found on the 17 August, two weeks later. The media became heavily embroiled in the search for the girls and then their killers, to the extent that their reports were deemed to be threatening to justice:

> The Contempt of Court Act 1981 makes it an offence for media organisations to report anything that would cause a 'substantial risk of serious prejudice' in any future trial … [yet] On Friday the Cambridgeshire coroner, David Morris, said the media 'invasion' of Soham and the offer of substantial rewards by newspapers placed extra pressure on the police and upset the girls' families. The *Express* offered £1 million for information leading to an arrest while the *Sun* offered £150,000. (Ahmed 2002)

News reports raised the spectre of the dangerous stranger when actually the girls had been abducted by someone they knew and trusted.

After feverish speculation that the girls had been 'groomed' by an internet paedophile, the police announced that their last session on the internet was innocent. They had not visited chatrooms or sent emails. But rumour still crackled like wildfire. One was that a sex offenders' hostel had been secretly opened nearby. Another said Terence Pocock, sentenced to life imprisonment in 1985 for the rape and stabbing of two 13-year-old girls nearby, had been released back into the area. Neither was true (Harris et al. 2002).

This kind of account exemplifies the way in which assumptions about crimes against children are readily directed away from suspicion of those they know and those who are supposed to care for them, by the news, because journalists seek rarity and drama. The costs may be multiple: actual offenders may be overlooked and even escape justice; wrongful arrests may be made; police time can be wasted; the public may act as vigilantes; trials may be prejudiced by misreporting and payments for stories; and the very real harm that happens in close-knit communities and families is under-recognised.

Media accounts, and the false leads prompted by them, deflected police and took huge amounts of time and resources to investigate, to no avail. Attention was 'focused on local sex offenders. Cambridgeshire had 266 registered and 433 others known to be resident. Five profilers drew up a picture of a suspect' (Harris et al. 2002). On Monday 12 August, a taxi driver's account of two children being driven erratically meant a massive search for the suspect vehicle 'throughout Britain, the numbers are 8,992 Peugeot and 2,500 Vectras' (Harris et al. 2002) until it transpired that the taxi clock was an hour ahead and the girls had still been at home when the sighting occurred. A jogger's anxious report of finding fresh mounds of earth led to hours of work digging up a badger set. 'By Wednesday morning it was clear that 10,000 phone calls, 400 door-to-door interviews and 700 cars stopped had produced nothing.' (Harris et al. 2002). On Thursday 15 August the police finally excluded the media and held a town meeting at which people volunteered to open their homes for searches (amazingly this had not been done, perhaps because of the abduction by stranger assumption) and to think about the activities and behaviours of neighbours, friends and family. Whatever information was offered is unknown but the afternoon of the next day 'two cars of plainclothes policemen pulled up outside the house of Huntley and Carr' (Harris et al. 2002). Huntley had already been questioned by police and been on television that morning. On that GMTV breakfast programme:

> Mr Huntley repeated his anguish at being possibly the last person to speak to the girls. He had broken down in tears when he told reporters – five days after the girls disappeared – that he was probably the last person to talk to them. At about 6:15pm on the Sunday Holly and Jessica had asked after Ms Carr, he said, after she failed to get a permanent job at St Andrew's Primary School. In an emotional interview, he said: 'How can two girls go missing in broad daylight, then nothing? No sighting. No nothing. It beggars belief.' (Mcveigh 2002)

On the morning of Saturday 17 August just two days after turning their attention to the close community:

> Police announce that a 28-year-old man and a 25-year-old woman have been arrested on suspicion of murdering Holly and Jessica. The man was detained on suspicion of murder and abduction and the woman on suspicion of murder after 'items of major importance' had been recovered during a search of Soham Village College. (Timeline for the search 2002)

Ian Huntley lived in a cottage overlooking college grounds with Maxine Carr who had worked in the girls' school, where Huntley was caretaker, as a temporary classroom assistant. It was her failed application for a permanent post he had referred to in the GMTV interview. At 1 p.m. on the same day two bodies were found just 10 miles from Soham at Mildenhall. The little girls were naked and Huntley had doused their bodies in petrol and set them alight.

In December 2003, Ian Huntley was convicted of murdering Jessica and Holly at his home. The motive was thought to be sexual but as the girls' bodies were partly decomposed and burned this was not a feature of the case. His partner, classroom assistant Maxine Carr, was found guilty of perverting the course of justice for providing Huntley with a false alibi. Throughout the press coverage of the trial and that which that followed his conviction, Huntley was demonised as a 'beast', 'monster' – the other. The press examined in detail his background: abusive father, broken home, the school weirdo and finally lesbian mother, 'She left home and began a lesbian relationship with a workmate from Ross foods' pizza factory' (*Sun* 18 December 2003: 4) to explain his difference and deviance. Also Huntley had changed his name to move to Soham and this was interpreted as indicative of an odd relationship with his mother: 'There's also an extreme psychological neatness in Huntley moving closer to his mother by adopting her surname' (Buzzle.com 2003). What the media barely acknowledged was that he was a man living in a heterosexual relationship who was part of a close community and who was well known and trusted by local children.

In a tape made before a failed suicide attempt in prison, Huntley implicated his partner, Maxine Carr as the mastermind of the cover up:

> She basically told me to get the car cleaned, change the tyres, go to the police over in St Andrews and tell them I've seen someone on the school grounds, carrying a black bag, looking suspicious. I was not thinking straight. She did most of the thinking for me. (Cambridge News 18 September 2006)

This attribution fitted neatly with most of the press coverage of the woman Huntley lived with, Maxine Carr. Her role and character were routinely seen in the press as somehow the cause of his violence, so once again women (his mother and partner) were implicated. Carr had backed Huntley's account of the events on Sunday 4 August, saying that she had been in Soham with him at the time of the murders. She claimed she had given him the alibi as she genuinely believed he did not kill the girls. In fact she was a hundred miles away in Grimsby, as her mobile phone records indicated. Even so she was widely viewed as an accomplice, either grooming the girls prior to the crime or helping to clear up afterwards. Quickly she was compared to Myra Hindley and even acknowledged in the witness box that fellow prisoners called her 'Myra Mark II'. She spun a 'complex web of lies' (*Guardian* 18 December 2003) about what she and Huntley had done together on the Sunday evening that was quickly exposed by mobile phone evidence of calls from Grimsby. She does seem to have believed in his innocence until he took the stand and started to explain how they had accidentally died in his bathroom, when she was heard to mutter: 'I don't believe a word of it', implying it was no accident (*Guardian* 18 December 2003: 5).

Carr was demonised as a 'snivelling, selfish liar' (*Sun* 18 December 2003) and there was as much coverage of her part in the crime as of his, even though she was finally only charged with conspiracy to pervert the course of justice and given three and half years, to serve half and then be on licence. Even her lies in the end did little damage. She didn't get the St Andrew's permanent job, with a CV riddled with invention. Moreover:

> Carr did indeed initially mislead a police investigation ... but it cannot be said that this caused significant delay ... and, according to a survey conducted by the Risk Advisory Group, two-thirds of the job applications they examined were 'inaccurate' in some way. (Law in a box 2008)

The *Sun* accused her of posing as another of Huntley's victims by claiming he was abusive. Yet the catalogue of claims against him that had never been brought to court and emerged after the trial suggest she may have indeed been terrified of him. However, her worst crime seems to have been being out at a night-club whilst the girls died, drinking, kissing another man and being photographed doing so. The *Sun* revealed all, with a whole page devoted to the image as the trial finished:

> THE KISS OF DEATH. On the night Huntley murdered two girls, Carr was out partying. Here is Maxine Carr snogging a man on a wild night out – the same evening that Ian Huntley killed Holly and Jessica. It is believed the very image of Carr going out on her own may have pushed Huntley over the edge. (*Sun* 18 December 2003)

This claim was made despite the fact that the kiss happened at 10pm, long after the girls were dead, and 100 miles away. The *Sun* quoted Huntley's mother as saying she was 'very flirty. She openly chatted to other fellas and wore tops with plunging necklines' (*Sun* 18 December 2007) and that his anger that Maxine was going out 'flipped' him.

Carr was released from jail in May 2004 but given a new identity because 'it was necessary to protect "life and limb" as well as Carr's psychological health' (BBC News 24 February 2005). The order included a secrecy clause banning the media revealing her name or whereabouts after death threats from the local community. She was vilified as if she was as guilty, maybe more guilty, than Huntley, for no better reason than as a woman the expectation of her was to be with her partner and so keep him safe.

More than anything, what Carr was perceived as doing wrong was not to be at Huntley's side taming his sexuality at 6.30 p.m. on that Sunday evening as a 'wife' should be, for the reason that she was going to go out and enjoy herself, drinking and dancing and not being very 'respectable'. The treatment of Carr as if she was as accountable as Huntley, demonstrated more than anything the institutionalised misogyny of journalists directed at any woman who transgresses the conventions of femininity, the acceptability of that to very large numbers of the public and, perhaps worse, how that diverts attention from the heterosexual, adult, white man who killed two little girls who knew and trusted him.

The case also indicated other institutional aspects that raised issues around gender and crime and the level of seriousness that crimes such as rape and domestic abuse attract in the police. After Huntley's conviction and sentence of 40 years, it emerged that there were previous domestic violence, rape and under-age sex allegations against him – charges had been dropped, there were no convictions and data had been erased. His appointment to a school caretaker's job in Soham seemed incredible in retrospect. Following the case, serious questions were raised about the response to these many allegations from child protection services in the area, Humberside police and other local services. Further, both the Humberside and Cambridgeshire police services faced considerable criticism about their procedures around recording and exchanging information on unproved allegations. The trial judge was highly critical:

- With regard to Cambridgeshire police, he said they were responsible for recording Huntley's birth date incorrectly and for checking only his alias, Nixon, on the Police National Computer (PNC), but added their mistakes 'were not systemic nor corporate' and the specific errors had only limited consequences.
- He said Humberside Police, not the Data Protection Act, was to blame for the fact Huntley's records had been deleted.
- He said he had 'misgivings' over the way social services handled the issue of Huntley's under-age sex allegations.
- He consequently urged the government to reaffirm its existing strong guidance on sex between 15-year-olds and older people. (BBC News 22 June 2004a)

In 2004, the Bichard inquiry looked into the 'key errors of police, social services and the education system' which allowed Huntley to be employed at a school despite 'nine allegations of rape, indecent assault on an 11-year-old girl and sex with underage girls while Huntley was living in Grimsby' (BBC News 22 June 2004b). The findings were simple enough: 'He was not identified as a risk to children because he had never been convicted and so did not have a criminal record' (Yates 2005: 286). Why there were no convictions despite the string of complaints about him raises many questions about the way police deal with gendered crime (Gregory and Lees 1999), the culture of policing (Reiner 1985; Fielding 1994) and the law and courts as discussed in Chapter 7. An example of each of those is evident in a final twist to the Soham story. This was the arrest of the police officer acting as family support officer to the bereaved parents, on allegations of sexual assault and downloading child pornography. He had 'comforted Jessica's family throughout the inquiry' (Hall and Vasager 2003). The CPS brought no charges even though indecent images were found on the officer's laptop as it had not been in his possession at all times and they might have been downloaded by someone else! The murder of Jessica and Holly still features in the press, most recently when the team investigating their deaths was assigned to tracking down the killer of five women working as prostitutes in nearby Ipswich.[5] Huntley's suicide attempt in 2006 drew a large mailbag insisting that he be kept alive (mirroring attitudes to Moors murderer Ian Brady who has asked to be allowed to die): 'If there is such a place as hell, then Huntley should not be allowed to arrive there quickly' (Cambridge News 18 September 2006). There are many websites featuring Maxine Carr and her whereabouts filled with much fear and vigilantism. This one features a petition to force a suspected woman out of the village:

> We cannot allow this to carry on – our children are at risk. With facial surgery and a new identity – we are not to know who we can trust and who we cannot. There is a lot of hearsay about where she actually is now. (Go-petition 22 June 2007)

During the trial and in its aftermath, Huntley and Carr seemed equally loathed and demonised as if the crimes of murdering two small girls, and telling lies to protect the man you loved and thought was innocent, were comparable. The only explanation for that equalisation can be that the expectations and requirements of men and women are very different and that those made of women are far less forgiving.

Conclusion

Soham's narrative constituents included many common to other accounts of gendered crime: sex; violence; the internet; agency errors; policing misdirection; blame of women; family; and searches for strangers. What features little in the accounts is the men, not as 'beasts, paeds, strangers and psychos' but the men who know and purport to care for their victims, who have roles in women's lives, families and communities. Very few of the most publicised crimes against women in the last 20 years have featured unknown assailants. Of the two stranger murders mentioned here, Rachel Nickell and Jill Dando, both now remain unsolved. Similarly crimes against children are rarely committed by strangers (Grubin 1998), as is discussed fully in Chapter 6, though it is these stranger killings that feature in the press. To some extent the shock of Soham was being forced to face the reality that the trusted, respectably coupled school caretaker did not care. There was no stranger to blame, just one of the community's own.

At the close of the twentieth and opening of the twenty-first century, most criminals were men (64,103 of those serving immediate custodial sentences in England and Wales compared to 5,770 women – ESRC 2002: 41); most homicide was committed by men (89% between 1995 and 2000 in England and Wales – ESRC 2002: 30); 60% of homicide victims were women killed by men (ESRC 2002: 30); most women were raped by men they know (73% of women contacting Rape Crisis had been assaulted by men they knew – ESRC 2002: 16); 77% of callers to Childline are girls (ESRC 2002: 15). Most violence against women was actually committed by husbands, fiancés and male family members (68% of murdered women were killed by spouses, lovers or family members in 1997 – Home Office 1999: 16). Little has changed.

Simplistically, men still appear in crime statistics mostly as perpetrators, against men and women; women appear mostly as victims of men, but more often than not as victims they simply don't appear at all. Much of this crime is systematically unreported in the press: its ordinariness and resolvedness removes it from journalism's newsworthy agenda but also its familial and domestic nature presents it as a problem for a profession still largely constituted in, and dependent on, exactly those conservative gender relations and values. Traditional gender norms and values are collapsed in such cases of familial violence. As a consequence, not only are many 'ordinary' women as victims of men 'annihilated' from the news but so are many 'ordinary' violent and sexually abusive men. But also when such intimate cases demand reporting because they are extreme, or there is no immediately found victim or perpetrator, or a celebrity is involved they are framed within consensual and conservative models of gender organisation. They are discursively oriented towards the interests of power not through overt conspiracy but through the cultural loading of meanings in language, the way stories make sense and through the ideologies informing those who have the power to disseminate them.

Things are very slow to change culturally. When Tuchman (1978) looked at women as featured in television drama, advertising, women's magazines and newspapers she found that, as a consequence of commercial pressure and sexism, women were systematically 'annihilated' unless they could be portrayed in traditional and stereotypical feminine roles. In reportage:

> On the whole, despite coverage of women being forcibly induced by the legitimation of the women's movement ... newspapers ... engage in the symbolic annihilation of women by ignoring women at work and trivializing women through banishment to hearth and home. (Tuchman 1978: 183)

The implications of that trivialization, denigration and annihilation of women in news is very evident in the news about gendered violence today. In many of the cases, whether women were perpetrators, victims or just linked by association, violence was explained by their inappropriate feminine behaviour, most frequently sexual but also social. In contrast, male violence was accounted for primarily as breaking the law, rather than as breaking any taboos of masculinity, or due to 'brain damage', the internet or of course a *bitch*, as O.J.'s net-fan so succinctly explained male violence. Thus, press accounts manage to perpetuate the legitimacy of male violence in gendered terms (by not mentioning it unless it can be pathologised) whilst also castigating it in legal terms. The accounts thus resolve the ideological contradiction of restoring both law and order and patriarchal power. In contrast, women were depicted as breaking the law, or causing men to break the law, because they had broken taboos of female behaviour. The net effect is to promote marriage, monogamy, maternity and modesty as safe, normal and responsible. In contrast feminists, *femmes fatales*, foreigners and feckless women drive men to badness and themselves to madness.

These cases demonstrate some terrible violence against women and children, mostly inflicted by men they know and should be able to trust. That in itself is a reason to be deeply concerned about violence and gender. They also show some serious injustices, specifically legal but also discursive – when so much violence is not publicised and when what is can be so routinely blamed on women themselves or can be diverted from real men to representations and *others*. The next chapter focuses closely on that legal context in terms of the volume and nature of real, ordinary, gendered crime rather than the extremes we regularly read about in the papers, before Chapter 4 looks critically at explanations for the relationship between crime and gender.

Notes: Issues for Reflection

1 This was entirely inappropriate as the fictional popular film of that title features a violent, obsessive, murderous, childless career woman.

Assess the effect of using it as an analogy in the McLean case.

2 The murder of James Bulger by two 10-year-old boys led to a media meltdown in the search for blame that focused on violent videos, faithless schools, failed families and inner city communities. (See A. Young (1996) *Imagining Crime: Textual Outlaws and Criminal Conversations*.)

Analyse the accounts of mothers and families in news stories about the case and evaluate their impact.

3 Rose West remains in prison. For a full account see M. Wykes (1998) 'A family affair', in C. Carter, G. Branston and S. Allan (1998) *News, Gender and Power*.

Research the case and subsequent events relating to it and compare and contrast the account to the Soham case.

4 This diversion towards blaming institutions rather than men and the family system also happened after the Cleveland child abuse (B. Campbell (1988) *Unofficial Secrets*.)

Consider the implications of 'blaming institutions' for men's crime against women and children.

5 Wright managed to blame his partner for his visits to prostitutes that ended with his killing spree: 'Their relationship dwindled and their sex life had petered out' (C. Milmo, *Independent* 8 February 2008). The case also raised a discussion about the description of the murdered women used in the news.

Research the story and consider the relationship of women's naming to each of violence, gender and justice.

Complementary Readings

H. Benedict (1992) *Virgin or Vamp: How the Press Covers Sex Crimes*. (New York and Oxford: Oxford University Press), includes the William Kennedy Smith rape trial and the Mike Tyson case and focuses on myths and journalistic attitudes.

K. Boyle (2003) *Media and Violence* (London: Sage), ch. 3, pp. 57–93 looks at violent male celebrities including O.J. Simpson, and ch. 4, pp. 94–112 includes accounts of news about Rose West and Myra Hindley.

Y. Jewkes (2004) *Media and Crime* (London: Sage) is an accessible textbook that explains very clearly why crime is so newsworthy.

M. Wykes (2001) *News, Crime and Culture* (London: Pluto Press), ch. 1, pp. 8–29 explains the importance of the news for criminology. Ch. 6 and ch. 7 look at intimate killing and sex in the news.

C. Carter and K. Weaver (2006) *Critical Readings: Violence and the Media* (Buckingham: Open University Press) includes sections on theory, production, representation and audiences.

For an analysis of some of the press coverage of the Soham case see P.J. Jones and C. Wardle (2008) '"No emotion, no sympathy": the visual construction of Maxine Carr', in *Crime, Media, Culture* 4(1): 53–71. This journal is a great source of articles on the media and crime.

3

INTIMACY, SECRETS AND STATISTICS

Chapter 3 reviews the actual data on violent and sexual crime. It looks in detail at the empirical evidence, extricating details about both victims and offenders and critically assessing the relationship between victim and offender in violent, sexual crimes. It draws on local and national crime/victimisation surveys and compares the UK data to that available internationally in order to establish the predominant patterns for crimes of violence and sexual offending. More than anything, it seeks to reveal the nature of the relationship between victim and offender that is so often characterised by intimacy in such crime but most frequently publicised as anything other than intimate.

The chapter explores the main sources of information about gendered violence before examining difficulties these sources face as a measure of such violence. In examining these difficulties, domestic violence is used as a case-study. This discussion provides an important context without which the evidence that follows cannot be properly understood. Once the problems and, indeed, possibilities in measuring gendered violence have been covered, the chapter moves on to consider the measures revealed. It discusses the evidence about sex and violent crime, detailing the patterns of offending shown therein. Indeed, having presented this evidence, the chapter moves on to problematise the familiar assumptions about the 'dangerous stranger' and the 'home as haven'. Contrasting these assumptions to both national and international evidence, the chapter considers just *who* presents the most common threat to women and their children and *where* this threat is encountered. Consideration is also given to whether or not the same threats are presented to men.

Crime Measures and Gendered Violence

Information about gendered violence can be obtained from three main sources – records from the police and other (criminal justice) services, national crime or victimisation surveys and local surveys. All encounter problems in measuring crime more generally (see Maguire 1997, 2002) and these problems are repeated as each is used to measure gendered violence in particular.

National recorded crime statistics could be used to measure violence that has been reported to, and recorded by, the police, in order to measure gendered violence nationally. Locally, the police also produce their own statistics and these could be used to measure such violence in a local area. Records from other service providers also provide information that assists measurement in relation to gendered violence. Indeed, domestic violence, rape and so on could all be measured through examining information about victims' use of hospitals, sexual health services, housing services, telephone helplines, refuges, etc.

Stanko (2000) provides a variation on using service providers' records as a measure. Stanko's research focused on domestic violence and sought to estimate the routine demand for domestic violence services. Stanko collected information from several services about their domestic violence provision on one day in 2000, Thursday 28 September. She then used these findings to generalise demand and, in doing so, produce a 'snap-shot' of domestic violence nationally.

Stanko and colleagues (Stanko et al. 1998; Stanko 2000) provide a further variation on using service providers' records as a measure. Focusing on the London Borough of Hackney, these researchers explored the records of certain agencies and organisations and estimated the proportion of domestic violence in these records. Using findings from other research (McGibbon et al. 1989), Stanko and colleagues developed a prevalence measure and, from this, arrived at a possible prevalence for one year in Hackney. For example, they estimated that around 1,250 women throughout Hackney in 1996 reported at least one incident of domestic violence to the police that was recorded as a crime. Drawing on McGibbon et al.'s (1989) finding that 24% of women experiencing domestic violence would have contacted the police, Stanko and colleagues applied the prevalence measure to estimate how many women aged 16 and over in Hackney experienced domestic violence in 1996. Based on information about Hackney's female population, these researchers then arrived at a possible prevalence. Stanko and colleagues applied the prevalence measure to information collected from each agency's records.

As we describe in the next section, however, police records or records from other services provide only a limited measure in relation to gendered violence. Thus, other measures are needed. Since the first survey in 1982, the British Crime Survey (BCS) has sought to provide this alternative. The BCS asks samples of the public – private householders aged 16 and over – to describe crimes committed against them within a given recent time period. Over 50,000 interviews take place each year. The number of respondents has increased five-fold since the 1980s and, in 1994, the BCS moved to Computer Assisted Personal Interviewing (CAPI).

Very soon after it developed, though, it became clear that the BCS was not without its problems in measuring gendered violence. Early British Crime Surveys, for example, asked about sexual offences, but, because so few were reported, were unable to produce reliable estimates of their prevalence. Those estimates that were produced suggested that less than 1% of women were subjected to rape and other sexual assault each year – a staggering under-estimation of the problem, as became increasingly clear with the development of more sophisticated measurement around issues such as sexual violence (Percy and Mayhew 1997; Walby and Myhill 2001).

The first moves to deal more appropriately with sensitive topics such as sexual violence came in the 1992 BCS, with the introduction of a self-completion component. Initially, this self-completion component was in pen-and-paper style – respondents completed the questions in private and then put their completed answers into a sealed envelope. The 'second generation' (Walby and Myhill 2001) surveys that have developed in the last decade have gone further in both challenging the traditional BCS focus and adopting increasingly sensitive survey methods. The 1996 BCS, for example, included for the first time a dedicated domestic violence 'module', which introduced a special set of questions on domestic violence, and a specially designed computer-assisted self-interviewing component (CASI). Here, the respondent operates a lap-top computer themselves and much greater emphasis is placed on respondent anonymity and confidentiality. These developments led to more than a doubling of the rate of domestic violence reported against women, when comparing the 1992 survey with that conducted in 1996. Indeed, the 1996 survey was described at its publication as providing 'the most reliable findings to date on the extent of domestic violence in England and Wales' (Mirlees-Black 1999: iii). Subsequent British Crime Surveys have included dedicated modules on stalking (1998), sexual victimisation (1998, 2000), interpersonal violence (2001) and intimate violence (2004/05).[1] All have been explored through the use of CASI.

Other countries have gone even further in attempting to measure gendered violence and have introduced separate and specialist surveys on national violence against women. Unsurprisingly, these surveys have succeeded in uncovering violence untouched even by existing national crime surveys. National violence against women surveys began in Canada in the Statistics Canada Violence against Women Survey (Statistics Canada 1993) and have since been conducted in Australia, Finland, Iceland and the US, though not in Britain (Walby and Myhill 2001; see Dobash and Dobash 1995). In some countries, surveys have further developed to examine personal violence against both women and men.

These national surveys, though, are not the first surveys to be dedicated to the measurement of violence against women. Indeed, dedicated violence against women surveys first developed in the mid to late 1980s, conducted by feminist researchers and activists. At the time these surveys were pioneering, lifting the lid on a whole range of behaviour that had hitherto remained hidden from view. These dedicated surveys set out to reveal not just the regularity of the abuse that women experience from men but also the *range* of such abuse (Hanmer and Saunders 1984; Radford 1987, McGibbon et al. 1989). Dedicated violence against women surveys developed from, and have been designed around, concern to explore women's lived experiences, inviting women themselves to name the abuse rather than imposing on them categories to be measured.

This is also true of surveys that have focused on certain categories of gendered violence, such as dedicated 'domestic violence' surveys or dedicated 'rape' surveys. The classic dedicated domestic violence survey, for example, was conducted by Jayne Mooney in North London. Mooney (1996, 1999, 2000) also set out to establish women's own definitions of domestic violence. Other prominent (Mirlees-Black 1999) dedicated domestic violence surveys include Dominy and Radford's (1996) research in Surrey, and Painter and Farrington's (1998) national survey. One of the earliest local surveys on rape was that conducted in London by Ruth Hall (1985). With the help of the campaigning group Women Against Rape, Hall conducted a Women's Safety Survey with 2,000 women. Internationally, the most famous dedicated survey is that conducted by Diana Russell into rape in marriage (Russell 1982).

Thus, many of the same measures that are used in relation to crime in general can be used to measure gendered violence in particular. In addition, research has been devised around these general measures and the measures themselves have also been developed in order to reveal more information about both the extent and experience of gendered violence. Notwithstanding these sometimes innovative developments, though, there remain problems in attempting to assess the incidence, prevalence, distribution, and so on, of gendered violence. Largely, these problems derive from the phenomenon being measured. Indeed, in the following discussion, we examine in more detail some of the problems in measuring gendered violence, before moving on to describe the possibilities in doing so.

Measuring Sex and Violent Crime – Problems and Possibilities

The first and most persistent problem in measuring gendered violence centres on definitional difficulties – how the phenomenon comes to be defined. There have been many definitions offered around women, gender and violence. All present problems for measurement. Where, for example, does Liz Kelly's pioneering 'continuum of sexual violence' leave efforts at measurement? Clearly, if we are measuring the extent of 'sexual violence', as defined by Kelly, a huge number of women will be affected. Indeed, Kelly herself suggests that using the concept of a continuum of sexual violence emphasises that 'all women experience sexual violence at some point in their lives' (1987: 59). Yet, does this render measurement pointless? Even if we limit our measurement to sex and violent crime, problems remain. Because, for example, rape is limited to penile penetration, a range of other abusive behaviours will be hidden from a measure which focuses only on the crime of rape.

In turn, these definitional difficulties affect the *sources* of measurement used. Efforts to measure 'sexual violence', as defined by Kelly, would have little, if any, success were they to rely, for example, on police recorded crime statistics, since much sexual violence is not criminal *per se*. On the other hand, efforts to measure rape, as defined in section 1 of the Sexual Offences Act 2003, would have little success if relying on dedicated violence against women surveys since popular assumptions about men, women, violence and sex mean that many women who have experienced 'rape' do not regard themselves as a victim of 'crime'.

More broadly, many of the same problems encountered in measuring crime in general apply equally to efforts to measure gendered violence in particular. Yet, there are certain aspects to much gendered violence that mean the main measurement tools used encounter further problems in this regard. In the following discussion, we demonstrate these problems using domestic violence as a case-study.

Case-study: measuring domestic violence.

Again, the first and most persistent problem in measuring domestic violence is how we define it. Does the word 'domestic' mean that we should restrict our measurement to intimate familial relationships, such as those within marriage or cohabitation? What about abuse of women by men with whom they have a sexual relationship but no joint living arrangements or by other male family members (such as fathers or brothers) or by male friends or colleagues? Should this abuse really be excluded from our measurement? Likewise, does the word 'violence' mean that we should restrict our measurement to violence and thus exclude other controlling or abusive behaviours? Yet, some would regard such behaviours as 'violence' and 'violent'. What does violence mean? In addition, whose definition of 'domestic violence' should we use? Relying on, for example, the Home Office's definition could allow changes in incidence and prevalence to be monitored over time and over different areas but relying on women's own definitions allows a much fuller 'measure' of the lived experience of violence in the home. Thus, as in relation to other problems, in relation to this phenomenon, definitional difficulties present measurement difficulties.

More broadly, records from the police, national crime surveys and dedicated surveys each encounter problems in measuring domestic violence. Police records do not include offences that do not come to police notice. A considerable number of those experiencing or who have experienced domestic violence will never seek assistance from the police (or, indeed, other service providers) or will seek assistance only following years of repeated and severe abuse and violence. These victims will therefore be excluded, either totally or partially, from police records. Between a half and two-thirds of women tell nobody when they first experience domestic violence – the average time taken to disclose is between one and two years (Mooney 1994, cited in Mooney 1999).

There are many reasons that make women reluctant to disclose their experiences of domestic violence. Women's terrible distress following the abuse can be compounded by feelings of shame and embarrassment – women often hide or minimise the harm they have suffered. Women's reluctance to disclose is also based on fear, supported by threats, that seeking assistance will provoke further violence and retaliation. Some women are unaware that assistance is available; others have concerns about not being taken seriously. Others fear that their need to make their own decisions

(Continued)

(Continued)

about the pace and process of escape from a violent partner will be undermined and their decision-making taken out of their hands when the police or other services become involved. Women also have tremendous fears that a domestic violence disclosure might lead to their children being removed from them. Others simply do not believe they are deserving of assistance. Years of abuse leave women feeling worthless and undeserving.

Women's general reluctance to report their experiences is compounded by their particular reluctance to report to the police. Research into domestic abuse has found that many women do not perceive that the police have a role in their situation – 'they do a good job generally, but this was a domestic – nothing to do with them' (Hoyle 1998: 188). In some cases, this is because women normalise their partner's abuse. This 'normalising' of abuse is described by Bush and Hood-Williams, who found in their research in London that women did not 'make the transition from seeing abuse as part of [their] everyday experience of life to defining [their] very identity in terms of the abuse' (1995: 17). Abuse that is seen as 'normal' is not seen as 'criminal' and is, thus, not perceived to be a 'police matter'.

The statistical attrition (Ferrante et al. 1996) in domestic violence that begins with women's reluctance to report to the police continues with the recording practices of the police. Police discretion means that police decision-making can determine whether and how a domestic violence case is recorded. The first point at which these cases can be 'screened out' is incident classification. Control room operators in Hoyle's (1998) Thames Valley research were asked about the classification they would give to a call from a woman claiming to have been assaulted by her partner. Hoyle (1998; Sorsby and Shapland 1995) found that fewer than half the operators agreed on a classification.

Decisions taken by attending officers can also screen out domestic violence. The police might decide that no 'offence' has occurred or that the incident is not worth recording. The offence might be recorded and then officially 'no-crimed' later. In pioneering research in the 1980s, Susan Edwards found that in one London police division, of all arrests made following an allegation of (domestic) violence, a crime sheet was opened in only one-third of cases. In the remaining two-thirds, charges were brought against the abuser for breach of the peace and drunkenness – not for assault or common assault, even though assault was the initial complaint (Edwards 1989). Repeated Home Office guidance since the early 1990s has warned the police against such practices in domestic violence cases. Nonetheless, police failures to regard (and thus record) 'domestics' as 'real crime' appear time and again in the literature.

As in relation to crime in general, since national crime surveys developed in Britain in the 1980s, their use in relation to domestic crime in particular has been to uncover violence otherwise hidden from police records or records from other service providers. Yet, surveys too have their own 'dark figure'. Clearly, women's fears and shame about having experienced domestic violence might make them reluctant to disclose their experiences. The limited amount of time available to the questioner means it is often hard to tease out details of traumatic events. Women may be reluctant to describe incidents when other people are present in the house or room at the time of the interview – they will be especially reluctant to describe incidents involving a partner or household member who is present. Also, not all incidents occurring within the relevant time-scale will be remembered and respondent fatigue (Ferrante et al. 1996) can be a problem where victims have many incidents to report – often the case with domestic violence. Another problem is that, after a series of questions about other crimes, a sudden change of emphasis to questions about a topic as sensitive as domestic violence may result in an almost knee-jerk response of 'no' (Walby and Myhill 2001).

Indeed, there remains a high probability that the BCS underestimates the real extent of domestic violence (Walby and Myhill 2001). Perhaps one of the most serious limitations of the BCS in this regard is that not all incidents will be defined by the respondent as relevant to a *crime* survey (Mirlees-Black 1995; Walby and Myhill 2001). A further problem the BCS encounters is its sampling frame. Limitation to those permanently resident in domestic households (to the exclusion of those in temporary or refuge accommodation) potentially excludes those suffering severe and repeated violence. Traditionally, the BCS has also concentrated on physical assaults and/or frightening threats between people who are in or who have been in an 'intimate' relationship, thus excluding measurement of psychologically controlling and emotionally abusive behaviour and/or measurement of violence between those not in a sexual relationship. The 2004/05 BCS moved to overcome some of these problems, for the first time measuring emotional or financial abuse between partners, in addition to measuring emotional/financial abuse, frightening threats and physical assaults by family members other than partners and by measuring sexual assault by partners or family members. Clearly, through including both sexual abuse and harassment as 'partner abuse', the 2004/05 BCS takes a much broader approach to measurement than that taken in previous British Crime Surveys and, in doing so, is better placed to reveal the combined abuse that women experience from their male partners.

Local and/or dedicated surveys are designed around concern to explore this combined abuse and to examine women's *broad* experiences, inviting women themselves to name the abuse rather than imposing on them categories to be measured. Yet, dedicated domestic violence surveys have also run into methodological difficulties. Although, as we discuss below, these surveys have succeeded in revealing the considerable violence and abuse that women face in their day-to-day lives, there remains a chance that they also underestimate the prevalence and incidence of domestic abuse, not least because, however sensitive the questioning used, the shame and embarrassment attached to domestic violence will lead many survivors to avoid disclosing their experiences. These surveys have also attracted significant criticism for *over*estimating the extent of domestic violence.

(Continued)

(Continued)

Numerous commentators criticise feminist researchers for promulgating 'myths' through using methodologies that exaggerate the prevalence and incidence of violence against women. These researchers are accused of 'advocacy research' and of choosing methodologies that enable them to promote their own ideological views. Certainly, men's rights campaigners have challenged feminist research on the extent of domestic violence, dismissing it as 'sheer drivel, devoid of any academic merit' (http://www.ukmm.org.uk) and of 'dubious quality ... involving samples that don't stand up to scrutiny' (Phillips, *Sunday Times* 15 November, 1998).

Thus, domestic violence presents some very particular problems for successful measurement. The problems here, though, are not exclusive to violence in the home. Domestic violence is a useful case-study to demonstrate how particular aspects cause difficulties in measurement but many of the same problems are presented by other gender violence issues.

Yet, although it is probable that the real extent of problems such as domestic violence and rape will be hidden from efforts to measure them, providing even a limited measure has value. Indeed, in relation to 'violence against women', Desai and Saltzman argue that:

Accurate measurement is essential if we are to identify high-risk populations, track changes in incidence and prevalence, monitor the effectiveness of programmes, identify and understand the consequences of victimisation, allocate resources and make policy decisions effectively to reduce violence. Only with accurate measurement can we determine whether resource allocations, programmes and policy decisions are having a beneficial effect on victims and reducing the magnitude of the problem. (2001: 35)

One value of measuring gendered violence is certainly that measurement enables a proper assessment of its distribution throughout the community to be made (Ferrante et al. 1996; Mirlees-Black 1999). This assessment can then inform the development of intervention and preventative programmes. Indeed, unless the possible extent of the problem is known, whether generally or in particular populations, it becomes almost impossible to begin the process of establishing programmes to address it or to assess the effectiveness of intervention and preventative measures.

Further, in order to understand the resource implications of gendered violence, it is almost imperative to know about its possible extent (Stanko et al. 1998). Measurement will certainly provide some understanding of the demand for services from both the voluntary and statutory sectors. In turn, estimating possible demand for services can provide a measure of the cost of providing those services and enable service providers to use resources effectively. It can also provide a measure of the number of workers needed to provide services – a particular consideration in the voluntary sector – the need for specialist workers and the need for the training of all workers.

Information about the possible extent of gendered violence can also be used to raise awareness about it in policy circles and so improve understanding in such places. Certainly, over the past three decades, feminists have endeavoured to uncover the extent of domestic violence, rape, incest, etc. and use their findings to encourage policy makers and others to take these problems more seriously. At the same time, policy initiatives responding to certain crimes are often supported by arguments based on numerical representations of the 'scale of the problem' (Maguire 1997). Indeed, the government's 'Living Without Fear' document, which heralded a flurry of activity on gendered violence in government circles in the late 1990s and early 2000s, describes the 'sheer scale of violence and abuse [against women]' (Women's Unit 1999: Foreword). It claims that the statistics it presents about the extent of domestic violence, rape, women's fear of crime and so on are 'unacceptable facts. We cannot live with them' (Women's Unit 1999: 4).

Finally, understanding the possible extent of gendered violence is valuable to understanding 'the problem' and, crucially, to *popular* understanding of the problem. In turn, understanding 'the problem' is valuable in challenging the assumptions that pervade popular representations and in creating an account based on women's lived experiences.

In the next section, we move on to do just that, by presenting the evidence about violence, sex and crime.

Violence, Sex and Crime

Before examining the empirical evidence on violent and sex crime in particular, it is first useful to explore what Braithwaite lists as the first 'key point' about crime in general – that '[it] is committed disproportionately by males' (1989: 44). It is certainly the case as put by Heidensohn (2002) that:

- women commit a smaller share of all crimes that men do
- women's crimes are fewer, less serious and less likely to be repeated, and
- in consequence, women form a smaller proportion of the prison population.

Indeed, in 2002, 316,000 or just 19% of 1.6 million known offenders were female (Home Office 2003). In the same year, 2002, males convicted of all offences at all courts in England and Wales outnumbered females by almost 4.5 to 1 (Home Office 2003). Home Office statistics consistently show that the proportion of women who have a criminal conviction is much lower than the proportion of men who have one. As regards the offences that men and women commit, in 2002 about the same proportions (30% compared with 28%) of men and women's known offending related to indictable offences (those which may be tried in a Crown Court). Importantly, though, there are significant differences between men's and women's offending *by offence*. In 2002, for example, the men to women ratio for theft and handling stolen goods stood at 2.6: 1. For violence against the person, the ratio increased to 5.5:1 – for sexual offences the ratio further increased to a massive 55:1 (Home Office 2003). It is also the case that men are far more likely than women to be murderers. In 2004/05, for example, 91% of suspects in homicide cases where proceedings had concluded were men (Coleman et al. 2006).

Even at this stage, then, patterns in the evidence are beginning to appear. These patterns, though, become more interesting as we move on to consider more detailed evidence about, first, violent crime and, secondly, sex crime.[2]

Violent crime

Violent offending is largely the preserve of men. Men are more likely to commit violence against the person and are much more likely to commit murder. Serious, violent offending is, it seems, 'a man thing'. Interestingly, violent victimisation is also largely a male phenomenon. Home Office measures, for example, reveal that, year on year, around 70% of homicide victims are male. In 2004/05, the percentage stood at 72% (Coleman et al. 2006).

Successive British Crime Surveys support the suggestion that most violent victimisation happens to men. In the 2005/06 BCS, for example, the risk of being a victim of violent crime was 3.4%. This risk more than trebled for young men (aged 16–24). Indeed, 12.6% of young men had experienced a violent crime of some sort in the year prior to the BCS and were the most at-risk group. For women, the risk of experiencing violent crime was much lower – 4.3% of men experienced violence, as compared to 2.5% of women. As an interesting introduction to the discussions that follow, domestic violence was the only category of violence where the risks for women were higher than for men (Jansson et al. 2007).

Internationally, these patterns remain consistent. The 2005 Personal Safety Survey in Australia found, for example, that men were just under twice as likely to have experienced an incident of violence (any incident involving the occurrence, attempt or threat of either physical or sexual assault) in the 12 months prior to the survey – 11% as compared to 5.8% of women. In the 12 months prior to the survey, 10% of men and 4.7% of women had experienced physical violence (Australian Bureau of Statistics 2005). Likewise, the 2000 American National Violence Against Women survey found that 3.4% of surveyed men and 1.9% of surveyed women reported having been physically assaulted in the previous 12 months (Tjaden and Thoennes 2000).

Thus, in addition to committing more violent crime, men are also more victimised through violence than women. This pattern starts to change, though, as our attention turns to *sexual* offending and victimisation.

Sex crime

Again, most sexual offences are committed by men. Indeed, it is in relation to sex crime that gender is *the* variable in offending patterns. It is also *the* variable in victimisation patterns. By far the greatest proportion of such offences are committed against women. Home Office statistics, for example, reveal that there were 14,449 recorded rapes in 2005/06 – 92% of which were of a woman (Jansson et al. 2007).

BCS findings support this gendering in relation to sex crime. The 2001 BCS, for example, included questions on 'inter-personal violence', designed to measure domestic violence, sexual assault and stalking, together in the same questionnaire (Walby and Allen 2004). In the findings, 0.5% of women said they had experienced serious sexual assault in the year prior to the 2001 BCS survey, including 0.3% who said they had experienced rape. A further 2% said they had suffered less serious sexual assault. Amongst men, 0.2% reported some form of sexual assault in this period. Further, 24% of women and 5% of men reported having suffered some form of sexual victimisation at least once in their lifetimes and 17% of women and 2% of men said they had been sexually victimised at least once since age 16. Further, 7% of women said they had suffered a serious sexual assault at least once in their lifetime – 5% said they had been raped and 3% said they had suffered some other serious (penetrative) sexual assault. Amongst men, 1.5% of men reported a serious sexual assault at least once in their lives, 0.9% reported having been raped (see Finney 2006).

Again, these patterns are supported in international comparisons. The Personal Safety Survey in Australia found, for example, that 1.6% of women and 0.6% of men reported having experienced an incident of sexual violence (including sexual assault and sexual threat) in the 12 months prior to the survey, and 19% of women compared to 5.5% of men reported having experienced sexual violence since the age of 15 (Australian Bureau of Statistics 2005). The 2000 American National Violence Against Women survey also found that women were around three times more likely to have experienced sexual victimisation in the previous year. Indeed, 0.3% of women reported having been raped (including forced vaginal, anal and oral sex) in the 12 months prior to the survey as compared to 0.1% of men. Further, 17.6% of women and 3.0% of men reported having experienced a completed or attempted rape at some time in their lives (Tjaden and Thoennes 2000).

Thus, men commit more crime than women. Men certainly commit more violent crime and are also more violently victimised than women. However, the prevailing pattern in the empirical evidence, in which men dominate both offending and victimisation, begins to change in relation to sexual crime. Here, men are the majority of offenders but are no longer the most victimised. Again, though, the evidence becomes more interesting as we move on to consider further information about patterns of offending.

Patterns of offending

Successive crime measures reveal that, in general, men who are violent to other men are violent to *strangers*. In contrast, men who are violent to women are violent to *known* women – commonly, their wives, partners and lovers. This pattern holds as regards sexual violence. For example, Home Office statistics reveal that, in 2004/05, 41% of male homicide victims knew the main or only suspect, while just 15% were killed by their partner or ex-partner. In contrast, 70% of female homicide victims knew the main or only suspect at the time of the offence – 64% of those female victims acquainted with the suspect were killed by a current or former partner or lover (Coleman et al. 2006).

These data are supported by BCS findings. Certainly, in the 2005/06 BCS, 77% of victims of violence classed as 'stranger violence' were men. In contrast, 80% of victims of violence classed as 'domestic violence' were women. Alongside this, 45% of violent incidents against men were incidents of stranger violence, as compared to 21% of incidents against women. In contrast, 31% of violent incidents against women were classed as domestic violence, as compared to just 5% of those against men (Jansson et al. 2007).

In relation to sexual violence, the 2001 BCS found that nearly half (45%) of those responsible for less serious sexual assaults against women (flashing, unwanted sexual touching and sexually threatening behaviour) that caused fear, alarm or distress were known to the victim. The more serious the sexual assault reported to the 2001 survey, the more likely it was that the perpetrator was known to the victim. The majority (54%) of rapes were committed by intimates (husbands, partners, ex-husband and ex-partners) – in just 17% of rapes and 18% of serious sexual assaults was the perpetrator a stranger.

Again, the evidence available internationally is consistent with the UK evidence. For example, in the Australian Personal Safety Survey, of the men who had been physically assaulted in the previous year, 74% were assaulted by a male stranger and 27% were assaulted by their current or previous partner. Of the women who had been physically assaulted in the previous year, 18% were assaulted by a male stranger but 38% were assaulted by their male current or previous partner. For physical assaults since age 15, men were more likely to be assaulted by a male stranger whereas women were more often assaulted by a male previous partner (Australian Bureau of Statistics 2005). The 2000 American National Violence Against Women survey also found that men were more likely to be victimised by a stranger whilst women were more likely to be victimised by intimate partners. Indeed, 50.4% of the men who reported being raped, physically assaulted and/or stalked since age 18 were victimised by a stranger – 16.2% were victimised by a female intimate partner. In contrast, 64% of women who reported being raped, physically assaulted and/or stalked since age 18 were victimised by a current or former husband, co-habiting partner, boyfriend or date – 14.6% were victimised by a stranger (Tjaden and Thoennes 2000).

Summarising so far, the empirical evidence reveals that men dominate both violent offending and victimisation – men are most violent and are most violently victimised. Men also dominate sexual offending, though women predominate in sexual victimisation. In examining patterns of offending, further details are revealed. Men who are victims of violence are likely to be victims of stranger violence. Women, on the other hand, are significantly more likely to be victims of 'domestic' violence. Central to violent sex crimes, then, is the relationship between offender and victim. In the next section, the centrality of this relationship is examined and the ordinary intimacy of much violent crime is explored more fully.

Stranger Danger or Home Dangerous Home?

The family man?

As is discussed more fully in Chapter 5, during the nineteenth century, marriage and family came to be seen as the 'proper' arrangement around which people were to organise. The home came into being as a distinct environment set off from work and, in principle, became a place of emotional support (Giddens 1992). Even in modern times, marriage and the family are promoted through various privileges and the family remains in the popular consciousness as a haven from 'the outside world' . Of course, this construction promotes and prioritises the heterosexual partnership, which is conceptualised as preserving this haven from outside dangers. Husbands at home are presented in direct contrast to the dangerous stranger who roams in dark alleyways. Further, women are encouraged to seek the protection of a known and trusted man to keep her safe from these 'monsters', 'beasts' and 'perverts' that lurk, indiscriminately attacking women.

Clearly, the evidence already detailed presents an immediate challenge to these assumptions. In the following discussion, we explore further the discordance between the popular consciousness about female and male relations and the empirical evidence about the dangers women face from their male partners. This section offers further information from police records, BCS 'modules' on domestic violence and other dedicated domestic violence research.

Dangerous love

Police records, records from other service providers and court records provide some measure of the dangers women face from their male partners. This measure can be either local or national. In her research, in which she attempted to provide a 'snap-shot' of domestic violence on one day in 2000, Stanko (2000; see also Stanko et al. 1998) found that one in four crimes of violence (including sexual offences, assaults between men, football, racist and homophobic violence) in the Metropolitan Police's records were domestic. From the information collected from police records, Stanko estimates that every minute in the UK the police receive a call from the public for assistance in cases of domestic violence and that an average of just under 3% of all calls to the police are for such assistance. Stanko also found that on the 'snap-shot' day one in 15 referrals to Victim Support Schemes in England were for domestic violence. She also found that on this day the domestic violence organisation, 'Refuge', housed 110 women and 102 children in London alone and were unable to house a further 32 women. Refuge also received 200 calls to their National Helpline – the Women's Aid national helpline received 127 calls and a further 941 calls could not be answered. Finally, Stanko found that almost one in five *Relate* couple-counselling sessions held on the day mentioned domestic violence as a problem in the marriage.

In her research in London (Stanko et al. 1998; see Stanko 2000), Stanko calculated possible prevalence using different services' records. The highest possible prevalence was based on information taken from a doctors' waiting room. This prevalence was one in nine – in other words, that a staggering one in nine women were experiencing or had experienced domestic violence in *one year* in Hackney.

National and local crime surveys support the suggestion that male violence in the home is far from an uncommon occurrence. Of the women surveyed, 23% reported to the 1996 BCS that they had experienced an assault from a current or former partner at some time in their lives – 26% said they had experienced an assault and/or frightening threats (Mirlees-Black 1999). Further, 4.2% of women said they had been assaulted by a current or former partner in the previous year – 5.9% said they had experienced physical assault and/or frightening threats. Importantly, the 1996 BCS also reveals the *repeat* nature of much of this domestic victimisation. Indeed, half the women who reported to the BCS that they had been assaulted by their partners in the previous year had been assaulted three or more times.

At the time of writing, the most recent BCS findings about violence in the home are from the 2004/05 BCS (Finney 2006). The 2004/05 BCS found that 28% of women reported having experienced one or more incidents of *non-sexual partner* abuse (emotional or financial abuse, threats or physical force by a current or former partner) since age 16. Further, 28% of women had experienced one or more forms of any partner abuse (*non-sexual abuse*, sexual assault or stalking) since the age of 16. Amongst victims of any partner abuse, 16% of women experienced sexual assault and 24% of women experienced stalking by a partner since age 16. A significant minority (29%) of victims of any partner abuse experienced more than one form of violence (non-sexual abuse, sexual assault or stalking) – 6% of women had experienced all three forms. About one in 20 women (6%) had experienced one or more incidents of any partner abuse in the previous year.

The classic local domestic violence survey is that conducted by Jayne Mooney in North London. Mooney summarises the findings from her survey:

> Violence from a partner is scarcely a rare phenomenon. Whether it is defined as mental cruelty, threats, actual violence with injury or rape, it has occurred to at least one quarter to a third of all women in their lifetime. (1999: 31)

Mooney (1999) found further that 12% of women had experienced actual physical violence from their partners in the previous 12 months, 8% of all women had been injured and 6% raped by their partners (see Mooney 2000). Other local surveys find the same proportions. Painter and Farrington (1998) also found that numerous women had been coerced into sex:

- 58.1% had had sexual intercourse when reluctant or disinclined
- 13% had had sexual intercourse clearly against their will

- 5.1% had been threatened with violence
- 4.3% had been the victims of sexual violence.

Altogether, 13.9% of women had been raped – of whom nearly half had been raped as a result of threatened or actual violence. Most of the raped wives in Painter and Farrington's research said that they had been raped more than once in marriage – only 14.5% had been raped once – 39.7% had been raped two to five times and 45.8% had been raped six or more times.

Internationally, national violence against women surveys support the suggestion that violence from a male partner is a common occurrence in women's day-to-day lives. The Women's Safety, Australia survey (Australian Bureau of Statistics 1996) measured the incidence of physical and sexual violence against Australian women (aged 18 and above) during the 12 months prior to the survey and over their lifetimes. As regards violence (whether physical or sexual) from partners, the survey found that 2.6% of women who were married or in a *de facto* relationship had experienced an incident of violence from their partner in the previous year, while 8% reported having experienced an incident of violence at some point in their current relationship. Half of all women experiencing violence from a current partner had experienced more than one incident of violence – 12% of women experiencing violence from a current partner said they were at the time living in fear. Of the women who had ever been married or in a *de facto* relationship, 23% had experienced violence from a partner at some time in the relationship. Of the women who had been in a previous relationship, 42% reported violence from a previous partner.

The 2000 American National Violence Against Women survey (Tjaden and Thoennes 2000) found that 22.1% of women reported having been physically assaulted by an intimate partner at some time in their lives, with 1.3% having been assaulted by a current or former intimate partner in the previous year. The survey approximated that there had been around 4.5 million physical assaults committed against American women by intimate partners in the previous year. The survey also found that 7.7% of women had been raped (classed as forced vaginal, anal or oral sex) by a current or former intimate partner at some time in their lives – 0.2% had been raped by a current or former partner in the previous year.

The evidence from both national and local measures, and comparing the UK evidence to that available internationally, demonstrates that, for many women, the heterosexual partnership is not a safe place. Nationally and internationally, many, many women are living in or have escaped from heterosexual partnerships in which they experience or have experienced repeated violence, abuse, harassment and intimidation. Assumptions about the 'home as haven' as compared to the 'dangerous stranger' do not hold. Rather, women are more likely to be murdered, assaulted, threatened and raped by men they know and, in particular, by men with whom they are having or have had a 'romantic' attachment. The single most significant risk to women's safety and the safety of their children[3] is entering into a heterosexual partnership arrangement.

Are men victims too?

From time to time in popular, policy and literature discussions, the question of men's domestic violence victimisation is raised. In newspapers and gossip magazines, we read about famous men who have been abused by their female partners. In policy discussions, we hear the government using much more gender-neutral language in relation to domestic violence and other such matters (Welsh 2008). In literature discussions we see 'periodic revivals of interest' (Gadd et al. 2002: 1) in the debate about men's victimisation. In the literature, the most obvious support for the suggestion that men also face extensive domestic victimisation comes from the so-called 'Family Violence Research', associated with the Americans, Murray Straus and Richard Gelles. The most common interpretation put on this research has been that male and female partners use similar levels of violence to each other and that men and women are 'equal combatants'.[4] But do men really face the same domestic violence victimisation as women?

In the 1996 BCS, 15% of men reported they had experienced an assault from a current or former partner at some time in their lives – 17% said they had experienced an assault and/or frightening threats (Mirlees-Black 1999). Further, 4.2% of *both* women and men said they had been assaulted by a current or former partner in the previous year – 5.9% of women and 4.9% of men said they had experienced physical assault and/or frightening threats. The 1996 Scottish Crime Survey also found that comparable proportions of women and men reported that they had experienced force or threatened violence in the past year – 6% of women and 4% of men (MVA 2000). These findings do appear to suggest that women and men face equal domestic violence victimisation.

However, the 1996 BCS also found considerable differences between women and men's *experiences* of domestic victimisation. Women certainly reported higher levels of repeat victimisation over the previous year – 12.1% of women compared with 5% of men had been assaulted three or more times and were termed 'chronic female victims'. Women were also twice as likely as men to have been injured by a partner in the previous year (2.2% compared with 1.1%) and women were three times as likely to have suffered frightening threats (3.8% compared with 1.5%). Women were also more likely to report feeling 'very upset' on the last occasion they were assaulted and found assaults considerably more frightening. The effects were also longer lasting for women than men – 38% of chronic female victims said they were still upset at the time of the BCS survey, compared with 11% of chronic male victims. Finally, almost no men defined their experience as a crime but 39% of chronic female victims defined their most recent experience as a crime.

It appears, then, that even in research suggesting that *extent* is comparable between men and women, the *experience* of domestic victimisation that is revealed remains very different. Successive research findings certainly support the suggestion in the 1996 BCS that the outcomes of domestic victimisation are less serious for men. Gadd et al. (2003) questioned 22 men who had reported domestic victimisation to the 2000 SCS about their experiences of abuse. Gadd et al. (2003) found that just four of these 22 men said they lived in fear of their partners and just nine of the 22 considered themselves to be 'victims of domestic violence'. Likewise,

Dobash and Dobash (2004) conducted 190 interviews with 95 couples about the violence that each partner had used against the other in the year preceding the research. These researchers found considerable differences between women and men's reactions to the violence that each had experienced. Women's reactions to violence from a male partner were feeling frightened (79%), abused (65%), alone (65%), helpless (60%) and trapped (57%). Men's reactions were much less negative. Most men who described their response to violence from women partners were 'not bothered' (26%). Just 6% reported feeling victimised – 3% were *impressed* that their partner had managed to respond.

Reflecting on the 1996 BCS findings, the Home Office researcher Catriona Mirlees-Black (1999) suggests three explanations for women's and men's seeming comparable prevalence but non-comparable incidence and experience. First, it might be that prevalence *is* comparable between men and women but that the outcomes are less serious for the former because men are, in general, bigger and stronger. It might, as Mirlees-Black suggests, be that men's different experiences are based on greater strength. It is certainly the case that most men are better placed than women to *leave* abusive partners since they are in a stronger economic position and commonly do not have the same childcare responsibilities as women. Indeed, in research in Scotland (Gadd et al. 2002, 2003), of the nine men who had experienced serious violence from women partners, *none* was still living with his abuser. Mirlees-Black's second explanation is that prevalence is comparable but that men do not admit to more serious outcomes because of shame and embarrassment. Again, it might be the case that men do not admit to more serious victimisation. Certainly, in Gadd et al.'s (2002, 2003) research, many men mentioned embarrassment and humiliation at having been abused.

Mirlees-Black's third explanation is that it might be that men are more willing to report less serious victimisation to crime surveys that women feel is inappropriate to mention (Mirlees-Black 1999). On this last point, in a valuable piece of research, David Gadd and his colleagues conducted a follow-up study to the 2000 Scottish Crime Survey (SCS), in which 90 men had reported experiences of force or threat from partners. Gadd et al. (2002, 2003) questioned 46 men about their experiences of abuse. Of these, 31 said their report to the SCS was accurate but 13 said that they had not experienced violence from their partner (in fact, two of these men had never had a partner). A further two men refused to confirm or deny their report to the SCS that they had been abused by their partner. Most of the 13 men who denied experiencing abuse were surprised, even annoyed, that they had found their way into statistics about domestic violence. As it turned out, many had misunderstood the meaning of the term 'domestic violence' – one man had reported being attacked by his girlfriend's other partner, another talked about an argument with a friend about his marriage and another included a 'trick-or-treat' incident.

Furthermore, of the men who confirmed their report to the SCS (22 of the 31 agreed to be interviewed in the follow-up study), Gadd et al. suggest that many:

Presented accounts of abuse that were so contestable and contradictory that a persuasive case could be made for placing these men in categories which contravened the terms they used to describe themselves. (2002: 44)

More specifically, Gadd et al. suggest that:

> In short our suspicion was that at least half of the partners of the men who had experienced some form of force or threat would have also been able to offer accounts of repeat domestic abuse perpetrated against themselves. We suspect that these partners would have described abuse that was criminal. (2002: 44)

Interestingly, other research in this area has also found contradictions and inconsistencies in men's accounts of violence within their relationships. The Dobashes, for example, conducted interviews with couples about each partner's violence. The men in the research had all been convicted of an offence involving violence against their partner (Dobash and Dobash 2004). These researchers found that men reported significantly fewer violent events against their woman partners than were reported by the women themselves. Indeed, no direct physical violence was reported by 21.1% of women and 30.5% of men – notwithstanding that 80% of the men had been arrested for and convicted of an assault! Again, there was a difference between men and women's reports of the frequency of male violence: 31.6% of women reported five or more incidents perpetrated by their male partner – only 13.7% of men agreed that they'd perpetrated this number of incidents. Finally, the couples disagreed about the injuries inflicted by men upon women – again, men reported much less of their own violence than their women partners described.

One area in relation to which men and women were much more in agreement was women's use of violence. Just below half the men (46.3%) and women (40%) agreed, for example, that there had been *no* physical violence perpetrated by the woman against the man. Men and women also agreed about the frequency of female violence – 9.3% of men and 9.5% of women reported that women perpetrated five or more incidents.

Clearly, it might simply be that women and men's experiences are different because the violence and abuse that women experience *is more serious*. Certainly, in Dobash and Dobash's (2004) research, couples reported that men committed a much wider range of violent physical and sexual acts against women than women committed against men. Couples reported that many more men had committed *every* type of violent or threatening act than women had. They also reported that there were certain acts (choking, threatening to damage property and threatening to hit) which a large proportion of men had committed but which women seldom committed. Couples also agreed that there were some acts (most obviously, forced sex) which women *never* committed. Furthermore, Dobash and Dobash (2004) found that couples reported that many more men inflicted every type of injury against women that women did against men. Again, there were some injuries which a good proportion of men inflicted but which women rarely inflicted. Overall, the couples agreed that injuries which women inflicted upon men were less frequent and less severe. Most importantly here, Dobash and Dobash (2004) found that couples generally agreed that men's violence was 'serious' or 'very serious', but that women's violence was 'not serious' or 'slightly serious'. The vast majority of men (66.1%) and women (82%) described men's violence as 'serious' or 'very serious' – only 36% of women and 28.5% of men described women's violence in the same terms.

Clearly, some men do experience domestic violence and, further, experience violence that is profoundly distressing and potentially devastating (see also Grady 2002). However, the empirical evidence suggests that it is incorrect to claim that women and men face the same domestic victimisation. Certainly, one of the main concerns about this claim is that it fails to recognise the 'constellation of abuse' (Dobash and Dobash 2004) that commonly characterises women's but not men's domestic violence victimisation. In most cases, women's victimisation in the home is more repeated, more sustained, more serious, more frightening, more upsetting and more varied than men's. As we have demonstrated throughout this chapter, it also takes place in a context in which male violence is routine.

Conclusion

This chapter has explored the main sources of information about gendered violence before examining difficulties these sources face as a measure of gendered violence in particular. The most obvious problem in this regard appeared to centre on the definitional difficulties. Other problems were examined using domestic violence as a case-study. The chapter suggested, though, that, notwithstanding the problems in measuring gendered violence, there are important possibilities in doing so.

The chapter set out empirical evidence revealing that men dominate violent offending, violent victimisation and sexual offending, *but not* sexual victimisation, in which women predominate. Further, the evidence presented revealed that male victims of violence are likely to be victims of stranger violence whereas female victims are more likely to be victims of 'domestic' violence. Indeed, to close, the chapter turned to present further evidence about the ordinary intimacy of much violent crime. The popular consciousness depicts the home as the place to which most people run to get away from fear and violence (Smith 1989). As the chapter has demonstrated, though, the home and the heterosexual partnership is, for many women, the context of the most frightening violence of all.

The following chapter shifts from documenting the evidence for a relationship between gender and violence that has emerged so clearly since the 1980s, towards considering how criminology as a discipline developed largely devoid of any concern for gender until the later 1970s. It traces a shift towards 'gendering' crime largely as result of feminists' interest in women's lack of offending, and critically assesses emergent theoretical trajectories in the face of evidence detailed here of so much male violence against women within the intimate relationships of sex and family. Chapter 6 returns to some of the points raised here about family and home to try to better understand why violence is so gendered behind closed doors.

Notes: Issues for Reflection

1 How, why and with what effects have the BCS measures into gendered violence changed over time?

2 The focus of this book is not on women and crime but on gendered violence. Research more information about women, crime and justice.

What crimes do women commit? How do women offenders encounter criminal justice processes?

3 What are the implications for children of living in a domestic violence situation?

4 Critically examine Family Violence Research into domestic violence. As a starting point, see Dobash and Dobash (2004) and Grady (2002).

Complementary Readings

C. Mirlees-Black (1999) *Domestic Violence: Findings from a New British Crime Survey Self-Completion Questionnaire.*

Home Office Research Study 191 (London: Home Office) considers the data arising from the British Crime Survey on domestic violence.

S. Walby and A. Myhill (2001) 'New survey methodologies in researching violence against women', in *British Journal of Criminology*, 41: 502, offers new and more sensistive ways of researching women's experience of violence.

E.A. Stanko (2003) *The Meanings of Violence* (London: Routledge) considers the meanings of violence and includes studies of violence against children, prostitutes and in domestic contexts.

R.E. Dobash and R.P. Dobash (2004) 'Women's violence to men in intimate relationships, working on a puzzle', in *British Journal of Criminology*, 44: 324–49, considered men's experience of abuse by women partners.

4

GENDERING CRIMINOLOGY?

Much publicity about sex 'n violence relates to cases where a male stranger is the danger, such as the Yorkshire Ripper and Jill Dando's murderer. Alternatively, cases are reported in the media in ways that discursively deflect from or obscure the marital or familial context of gendered crimes, such as news coverage of the West Case (Wykes 1998). Yet, as the last chapter evidenced, most male crime against women and/or children occurs through 'intimate' relationships: victims are known to and by offenders, often within families or close communities. This chapter considers the roles of criminology and feminist politics in theorising such gendered crime. It critically assesses the contribution to criminology of feminism, which highlighted women's place in crime (Smart 1976, 1995; Heidensohn 1985; Allen 1987; Carlen and Worrall 1987). It examines a perhaps consequent diversion of attention from offending, which, as has already been discussed, is overwhelmingly male, and hence to the masculinities implicated in offending because of the overdue recognition of, and significant concentration on, the very often female victim. It assesses the extent to which this lack has not only impoverished theory, which remains slight on the strong link between masculinities and crime, with a few valuable exceptions (Newburn and Stanko 1994; Collier 1998; Goodey 1997; Messerschmidt 1993, 1997, 2000; Gadd and Jefferson 2007), but how the lack in theory also supports a diversion of resources in practice away from the real sites of violence towards the rare and extreme cases that comply with news values, political interests and public prurience.

The evidence for the intimacy of much violence is detailed in Chapter 3 and is well documented. In London alone: 'The Met receive 104,000 calls a year about domestic violence, about one every six minutes' (Cowan 2004). Yet the more evidence there is of intimate crime, the less successful seem the attempts to prevent or punish it. For example: 'Although reporting of rape continues to rise – by 20% in 2002, convictions in England and Wales are at a 30-year low' (Cowan 2004). Chapter 7 discusses this in detail. The price of such damage is not just physical or emotional but economic (see Walby 2004 and Chapter 9 below).

Crimes such as these are part of a familiar, repetitive contemporary trope serving a range of evaluative discursive genres, from law through media to gossip, with the effect that the relative modernity of crime *per se*, let alone any concern with gendered crime, is often forgotten. In many ways ordinary gendered crime is so common in our culture (Stanko 1990) it is part of the fabric and only the extraordinary merits attention. Yet, the recognition and prosecution of crimes (even if often unsuccessful) that occur between intimates or within families is relatively modern. In England, for example, incest was not a crime before the Punishment of Incest Act in 1908 and rape in marriage was only made illegal from 1991. Another crime, 'stalking', was a deviant and sometimes dangerous behaviour usually associated with men and often with a sexual element that was well documented within psychology and psychiatry (Zona et al. 1993, 1998; Mullen 1999) until the early 1990s, when it became criminalised through a series of harassment acts in the US, Canada and Australia and then in the UK in 1997 in the Protection from Harassment Act. The change in status from nuisance to crime not only illuminates the constructed nature of crime but also the impact of power, media and politics on that process, because arguably the mediatisation of several high-profile, that is newsworthy, celebrity stalks alongside increasing feminist concerns with women as victims impelled the legislative change (Wykes 2006). So, in practice, specific cultural and historical contexts inform what is considered criminal and therefore must also inform how crime is explained, punished and prevented. This chapter begins by culturally historicising the way in which knowledge about crime emerged, and then traces how it turned to gender.

Theoretical Histories

Crime and science

Criminology is a 'science' in that it emerged during the period of Victorian fervour to know the world; a fervour underwritten by knowledge from the natural sciences with their empirical base in discovery, identification, labelling, classification and, where possible, controlled utilisation and even improvement. During the nineteenth century the new 'sciences' of psychology, sexology and anthropology emerged as efforts to deal with humans as subjects of study, with much the same goals in mind. Criminology developed in this context and in a political context of an increasing turn to law as a means of social organisation. It has been:

> A story of constant reformulation in response to shifting political pressures, changes in institutional and administrative arrangements, intellectual developments occurring in adjacent disciplines and the changing ideological commitments of its practitioners ... As a discipline criminology is shaped only to a small extent by its own theoretical object and logic of inquiry. Its epistemological threshold is a low one, making it susceptible to pressures and interests elsewhere. (Garland 2002: 17)

The new science emerged in a very particular UK framework of burgeoning governance that sought compliance, productivity, security and order within the newly urbanised industrialised economies. The city landscapes of the nineteenth century were rapidly becoming vast, poor, filthy, chaotic and deadly. They were ungovernable and unsuited to the needs of factory systems with their structures, shifts and skills requirements. The imposition on this of the new knowledge of 'criminology' was a significant contributor to what E.P Thompson (1970) would term *'the making of the English working class'*. The lewd, violent drunks, mobs, thieves and vagabonds made the cities dangerous and disorderly, so inhibiting trade and transportation. Controlling the criminal necessarily became central to the project of embourgeoisement, and prevailing secular, humanistic, philosophical ideas about crime being a matter of individual free choice were clearly as insufficient to the task as was the Church with its threat of hell and damnation. This failure of faith and philosophy was hardly surprising because the prevalence of appalling poverty made it obvious to many that 'crime would yield more rewards than would conformity' (Arrigo and Williams 2006: 11).

In this context, the paradigmatic shift in the nineteenth century was substantial, moving away from a philosophical exploration of the ideas and subjective reasoning leading to *crime* towards a concentration on the empirical substance of crime and the criminal. Yet, criminology's positivistic Victorian *naissance* did little to obliterate the pre-modern concepts of evil, original sin, possession, lust, animalism, fatalism and sorcery which survived comfortably alongside 'science'. These explanations for 'wrongdoing' entangle Christianity, paganism, witchcraft, Satanism and cosmology but are evidenced throughout contemporary popular culture and frequently applied by journalists to the most extreme violence when no other account seems available, plausible or bearable. Extreme offenders are often dehumanised: The *Sun* offered a front-page account of Huntley's crimes after Soham: 'From Boy to Beast' (18 December 2003): Glitter was not only a 'monster' (*Daily Mail* 18 November 1999) but also 'illegitimate' (*The Times* 13 November 1999), a deeply Christian assessment of the cause of crime. After 9/11 The *Daily Mail's* front-page headline on 12 September 2001 echoed such religiosity with: 'APOC-ALYPSE'. Scientism largely obliterated any rationalistic, philosophical discussion of crime as a matter of individual conscience and reason under a wealth of material data but left intact many moral, mystical and symbolic interpretations. Rather, the anarchy of the new urban communities of the nineteenth century suggested that absence of any reason or conscience might explain crime, and the emerging discipline of psychiatry enabled some connections to be made between unacceptable behaviours and mental abnormalities.

One result was an increasing tendency to lock up minor criminals or the morally problematic in asylums. In Italy, Cesare Lombroso, a doctor with an interest in anthropology, developed a typology of criminal types and published *L'Uomo Delinquente* in 1876. In the UK, the focus was on the more institutional aspects of crime and criminals, prisons, workhouses, courts and policing – effectively the criminal justice system. What linked the two projects was a new commitment to observable data, to the collection of evidence, to the counting of occurrences and the classification of action and processes whether institutional or human subjects. The division between these two, that remains a characteristic of modern criminology, was also perhaps evident here: governance and social subjects do not necessarily all or always share the same interests. In the late nineteenth century studying the deviating subject was seen as key to effectively controlling their actions. This was a criminology that aspired to be predictive through mapping patterns of behaviours against types and introducing means of prevention and deterrence. Should this fail, then the institutional systems were also redesigned to account for different kinds of crimes and offenders, hopefully to reform where possible and contain where not. The goal was to identify and eliminate the criminal – observation, classification and discipline epitomised the new prison regimes characterised by the panopticon-shaped building designed by Bentham, that Foucault (1977) identified as metaphoric for the broader political project of social control. These 'others' were contained and studied and rehabilitated humanely in order to make them fit with the requirements of the new 'us' – the moral middle classes, governing elite and industrial bourgeoisie.

The close links between medical knowledge and crime saw associations being made between mental health and crime (Maudsley 1895) and also physical shape and low intelligence. In 1913 Goring wrote *The English Convict: A Statistical Study* and called for regulation of the propagation of certain physical types. Such positivism was a powerful tool. The measurement and categorising of features slid across from the Darwinian approach used by anthropologists, keen to understand and so better manage the colonies, and so also racialising the positivistic account of crime. It also seeped in the reverse direction, criminalising racialised looks, actions and culture. Positivism offered 'verifiable knowledge or truth about events' (Smart 1995: 34) or 'a-theoretical pragmatism' (Garland 2002: 44) and left a profound legacy where people were stigmatized by biology:

> Lombroso's anatomical obsessions were part of the explosion of pseudo-science which justified colonialism and the privileges of the wealthy. No reform of society could help the lower orders and lesser breeds overcome biological destiny. It was pointless to try when God or Darwin had made them unreformable. The market for such excuses still flourishes among those rich, white Americans who are comforted by the belief that blacks are condemned by their genes to be poor and criminal, rather than, for instance, 250 years of slavery and racism. (Cohen 2001).

Positivism applied a standard against which those not conforming were evaluated. The standard complied with the characteristics of those who applied it because the goal of the project was to bring all those living *outside* acceptable social mores within them or safely contain them where they could pose no threat. *Inside* were middle-class, educated, white, heterosexuals and their families, and they wanted security, prosperity and a continuation of their lifestyle and beliefs. Their needs and interests were simply applied wholesale as if the desirable norm for all.

Positivism was a means of identifying those who didn't comply and, by studying them, to develop institutions to shape them to fit, or securely contain them. Many institutions were the result of changes designed to control and/or change the masses: libraries; schooling; public baths; policing and even cheap newspapers and magazines, all helped clean up, educate and regulate, whilst prisons and asylums removed the remainder to a secure place. Acts impacted on popular culture, enclosing space, limiting mass gatherings and licensing alcohol, all to produce a tame and present workforce and secure thoroughfares for goods. Arguably, even football was part of this process; taken off common land by the Enclosures Acts, and the streets by the Highways Act 1835, where it had regularly interrupted traffic, it was placed in stadia where the workers became paying audiences rather than participants, and leisure as industry began to emerge (Wykes 2001: 76–85).

Knowledge about crime and deviance was therefore constructed around particular sets of norms and interests that were middle-class, white and heterosexually familial, and also overwhelmingly, though unacknowledgedly, masculine. In the Victorian public sphere and within the privacy of the family, women's role was subordinate, maternal and passive. Women had no vote, no contraception and in law wives and children were the property of the husband. Only in 1882 did the Married Women's Property Act give women a right to own property and keep their earnings. Respectable women were idealised and seen as in need of protection by a husband within a family, or at risk of being corrupted. Legislation that appeared to be concerned with women's well-being was very often actually focused on men's welfare and/or on women's morals, such as the 1860's Contagious Diseases Act, because women were presumed to be susceptible to corruption because of their frail and emotional natures.

The early twentieth century saw the increasing influence of Freudian ideas alongside growing interest in the relationship between immorality and insanity. Jones noted that 'the end of World War 1 and the return of large numbers of shell-shocked and mentally disturbed men to Britain – some of whom would eventually end in prison' (2006: 3) marked a shift towards psychological profiling of deviance. The search was still for generic explanations, rather than the individual psychoanalysis of single patients. Early criminological publications were usually reports of prison-based studies such as Goring (1913) and reflect this effort (Smith 1922; Sullivan 1924). This work arguably constituted the origins of applied criminology within prison psychiatry. Also influential in this new knowledge was Burt's (1925) study of 400 schoolchildren, which sought to identify psychological characteristics that might be criminogenic. Crucially his case histories identified issues such as family and discipline as contributing to such characteristics. Although he sought genetic explanations for his findings he also shifted the narrow parameters of British work on crime and criminals towards the work being done on deviance from a social perspective in Europe and the US.

Crime and society

Theory began to turn towards mapping the patterns of the socio-cultural context of criminality, including concern for aspects like family and education that Burt had alluded to in 1925, but the effort was still to document the facts about crime and criminals as out there to be collected and understood. US work on crime in the 1920s had tended to focus on the city rather than the criminal citizen (though for much the same reasons of urban disorder as criminology had developed around the criminal in the UK 50 years previously). The impetus in the US was that effective urbanisation and industrialisation were being compromised by crime. Park and Burgess (1925) analysed Chicago in terms of zones of work, living and crime and argued that most crime occurred in the 'zone of transition' between work areas in the centre and respectable residential areas. Shaw and Mackay (1942) explored this further in the early 1930s and identified such crime as male, juvenile, mobile, poor and culturally heterogeneous. Explanations hovered around concepts such as alienation and anomie, and the juvenile, mobile and heterogenic aspects of urban crime became the subject of welfarist interventions, youth crime initiatives, environmental and housing improvements and civil rights, with a focus very much on the context as causal of crime. In the US such moves were arguably a government-led appeasement to try and contain the spread of communism amongst the poor and disenfranchised.

Youth, cities, and later race, became the focus for criminologists in the latter part of the twentieth century, though theory focused closely on social structure and order rather than conditions. Merton (1968) offered a typology, not of people, or the environment, but of the norms and values of society, with citizens differently placed in relation to these: at 'best' conforming and at 'worst' rebelling. It was argued that differential access to the means of achieving success through conforming leads to strain amongst those with less opportunity, and that strain was likely to generate non-conformist methods of gaining symbols of success. As those with least access were often the poor, class became a major variable to consider in theorising crime. Moreover such differentiation in access to social success was also theorised as not just structural but cultural, in that some groups were perceived to have less possibility of even understanding the norms and rules than others simply because the rules were constructed, represented, disseminated and applied by a group or groups of which they were not members. In *Outsiders*, Becker wrote: 'Social groups create deviance by making the rules whose infraction constitutes deviance' (1963: 9). Deviant groups were seen by some as sub-cultures with their own identifying names, rules and processes (Cohen 1955; Downes 1966). Merton's strain and Becker's labelling theory identified power, both structural (occupying the social position of dominance), and cultural (having the means to represent and disseminate ideas), as key to understanding crime and offending. The one aspect that seemed little recognised or addressed in the work of criminologists and sociologists on urban crime patterns was that although often young and ethnically non-Caucasian, it was almost always men offending.

In Britain, much of the latter half of the twentieth century saw criminology as an academic discipline extend the empirical footprint of the nineteenth, beginning politically with the 1948 Criminal Justice Act's recognition of the potential of criminological research, which added governmental support to the project. Policy-led research began at the Home Office in the late 1950s and the establishment of the Cambridge Institute of Criminology in 1961 consolidated its presence in the academy. Early work focused on statistical data collection to inform policy and improve correctional institutions and processes. But in the UK, criminologists seemed determined to resist the US administrative approach to crime. When critiques emerged from the radical political thinking of the later 1960s and 1970s (Cohen 1972; Taylor et al. 1973; Hall et al. 1978) they were deeply sociological and contrary to the scientific and governmental interests that shaped the new discipline. Social conditions were seen as effectively causal of crime rather than individual choice. Such perspectives generated deeply politicised critiques of the status quo, both within the state and within criminology, and became the impetus for a turn to Marxism. Yet, men were missing too from the Marxist accounts of deviance that characterised the 1970s when class was the dominant variable; yet it was men behind social problems such as football hooliganism, disorderly demonstrations and rampant youth. Marxist scholars, influenced by the less reductionist work of Gramsci (1971) and Althusser (1977), saw the power of capital being imposed not directly by the state but hegemonically via the law, education and the mass media. Representations of deviance were seen as disseminated by dominant institutions sharing mutual interests and so ensuring that the preferred and legitimate behaviours were those conducive to their own interests. Pre-war models of offending were challenged as more than anything bourgeois, and most important crime was therefore seen as constructed rather than fact.

Politicising crime in this way also allowed the development of theories of offending that saw it as resistant to oppressive power rather than simply wrong. For example, Taylor argued that hooliganism was a class response to the commodification of football, with working-class fans seeking through violence an 'inarticulate but keenly experienced sense of control over the game that was theirs' (1971: 163). Murdoch, on the other hand, argued that much public disorder – 'urban guerrilla insurgency and bombing of Ulster; the occupation of workplaces; student sit-ins; squatting and rent strikes; together with militant industrial strikes and mass demonstrations' (1973: 206) – was a challenge to power, not crime.

Increasingly, the means of labelling *resistance as deviance* was identified as the mass media, initiating media analysis designed to ellicit evidence of media complicity with the interests of power and, explicitly, evidence of the construction of non-compliant subordinate groups: working-class; black; young or politically dissident as illegitimate (Cohen 1972; Murdoch 1973; Chibnall 1977; Hall et al. 1978). This was a new criminology (Taylor et al. 1973) with profound political and social concerns and goals and a new vision of crime as a construct largely serving the interests of power. It also underwrote a new and continuing direction of cultural criminology that was and is deeply concerned with identity, expressiveness and representation (Willis 1978a; Hall and Jefferson 1993; Ferrell and Sanders 1997; Presdee 2000). It did, however, still seek a causal explanation for crime, now in class or economic relations rather than biology, which still virtually never recognised the fact that crime was almost entirely committed by men, legislated against by men, studied by men and that the media reports were by male journalists. This was a criminology threatening to conservatism in all its manifestations of power except patriarchy.

Realisms

When in Britain the strike-ridden 'Winter of Discontent' of 1978 saw the sweeping to power of the Thatcher government with a law and order, nationhood, individualism and enterprise agenda matching the conservatism of the Reagan administration in the US, the problem of crime became central to the administration. Criminology, as an academic discipline, rapidly became realistic rather than revolutionary, as deep criticism of the failure of prior liberalism to prevent crime impacted on research and policy initiatives emanating from the Home Office. Research was heavily dependent on state funding, either from the government via the Home Office or via the major social research councils and with an overwhelming government manifesto commitment to law and order that was the kind of knowledge that was being financially and politically encouraged. Realism occupied both right and left positions politically, but more than anything it was about policy rather than politics. On the right, the individual rather than society or the state was held responsible for their deviance: 'Offenders seek to benefit themselves by their criminal behaviour' (Cornish and Clarke 1986: 1); and ideas complied with ideas of the Conservative government and moved towards an agenda of managing rather than explaining crime. Any theoretical abstraction was also abandoned by criminologists on the left who responded practically to the industrial and inner-city disorders of the 1980s almost as if in response to the recommendations of the 1981 Scarman report which, as a way of reducing disorder, had 'suggested more aid to improve living conditions in the inner cities; positive discrimination in education and employment; reform within the police, especially in relation to riot tactics but also legal changes' (Wykes 2001: 55).

Left realism argued for a multi-agency approach to crime, integrating the real concerns of offender, victim, state and general public with criminologists stepping down from their ivory tower and getting involved in practice. Surveys, particularly at the local level, were 'used as a social democratic instrument for informing the policy-making process' (Walklate 2003: 61), indicating a return to positivism and its assumptions that reality could be defined, labelled and collated unproblematically to inform change towards improvement. The left realist project in the UK was largely embraced and continued by New Labour, in government from 1997, but the problem of crime remained at crisis levels with prisons overflowing into police cells. On 13 October 2006, of the 79,714 people in UK prisons 75,205 were male (NOMS 2006), a phenomenon barely addressed within realism, from either political orientation.

So not only has the problem of crime apparently not in any way been resolved, but despite 30 years of effort from feminists in the areas of socio-political life, the academy and sexual relationships, the masculinity of much offending remains largely unacknowledged. Even though feminists within criminology and beyond have made significant changes by recognizing the gendered patterns of crime and placing women clearly on the agenda of justice, man remains a rarely used variable unless qualified by a racial or religious descriptor or by youth or poverty and deprivation. When it comes to the intimate and personal crimes that are the focus of this book, men are not disappeared but rarely called men, rather they are *beasts, evil, paeds, psychos and perverts* (Wykes 2002).

Criminal Women?

Carol Smart developed her MA dissertation into *Women, Crime and Criminology* to criticise a criminology that was failing to acknowledge its positivist and paternalistic past. In 1976 she wrote:

> The deviant, the criminal or the actor is always male; it is always *his* rationality, *his* motivation, *his* alienation or *his* victim. And this is more than a convenient choice of words; the selection of the male pronoun may be said to be inclusive of the female but in reality it is not; it merely excludes women and makes them invisible. (Smart 1976: 177).

Her point was that women were *symbolically annihilated* (Tuchman 1978) by such pronouns, and however different the crime configuration was for women, it deserved an account. However, that necessary, innovative and resistant recognition of the *atavistic man* at the centre of criminology did not also focus on the masculinity of the vast majority of crime and the criminal justice system as requiring study. Instead, in the 1970s' climate of passionate defence of women and in search of better experiences and opportunities for them, it concentrated on making explicit women's place in crime.

The irony is that the generic use of the male pronoun for all humanity not only disappeared women from the discourse but also made *men* invisible in that they are thereby undifferentiated from women and so unproblematised as a criminogenic variable. The fact that the early criminology Smart was criticising was 'written largely by men, on the subject of men, for an audience of men' (1976: 178) no more focused it on men than it did on women, as is evident from the voluminous history of work on physique, mental health, race, youth and class as criminal variables with no mention of gender. Certainly there was a subsumption of the feminine within language and therefore within the recorded knowledge of crime (and arguably within most recorded knowledge, the missing *herstory*) until second-wave feminism began to impact, but the masculine was not the focus of such knowledge either. Simply, criminology was blind to the masculinity at the heart of its discipline, at the source of its subject and as the basis of meaning. That lack of acknowledgement of men at the heart of social and cultural power meant men were (and still often are) metaphorically inextricable and therefore unaccountable.

Feminism is both philosophical and political as its goals are not merely to understand the world but to change it so that women gain power over themselves and their lives (Wollstonecraft 1792). It is not a unitary project but one with varying theories and practices which broadly espouse: (a) the creation of a separate feminine system; (b) change within the system; (c) or change of the system. During the 1970s the first approach saw no potential to change patriarchy and sought ways instead of eschewing heterosexuality and marriage in order to liberate women from the subordinate sex-class their bodies designate them to occupy; the second was broadly liberal and viewed change for women as a matter of evolutionary, historical progression achieved by legislation, education and egalitarian social aims; whilst the last effort viewed the existing political (capitalist and paternalist) system as supporting power bases that were deeply antagonistic to women's lives (and not always very good for men) and therefore this perspective advocated a reconstruction of the system to differently position both men and women in relation to each other and capital. The three broad approaches were quickly devolved by the concept of different femininities, but can be seen to relate to the three main trajectories in feminist criminology: women and crime; women and justice; and criminological theory. The impetus for feminist criminologists in the 1970s was the empirical evidence detailed in earlier chapters: why do women commit a smaller share of all crimes; why are the crimes they commit different – less serious, less professional, less likely to be repeated; how does this impact on justice processes and prisons; and how does it relate to gender roles and relations more widely (Heidensohn 2002)? Initial forays reviewed the early ideas about women and crime that had emerged from the positivistic origins of criminology.

The early criminologists, Lombroso and Ferrero (1895) were aware of women's place in crime. They focused on sexual biology, arguing that normal women's conservatism and passivity was a result of the fixity of the ovule and the post-partum housebound role of childcare. Women who did seriously transgress were therefore assumed to be unnatural and biologically deviant. Emotionality was also seen as part of women's biology making them maternal but also not rational, and therefore likely to succumb to temptations or be vulnerable to wrongdoers unless properly cared for and protected within marriage, which should ultimately be their goal. Wollstonecraft had fruitlessly criticised such ideas a century earlier:

mad, bad, or sad

> It would be an endless task to trace the variety of meannesses, cares, and sorrows, into which women are plunged by the prevailing opinion, that they were created rather to feel than reason, and that all the power they obtain, must be obtained by their charms and weakness. (Wollstonecraft 1792: ch. iv, line 36)

There is in positivist criminology a double bind for women, who at their most female are characterised by their biology as frail, dependent, emotional and illogical and therefore vulnerable to corruption or loss of control and in need of protection; whilst those appearing as neither frail nor emotional are necessarily therefore not *natural* women but rather masculinised. Either way women are biologically blamed.

Lombroso's focus was developed by Pollak (1950) to explain how premenstrual, menopausal and post-partum states might disrupt women's physiology and psychology, leading to deviance. The theory was that 'the generative phases of women are bound to present many stumbling blocks for the law-abiding behaviour of women' (1950: 157). The main problem with such theory is that the amount of menstruation, childbirth and menopause experienced by half the world's population would suggest that women should be much more significantly criminal than they are, and certainly more criminal than men who have no such disruptions, yet the 'hormone plea' remains popular, for example, in relation to infanticide (Wilcynski, 1995). The second bind of biologism informed Adler's view that if women became socially more liberated, that is more like men, they would also force 'their way into the world of major crimes' (1975: 13) – a view that supported backlashes against equal opportunities initiatives and helped entrench the most patriarchal men in their authority.

crime rates don't support this

Feminists within criminology queried biologism. Young (1988) found such positivistic accounts prevalent in explanations of the suffragettes in the early twentieth century. They were labelled 'victims of hysteria' (Young 1988: 282) and also 'unwomanly' and 'sexless creatures' (1988: 287). More worryingly the same kinds of terms were used again in press accounts of women Greenham Common protesters in the mid-1980s (Young 1990). Sex-biologised explanations for women's deviance remain entrenched in and beyond popular culture (see Chapter 2), despite 100 years of history and decades of systematic challenge by feminism. Such models of female offending stereotyped women as weak and irrational, or not real women, rather than viewing them as active and purposeful agents, some of whom had good reason for their offences and/or criminal careers (Carlen 1988).

Although the statistical differentiations between male and female crime were and are probably valid, little was known about women's actual experience of crime. Work on hidden crimes, particularly those within the family or home, where women were traditionally seen as having more authority, merely exposed further levels of male offending against partners or children, most often female (Dobash and Dobash 1979: Stanko 1985, 1990). Perhaps most crucially though, the focus on gender differentiation and crime, alongside a strongly radical feminist perspective, clarified for the first time the extent of women's victimisation by men and impelled a massively influential field of work.

Women as victims *Look up stats to include*

In the US in the 1970s, rape drew the attention of feminists who sought to rethink the old parameters of the crime which only recognised rape at its most extreme in terms of violation, unexpectedness, strangers and damage. In reality most rape occurs as intercourse *against women's will* by boyfriends, dates and acquaintances, rather than violent assault by an unknown man in a dark street (Furstenburg 1976). For many feminists, this emerging argument confirmed radical views of patriarchy, at the heart of which they saw the family, marriage and heterosexuality. Brownmiller (1975) in *Against our Will* was one of the first to identify rape as specifically a crime by men against women, not some violent result of a deranged mind. She also challenged the idea that rape necessarily involved violence; rather it was often a result of pressure by a known man, of fear and cultural myths such as that a women who says no actually means yes and that husbands have rights to sex from their wives.[1] She argued that 'women are trained to be rape victims' (Brownmiller 1975: 309), to be passive vaginas awaiting male penetration and that even those men who do not rape benefit from those who do because they keep all women in fear and subordination.

Thinking of women as sexual victims pervades much radical feminist thinking and characterises: a campaign against the eroticisation of rape, for example in pornography as reproducing violence against women (Dworkin 1981; MacKinnon 1987); efforts to criminalise male kerb-crawlers and pimps, rather than prostitutes, or legalise brothels to protect women and reduce their stigmatisation (Smart 1995); and much work to improve the policing of sexual crimes and treatment of women victims (Gregory and Lees 1999). Although admirable and effective in achieving better treatment for women victims, such radical work often leaves male offenders no better understood, controlled or treated, nor has it appeared to reduce offending against women (Home Office 2002/03). It also leaves in place, as if essential, the very model of sexual roles it views as problematic and if anything continues the very paradigm it opposes that women are at risk from male heterosexuality; its discourses continue the myth of male power and female passivity and change is rendered impossible. Woman-focused work has been called *standpointism* (Harding 1987) as it seeks to view the experience of crime from the standpoint of woman, often as victim. One problem with the approach is that by leaving men out of the picture change becomes impossible, because, as graffiti on a Sheffield phone kiosk stated in 2005: 'Only men can stop rape.' Standpointism has been influential in providing new insights into crime and deviance from a subordinate (feminine) view to counter the dominance of the taken-for-granted masculinism of mainstream criminology, and for encouraging '[t]heoretical and personal reflexivity in relation to knowledge and the process of knowledge production through research' (Gelsthorpe 2002: 123).

Clearly, awful damage is done to women and children by male sexuality but to treat that as inevitable condemns both men and women to stereotypes. Refusal to accept the inevitability of the state of things inevitably characterises the effort to practical change through law and policy and most closely constitutes a realist model of feminist criminology. Work on women and justice seeks less to explain patterns of offending and victimisation and more to resolve inequity and abuse in and through the legal system, institutions of justice and social policy. It evidences a liberal rather than radical feminism that in principle might look to develop egalitarian approaches within the Criminal Justice System (CJS) and the erosion of differential treatment, but in practice raises many complex theoretical questions for criminology.

Criminal justice for women

Liberal feminists took as their starting point an empirical approach when the turn towards data and survey-based research in the realist 1980s indicated differences and anomalies radicalism could not explain. More than anything the evidence posed the questions: what is known about women and crime; why

zapper

WE WILL BUY YOUR UNWANTED BOOKS FOR CASH

SPECIAL OFFER
EARN 5% MORE
WITH CODE: ZAP005

Text Books
Cook Books
Children's Books
Fiction
Fantasy
Romance
Biographies
Rare Books
Language Books
And many more

FREE POSTAGE

GET FAST CASH
today with...

zapper.co.uk

are women's offending rates so low when they are as likely to suffer poverty, racism and oppression as men, in addition to sexism; why do some women offend at all given that the vast majority do not, and how are those who do treated? In 1968, Heidensohn first raised these questions by focusing on the 'lack of interest in sex differences in recorded criminality and in female deviance itself' (2002: 517). First, women's place in crime needed to be mapped and counted both for women's sake and for criminology's, which was impoverished as a knowledge discipline by its lack of attention to gender (Heidensohn 1968; Smart 1976). Much of the evidence of crime is statistical data rather than facts (see Chapter 3), in that such figures are subject to the 'vagaries of reporting and recording behaviour' (Maguire 2002: 368). Also, such material focuses on offences rather than offenders or victims and is very often collected under political and policy directives rather than as an effort at getting at the truth. Not until 1982 did the British Crime Survey question the public about their crime experience and so begin to reveal levels of unreported crime as well as that recorded by the police. This focus drew attention to the 'dark' figure of crimes such as white-collar, corporate, domestic, vandalism and consensual that rarely came to the attention of the criminal justice system but nonetheless were usually committed by men. The plethora of surveys and research worldwide has done little to suggest anything other than that this remains 'true'. Work on women's offending found itself largely trying to account for an absence except in the areas of prostitution, TV licence evasion and shop-lifting.

In terms of offending rates three key explanations were offered for the low female figures – chivalry, hidden female crime and control of femininity. Chivalry might include non-reporting of women's offences by males; 'blind-eye' policing of female crime and leniency by the courts. Evidence of chivalry, though, was hard to find and often refuted by researchers, for example by Daly (1994). Work on policing, on the other hand, even suggested there was particularly harsh treatment of women as offenders, witness, for example, the harassment of prostitutes (Mcleod 1982). The idea that women hid their crimes, particularly in the home and family, led to work on the domestic area that actually exposed significantly unreported amounts of violence towards women by their male partners (Mirlees-Black 1999), rather than the deviousness and secretiveness claimed by Pollak (1950). Incidences when women offend were claimed to be likely to rise in the 1970s, with the onset of feminism empowering women's offending along with all other aspects of their lives (Adler 1975), but in practice women continued to deviate most from men by conforming, not just in the UK but throughout Europe (Heidensohn 2002). This conformity led to the concept of the control of femininity, that girls in fact *grow up good* (Cain 1990) as a result of learnt behaviour and are therefore less likely to commit crime. Girls were deemed to be more controlled by the family, less likely to occupy, or act in, public space and were more praised for passivity and obedience than boys (Hagan 1979). This theory of conformity was criticised for lack of methodological rigour, reproducing stereotypes of femininity and failing to address the reasons why some women do offend, but its strength, given how few women offend, is perhaps that it looks for explanations of gender and crime outside of criminology in broader socio-sexual relations, roles and values.

Conviction rates and the low presence of women in prisons seems to be related to the different nature of the crimes most women commit, which are very rarely violent or serious, and 'research on remand has found offence seriousness to be strongly correlated to remand outcomes' (Steward 2006: 130). In cases of shop-lifting, prolific offending might eventually lead to custody (Steward 2006: 134), whereas in prostitution the visibility of street-working women makes them vulnerable to prosecution but they are more likely to be imprisoned for non-payment of the resulting fines than for the act of soliciting. 'Up to 52% of female prison sentenced admissions are fine defaulters' (Scottish Office 1998), including for non-payment of TV licences. TV licence evasion, shop-lifting and prostitution are quintessentially feminine offences but are also closely linked to poverty. Arguably, resolving these kinds of gendered crimes has more to do with relieving poverty than with opposing patriarchy. Moreover, in terms of prostitution, the arrest of male kerb-crawlers, enabled in the UK since 2001, could theoretically turn this crime from one resulting in female offences to one of male offending. Such a drive has been supported by calls to prosecute men who use under-age prostitutes for child abuse (Phoenix 2006) and charge those who pay for sex with trafficked women,[2] on the grounds that such women cannot freely consent to sex (see Chapter 7). Such a shift reveals not just the mutability of crime as gendered but also the further victimisation of women and girls, usually at the hands of men in intimate and sexualised contexts.

Even when women do transgress and commit very serious crimes such as murder or manslaughter, not only is it very rare but it is even rarer that the act mirrors similar crimes as committed by men, though the very existence of such female offending does confound any generalisable assumptions about gender and crime: women can be violent and, of course, most men are not. Given the levels of violence directed at women in their most personal and intimate relationships, what is surely surprising is how few respond with like violence. On the rare occasions when women kill, rather than receive chivalry, they seemed, until recently, to be routinely more severely punished than men. Such inequity drew the attention of feminist criminologists throughout the 1990s and highlighted patriarchal practice in the law, courts and media, and ensuing injustice. The trials of Joseph McGrail and Sara Thornton[3] in 1991 provide a case-study:

Case-study: McGrail and Thornton

Joseph McGrail 'killed the bullying, alcoholic woman he was living with [and] was given a two year suspended jail sentence' (*Daily Telegraph* 1 August 1991). McGrail 'finally cracked on Feb. 27 when he came home from work to find her drunk and demanding yet more drink' (Daily Telegraph 1 August 1991). McGrail's reaction was described by prosecuting counsel as a 'sudden, temporary loss of control caused by provocation' (*Daily Telegraph* 1 August 1991), even though he did drag his wife into the bedroom and kick her to death (which takes some time and not a little 'thinking' surely). He was offered 12 months' psychiatric supervision to help him 'overcome his feelings of remorse'. McGrail's 'common law' wife, Marion Kennedy, was not violent, only verbally abusive. The press barely covered the case at all and seemed to agree with the Judge, Justice Popplewell, that the murdered woman would have 'tried the patience of a saint'. None mentioned McGrail's sex-life or underwear, both of which featured significantly in accounts of Sara Thornton's appeal at exactly the same time.

In the Sara Thornton case, she had killed her partner in 1989 and pleaded guilty on the grounds of diminished responsibility. She was found guilty of murder and sentenced to life but appealed on the grounds of provocation in 1991. Malcolm Thornton had been an 'ex-policeman working as a security consultant'. He was also an 'alcoholic and violent husband'. 'She had called the police to her house at least 5 times because of Thornton's attacks on her and he was in fact due to appear in court on a charge of assault 10 days after he died' (Justice for Women 2006). The judge commented of Sara that there were 'other alternatives available such as walking out or going upstairs' (*Guardian* 30 July 1991). The newspaper reports referred to Sara's sexual history and mental health. Sara Thornton was, herself, acutely aware of being tried not only as a criminal but as a woman who was too liberal, too independent, too *feminist*. Her appeal was rejected 'on the grounds that the 60 seconds it took to get the knife did not constitute "a sudden and temporary loss of self-control"' (*Guardian* 30 July 1991). After a long campaign to establish that a history of battering could 'provoke' violence, a further appeal was granted and in December 1995, Lord Chief Justice Taylor, quashed her murder conviction. She had served five years in prison.

The anomalies between the cases are obvious enough: women are rarely strong enough to kill with their bare hands as provocation usually requires, so the law is masculinist. Why can't provocation be 'slow-burn'? Is 'nagging' a reason to kill?[4] Why wasn't McGrail told he could have walked out? Why was he not criticised for his sexual history or clothing preferences? As has been found in other cases (Wykes 2001: 138–63) women who kill are doubly damned for going against the law and femininity and, until recently, frequently apparently more profoundly punished than men committing similar crimes. Worrall (2004) found similarly harsh treatment of violent girls in court and the media in the 1990s. The construction of femininity in crime discourses works twice to oppress women; it maintains as normal, respectable, traditional feminine passivity and modesty (and women who deviate from this norm either *become* violent or *cause* men to become violent). The representation of crime, 'normally', fails to address ordinary masculinity whilst perpetuating models of femininity that support Heidensohn's (1985) claim that, in our culture, women are represented as either *good and placed on pedestals or bad and given their just deserts* and, further, women are responsible for men's badness.[5] Crime discourses are less chivalrous than they are doubly punitive: punishing women for their crimes but also for not being good enough women as discussed in Chapter 2, the latter applying even when they are victims.

These kinds of accounts alongside ever increasing data on the violence suffered by women and the lack of effective prevention and prosecution seem to suggest that, despite all that knowledge, feminist criminology has done little to either solve the problem of crime or of patriarchy, however the relationship between the two is theorised, research practised and policy and legislation put in place. It is hard to counter Heidensohn's claim that a 'long journey hasn't taken us very far' (2002: 524), when not only do old crimes against women continue to go unpunished (Kelly et al. 2005; BBC News 25 February 2005; Fernandez 2006) but new ones emerge, such as women-trafficking (Metropolitan Police 2006) and dowry/honour killings (Paterson 2005).

Areas that need critically addressing in relation to the failure to impact on such violence by men against women must include feminism and criminology, because the knowledge they have developed and publicised about gendered crime seems not to have changed the relationship between gender and crime, despite better instances being recorded, damage acknowledged and help made available. Something is inadequate in the addressing of gendered crime through feminist criminology. What it has done extraordinarily well, is to achieve better mapping of women's place in crime, and political concern about and practical aid for victims. This latter practical aspect is explored with illustrations in Chapter 5.

Theorising women and crime

Radicalism and liberalism have shown clearly the high of levels of violence against women and children in intimate contexts and the failure of the justice system to properly punish, let alone prevent, such violence, but have done little to achieve either effective punishment of male offenders or prevention. Rather, they have dramatically changed the managing of the impact of such violence after the event, with support for and belief in women's experiences, changes in treatment of victims in the CJS and improvements in legislation and policy, even if the latter is frequently stymied by procedure in practice. Important issues are that a radical feminist approach cannot change male violence, a change it sees as essential, and that it can only seek to protect women by eschewing men or repairing women who have not done so. Alternatively, liberal feminist criminology works for change within the CJS system, when many of the problems that bring women into a criminal context lie outside of that system: poverty and patriarchy, for example. Without addressing such meta-contexts, they are simply left in place to underwrite future generations of gendered identity and experience, men's and women's. So women's place in crime becomes better and perhaps more fairly managed, whether as victim or offender, but *remains the same place* in crime as, problematically for women, does men's. In consequence, some feminists have argued that criminology itself cannot address the problem of crime. Carol Smart (1990) who arguably launched the feminist criminology agenda now concentrates on policy, and Cain (1990) has argued that the questions that need to be addressed are about women and require a feminist politics rather than a narrow criminological investigation.

However, it is not just criminology that cannot deliver the knowledge to change crime's gendered quality, but feminism. Once it becomes clear through feminist work within criminology that women's place in crime is largely due to their lack of economic power and their place in sexual and familial relations, and often both in conjunction, then criminology becomes largely a redundant source of explication. Further, in terms of the intimate violence that is the subject of this book and the most extremely gendered form of crime, it is the victimisation of women by men that requires explanation and change, but feminism has always focused, quite rightly, on women. It is fruitless to try to change only one half of the equation of gendered crime, particularly when the most active and destructive half is the one left unaddressed, so masculinity as criminogenic must be addressed. Just as race is a white problem and, as Dyer (1997) argued so cogently in *White*, must be addressed by dealing with the problem of whitism, so male violence requires an address of masculinism. Just as all whites are not overtly racist, this is not to suggest that all men are actually violent (and some women certainly are) but that is also no reason to avoid the fact that most crime and nearly all violence is committed by men.

More, to understand women's place in crime it is crucial to focus on the men who very often place them there, directly or indirectly. Indirectly because so many accounts, factual and fictional, of women and crime blame their femininity for their experience. Inversely, qualities of masculinity are rarely part of any crime discourse. Despite men's overwhelming domination of offending, explanations for their crime tend to focus on youth, race, religion or *inhuman* (beast/animal/devil) characteristics rather than male gender. This is perhaps unsurprising as masculinism is the invisible bedrock of understanding about our world: it is the place from which things are viewed, categorised and defined, but it is not the subject of its own gaze; it does not see itself whilst measuring all against its norms and expectations. It collates human and man as one and so presents 'the falsely universalising perspective of the master' (Harding 1987: 188). The knowledge disciplines of the twenty-first century continue to trail the scientific enterprises of the nineteenth-century patriarchs without apparently realising that fathers/husbands are very often the problem for women and children.

Once it becomes possible to see knowledge as constructed by power and applied by power it is easier to see why it isn't truth but myth, and therefore inadequate or diversionary if the goal is to bring about real change. It also becomes clear that power itself has to be subject to scrutiny if any adequate understanding of the world is to be possible. 'Analysing the power effects that claims to truth entail' (Smart 1995: 45) is part of a post-modern approach to knowledge that challenges the fixity embraced by the modernist project by deconstructing and revealing the processes that generate meanings. For criminologists this entails uncovering the means by which acts become crimes; for feminists it means exploring how the sexed body acquires the meanings of gendered subjectivity. In order to understand gendered crime, then, it becomes important to think of where power is and how it is used to construct meanings about subjects and acts in ways that enable men either to be violent or to gain power vicariously through other men's violence. Clearly it is in intimate relationships, familial and sexual, that most violence occurs: in the intimate spaces of the home and the body. The family and the body are also pivotal to subjects gaining gendered identity and are the focus for Chapters 6 and 8.

Conclusion

Criminology has not been well gendered, although arguably it has been well feminised. There are two key areas for any *violence* and *justice* study: the private sphere where violence is overwhelmingly acted by men against women and/or children in intimate familial relationships, and the public sphere where peacetime interpersonal violence is usually acted by men against other men[6] (Taylor 1971; Pearson 1983; Maguire 1996). It is the former private arena that is the focus of this book essentially because it is here that crime is acutely *gendered* in that it is differentiated in terms of roles, motives and outcomes between male and female. In public space interpersonal violence is most often masculinised rather than gendered in that men attack men – although there may well be differentiations in relation to identity such as age, class, ethnicity, work, football team, sexuality, gang membership (discussed in Chapter 8).

The key question should be not why is women's offending rate so low, or what is women's experience of being victims, or is the CJS biased, but why is men's offending so high? What seems necessary is a critique of masculinity – not blackness or gayness or youth or any other diversion, but the attributes of male identity shared by all men in that men as a 'class' continue to benefit from power much more substantially than women. The male body enables a violent script to be written into its identity as it acquires maturity. Somehow the male body is sexed around power – physical strength, sexual potency and, with adulthood, patriarchal authority and public presence and purpose. Yet these are also the places where male power can become dangerous.

Omissions in theoretical studies mean that whilst attention is paid to women as victims little is paid to the family or heterosexuality as the context of that, nor to the fact that the offenders are men in those intimate contexts. Massive gaps have been left: directly, by the focus on women as victims in feminist criminology and, indirectly, by the lack of theoretical focus on the family as a dangerous space. Both of these leave men – husbands, lovers, fathers, boyfriends – out of the picture and so ordinary masculinity is poorly understood. There are many reasons to address this: violence by men against women and children remains high; the family remains secure and within it male power; *evil beasts* rather than everyday men are blamed for sexual violence in popular mass media accounts, and practical help and resources for both victims and offenders remain paltry and rarely statutory – worse, if anything, resources are actively diverted away from real sites of danger to women and children. For example:

> Sexual abuse by a stranger is what tends to be of most concern to the general public and is of most interest to the media, it is actually abuse within the family, or by an individual who has a relationship of trust with the child, that is not only more common but also on the whole more damaging. (Grubin 1998: 13)

Despite this evidence, at no time have the news media or the Home Office or the Serious Organised Crime Agency groups of vigilantes orchestrated a campaign around what should be the 'real' headlines of child abuse: 'DAD RAPES HIS BABY DAUGHTER'. Instead there are diversions and obfuscations, and annihilations of the fact that mainstream masculinities are 'deviant' and 'dangerous' and that danger-ousness is very often directed toward the women and children of their families.

In many ways this chapter has come full circle by returning to the bourgeois patriarchy and sexism of the Victorian period, not as a useful source of crimi-nological knowledge but as a remaining major source of crime against women and children. The use of a particular model of masculinity as some kind of truth, and a whole epistemology modelled on it, has fostered both an *engendering* of crime and a failure to see crime as masculine. Sets of values inscribe gender on the sexed bodies of men and women. Those for women occupy many discursive spaces from religion through law to soap opera. In fact women are always under instruction on how to be women: 'Women are exhorted, cajoled and subtly coerced into conformity' (Heidensohn 1985: 108), not least by other women. Men, on the other hand, are rarely addressed as men at all, though a little wild-ness in 'boys' is seen as admirable, part of a rite of passage to maturity (Pearson 1983). Public toughness remains part of adult masculinity whether in the board-room or the bar or on the playing field or war zone. Yet it is those male bodies that inflict damage in families and sexual relations where the genders are most significantly in contact. Part of that subjectivity is what Collier (1998) calls becoming 'sexed' bodies. The use of the phrase 'sexed body' is important because it grounds gender on sexual difference without returning to simplistic biologisms, and because it retains *action*, sex is used as a verb, and allows for change. It also avoids the diversions afforded by other constituents of gender identity. Lastly, it is between sexed bodies that gendered crime occurs in the kinds of relationships that are about desire, reproduction and difference. So bod-ies and intimate relationships are crucial aspects of understanding violence and gender, which understanding is, in turn, necessary in any quest for justice.

Before looking closely in Chapter 6 at families as contexts for gender and crime, the next chapter focuses on that issue of justice by looking at the practical and pressing consequences of the failure to properly theorise gendered violence for the people, policies and institutions working in gendered crime and those who need them. The body is then centralised when Chapter 7 focuses closely on how the law operates in relation to sex crimes, whilst Chapter 8 looks to masculinity, identity and the body to try and understand better *why masculinity turns to such spectacularly destructive forms* (Campbell 1991) in gendered and intimate relationships.

Notes: Issues for Reflection

1 Rape in marriage was only made illegal in England in 1991 largely as result of feminist pressure.

Research rape in marriage in other cultures. What are the norms? Try to explain differences?

2 'The Metropolitan police believes trafficked women coerced into prostitution are often forced to see between 20 and 30 men a day' (Townsend 2005).

Read the article and search for more information about trafficked women. Critically assess their situation in relation to 'consent' as discussed later, in Chapter 7.

3 How did the press cover the cases of Joseph McGrail and Sara Thornton and does it matter?

Can you find any further cases with similar outcomes? Look up *Justice for Women* (http://www.jfw.org.uk/).

What would be gained and what lost by removing provocation as a plea in homicide cases?

4 At the end of July 2008 reforms were set in motion by the British Ministry of Justice to address the inequities (MOJ http://www.justice.gov.uk/news/newsrelease290708a.htm). Research the proposals and critically assess the consequences of such changes for violence, gender and justice.

5 When women are victims they are often blamed for their own demise in ways which suggest they either let down, betrayed or corrupted the men who killed them and so are responsible for men's violence (Wykes 1995).

How else are women deemed to be responsible for men's behaviour towards them?

6 The one exception here is gang rape which has been written about widely in the context of war (Brownmiller 1975; Allen 1996) and less frequently as a phenomenon of gendered crime, though there is a literature on gang rape on American campuses (Reeves Sanday 1991 & 2007).

Look up and analyse the gang rape in Britain that resulted in an 18-year-old girl being convicted in 2001. 'Girl, 18, convicted of canal rape' (http://news.bbc.co.uk/1/hi/uk/1225124.stm).

Why would the conviction not happen now?

Complementary Readings

S. Brownmiller (1975) *Against our Will* (Harmondsworth: Penguin) is a classic of early second-wave feminism which puts rape on the agenda of sexual politics.

M. Cain (1989) 'Feminists transgress criminology', in M. Cain (ed.) *Growing up Good* (London: Sage) explains why criminology cannot explain women's place in crime.

D. Garland 'Of crimes and criminals', in M. Maguire et al. (2002) *The Oxford Handbook of Criminology* (3rd edn) (Oxford: Oxford University Press, pp. 7–51) is an illuminating and thorough history of the discipline of criminology.

C. Smart (1976) *Women, Crime and Criminology* (London: Routledge) is perhaps the original feminist criminology book and C. Smart (1990) 'Feminist approaches to criminology or postmodern woman meets atavistic man', in A. Morris and L. Gelsthorpe (eds) *Feminist Perspectives in Criminology* (Milton Keynes: Open University Press) asks what has criminology has got to offer feminism.

L. Gelsthorpe 'Feminism and criminology', in M. Maguire et al. (2002) *The Oxford Handbook of Criminology* (3rd edn) (Oxford: Oxford University Press, pp. 112–43) reviews feminist criminology at the start of the twenty-first century.

M. Morash (2005) *Understanding Gender, Crime and Justice* (London: Sage) focuses closely on victims and the US context.

M. Silvestri and C. Crowther-Dowey (2008) *Gender and Crime* (London: Sage) focuses on control, and particularly on criminal justice institutions, to argue for a human rights approach to gender and crime.

5

CONFRONTING VIOLENCE

People, Policies and Places

Many agencies and organisations become involved and policies become applicable when violence has occurred. This chapter looks at the tools available for confronting violence and the inhibitions on any kind of resolution. It explores the development of feminist action against gendered violence and examines the involvement of the state in challenging such violence.

This chapter tracks the ways in which 1970s feminist thinking, described in the last chapter, was translated into action, particularly in relation to domestic violence and rape, through the founding of the first refuges and rape crisis centres for survivors of domestic and sexual violence. The chapter examines the expansion of service provision on domestic violence and rape and explores the extraordinary assistance that services such as refuges, rape crisis centres and other support organisations provide to women who are surviving male violence. Here we also consider, though, the financial difficulties that all such organisations face and compare their contribution to action against gendered violence to the government's contribution to them, their services and their funding situations. Why, for example, given the government's supposed commitment to fighting violent crime, does it leave to volunteers in refuges funded by the National Lottery a crime that one in four women experience in their lives and that kills more than two women every week?

Indeed, having examined the important role that organisations such as refuges assume in challenging and confronting male violence, this chapter goes on to explore the role that state agencies have assumed in this regard. It exposes state services' failure to take on gendered violence and their associated failure to recognise violence as *gendered*. The chapter suggests that, in the 1970s and 1980s, state responses to gendered violence were grounded in lack of interest and disingenuousness and that, in addition, state services around this time also denied its gendered nature through colluding in and continuing gendered assumptions in the response to it. The chapter goes on to suggest that, even though state services are increasingly taking on gendered violence, there remain considerable failings in this regard. The chapter also suggests that, even as the state has taken on gendered violence, the government's inclination to regard and respond to it as a crime problem, health problem, sexual health problem, drugs problem, etc, has increasingly denied its classification as a *gender* problem.

The chapter does not, therefore, set out to provide only an account of current responses to gendered violence. Indeed, without discussion of responses over the last 30 years, any such account would be without contextualisation and thus without meaning. An appreciation of the contrast between feminist praxis since the 1970s and state responses over the same time in challenging male violence is needed in order to even begin the process of reflecting on current policy and practice responses. The chapter therefore aims to provide some degree of context before moving on to consider more recent discourse and developments.

Challenging Male Violence: Feminist Action

In the late 1960s and early 1970s the women's liberation movement 'provided the base of membership and the overall perspective from which numerous issues could be addressed' (Dobash and Dobash 1992: 16). All centred on male domination and power (see Borkowski et al. 1983). As the Dobashes put it:

> Wage work and the economy, domestic work and the family, reproduction and medicine, mental health and psychology, knowledge and the university, sex and the double standard, violence against women and many others became the sites of protest against disadvantages historically constructed and maintained through economic segmentation, cultural beliefs and institutional practices. Male domination and power were fundamental to all. (Dobash and Dobash 1992: 16)

From women's liberation came the development of feminist analysis and action around gendered violence. Increasing recognition of men's power and domination and women's oppression and subordination enabled feminists to contextualise domestic and sexual violence – increasing recognition of gendered violence enabled further campaigning around, and challenge to, these gendered power relations.

From women's liberation also came the establishment of services to assist female survivors of male violence. Feminist politics and philosophies in analyses of gendered violence were translated in practice into action on the ground to respond to it. Largely, this action was focused around two movements – the refuge movement, which developed in the early 1970s to assist women escaping from domestic violence, and the rape crisis movement, which developed in the late 1970s to assist women dealing with the aftermath of rape and sexual assault.[1] As we detail in the following discussion, the feminist analysis that created both movements has continued to be central to their existence. For over 30 years in both movements, women have worked with women for women to provide services to challenge and confront male violence.

The refuge and rape crisis movements

The refuge movement – sometimes called the battered women's movement – began in Britain in 1972 when feminists established the 'Goldhawk Road

Women's Liberation Movement Centre' in Chiswick, London. This centre was like others that were being established by feminists in Britain and other countries to provide a 'focal point for mutual support, discussion and political action' (Dobash and Dobash 1979: 223). Women came to the centre to discuss their problems and find support from other women. It was here that they began to disclose the systematic and severe abuse and violence they were receiving from their husbands (Pizzey 1974; Dobash and Dobash 1979, 1987, 1992; Sutton 1978). When a woman escaping her abusive husband was allowed to use the centre as emergency temporary accommodation, the centre became a 24-hour refuge for battered women – by April 1973 it had an average daily population of 25 women and children. There was much overcrowding – 'the refuge was literally bursting at the seams' (Dobash and Dobash 1992: 63). Nonetheless, the overcrowding made a strong point about demand and generated considerable popular interest. Indeed, it is this *double role* that has made the refuge so important to action against domestic violence.

Refuges have provided women with accommodation. In doing so, they have also challenged the social order in which women are dependent on others for their basic accommodation needs. By their very existence, refuges have demonstrated women's oppression in the family and society and have demanded that domestic violence be seen in a social, economic, cultural and political context of male domination and female disadvantage. As the Dobashes put it, 'the refuge stands simultaneously as an essential aspect of supporting women subject to male violence and of rejecting patriarchal control of women' (Dobash and Dobash 1992: 63).

The Rape Crisis Centres that developed in Britain in the late 1970s were to have the same dual purpose (Anna T. 1988; Corbett and Hobdell 1988; Kelly 1988; Gillespie 1994; Zedner 1997). The first Rape Crisis Centre (RCC) in Britain opened in London in 1976, offering a 24-hour telephone counselling service run by and for women, in addition to individual support to survivors of sexual violence (see London Rape Crisis Centre 1984; Roberts 1989). Another RCC opened in Birmingham in 1979. By 1986, the Birmingham RCC was dealing with almost 2,000 cases of rape, sexual assault and sexual abuse each year (Anna T. 1988). Nonetheless, as refuges were more than just accommodation, RCCs were much more than just service provision. Rather, from its beginnings, the rape crisis movement campaigned to raise awareness about the issues around rape, challenging assumptions about both 'the rape victim' and 'the rapist'. The movement always sought to make the connection between practice and theory and demanded that rape be understood in a political and social context which encouraged, condoned and excused male violence to women – the experiences of women themselves became the focus for collective action and collective change (Foley 1996). As Foley puts it, 'RCCs were never just about service provision but about making the fundamental connection between practice and theory and translating that into campaigning for social change' (Foley 1996: 167).

In addition to discovering women's need for accommodation, in the 1970s the battered women's movement discovered that, by working with them in the context of their own problems and needs, refuges could empower women to take decisions about their circumstances and futures (Dobash and Dobash 1980; Hague and Malos 1998). Throughout, the refuge movement has had as 'foundation stones' principles grounded in 'self-help, self-determination and empowerment' (Hague and Malos 1998: 39). Self-help involves women working with women for women to establish services to deal with male violence (Sutton 1978). Self-determination is grounded in an understanding that women should be able to determine their own lives and futures and take control back from their abusers. Empowerment centres on assisting abused women to develop the resources, both emotional and economic, to make appropriate decisions about their circumstances and futures (Hague and Malos 1998). By their very existence, refuges encompass these principles.

Likewise, the RCCs that developed in the late 1970s and early 1980s sought to provide a service that 'responded to women's needs, rather than defining for them what [their] experiences and responses should be' (Foley 1996: 167). Again, throughout the movement, RCCs have operated within a women-centred model of service provision, aiming to empower women who have been raped or sexually abused by listening to them, acknowledging how they feel, what difficulties they face and what struggles they are engaged in and *believing* their accounts of sexual violence (London Rape Crisis Centre 1984; Stanko 1985; Mawby and Gill 1987; Kelly 1988; Anna T. 1988; Gillespie 1994). Above all, this women-centred model attempts to enable women to regain *control* of their lives by supporting them to make their own decisions.

Since the 1970s, both the refuge and rape crisis movements have expanded such that there are now more that 300 refuges and over 60 RCCs in Great Britain. Both movements are now organised through national groupings – the refuge movement through the Women's Aid Federation England (WAFE) and the rape crisis movement through the Rape Crisis Co-Ordinating Group (RCCG). The Women's Aid Federation first formed in 1974, bringing together 35 founding groups that had developed since the events in Chiswick. The 'National Women's Aid Federation' allowed activists to turn popular attention to and raise awareness about domestic violence through more co-ordinated campaigning. General tenets derived from the women's liberation movement were translated into its original principles (Sutton 1978; Dobash and Dobash 1987, 1992). For many years, the rape crisis movement resisted this more federalised structure. Only in 1996, did it first organise around a national grouping – the Rape Crisis Federation, which 'exist[ed] to provide a range of facilities and resources to enable the continuance and development of Rape Crisis groups throughout England and Wales' (http://www.rapecrisis.co.uk). In 2003, a funding shortage forced the Rape Crisis Federation to close (see Jones and Westmarland 2004) but, in 2006, a new co-ordinating group emerged. The Rape Crisis Co-ordinating Group was 'formed to provide organisation for the rape crisis movement' (http://www.rapecrisis.org.uk).

At a national level, Women's Aid has continually undertaken to raise awareness about the existence, extent and experience of domestic violence and has monitored and campaigned about legal, policy and practice measures and for comprehensive services to meet the needs of abused women and their children (Hague and Malos 1998). In addition to this general awareness raising, Women's Aid delivers advice, support and training to local domestic violence groups and other agencies and organisations. The Women's Aid National Domestic Violence Helpline was established in 1994 – it became a 24-hour service in 2001. In 2003, Women's Aid joined with the national domestic violence charity, Refuge (see http://www.refuge.org.uk), to launch a new 24-hour Freephone National Domestic Violence Helpline. In 2004, Women's Aid launched The Hideout (http://www.thehideout.org.uk) – the first dedicated UK website for children and young people experiencing domestic abuse at home and relationship violence.

At a local level, Women's Aid refuges provide emergency and temporary accommodation to thousands of women and children fleeing violence in the home – in England alone over 50,000 women and children escape to refuges each year (see Williamson 2006). Within refuges, Women's Aid also runs support groups for women and provides children with support and assistance through the work of specialist children's workers. Locally, RCCs work with thousands of women each year, providing crisis and counselling telephone lines, face-to-face services and support groups. The centres also work with individuals to provide information and support about and around medical processes, reporting to the police, court procedures and so on. Not all groups providing services on and around domestic violence and rape are associated to Women's Aid or the rape crisis movement. For example, in our own city, Sheffield, in addition to the Women's Aid refuge and Sheffield Rape Crisis, there are a further three refuges, a 'floating support service' and four community-based domestic violence groups.[2]

Since their development in the 1970s, a main challenge that all refuges, RCCs and other support services have encountered is obtaining funding. Certainly, the considerable contribution from these organisations to action against gendered violence has not been mirrored in their resourcing. In her 1989 survey of RCCs, for example, Terry Gillespie found most considered themselves to be 'over-stretched, under-resourced and facing an increasing demand for their services' (Gillespie 1994: 16). A decade on, writing about refuges, Hague and Malos concluded that, 'while Women's Aid and the refuge network as a whole does its best to provide responsive and empowering services for abused women and their children, the whole enterprise is hampered by inadequate funding and poor resources' (1998: 47). Indeed, most such services have traditionally not received direct funding from central or local government and have relied, instead, on submitting 'bids' to bodies such as the National Lottery Fund and other charitable organisations to obtain funding. Enormous amounts of time have been spent preparing these bids – time that could clearly have been spent responding to women or otherwise developing services.

In the last five years, things have improved a little. Since 2003, the Office of the Deputy Prime Minister's 'Supporting People' initiative, which funds housing related support services for vulnerable people, has been the main funding source for the provision of refuge-based domestic violence services. In Sheffield, for example, the city's four refuges have, for the first time, received this funding to provide their core services, and, nationally, Women's Aid has recognised Supporting People's 'significance' to refuge services. In addition, since 2004, the government's Victims' Fund has provided funding, recovered from the proceeds of crime, to support the development of community-based services for victims of sexual offending. Over 100 organisations delivering such services received funding in 2004/05 and 2005/06 and £1.25 million was made available in the 2006/07 funding round.

Nonetheless, the funding situation in many organisations responding to gendered violence remains uncertain at best. For example, the Supporting People initiative does not fund children's services in refuges. Indeed, more broadly, refuges face particular funding difficulties in relation to children's services. Children and young people comprise about two-thirds of the refuge population but refuges receive little or no funding to provide specialist children's services – many provide such services without dedicated funding to do so. Further, a characteristic of the processes by which organisations responding to gendered violence have obtained funding, whether through bidding to the National Lottery and so on, or, indeed, to the government, is that there has been an emphasis on funding new and/or innovative projects for time-limited periods. Not only does this challenge the consolidation and consistent provision of existing services, it also means that development and delivery of long-term services is difficult. Further, evaluation of services becomes almost impossible to achieve (see Refuge 2004).

Finally, organisations working around gendered violence depend, sometimes solely, on women who volunteer their time through dedication and commitment to the problem. The thousands of women and children who use the services of refuges, RCCs and other such organisations are mostly supported by other women, who, for little or no pay, take on the day-to-day responsibility of assisting abused women to rebuild their lives and survive male violence. From the beginnings of the refuge and rape crisis movements over 30 years ago, this reliance on women volunteers has remained unchanged. It, perhaps more than any other feature of the funding situation these organisations face, reveals the abdication of responsibility for tackling men's violence and the associated projection of this responsibility on to women.

We have discussed, then, the discovery of domestic violence and rape and the development of the refuge movement and the rape crisis movement. We have seen that feminist theorising about gendered power relations grounded the first responses to both domestic violence and rape. We have also seen that this feminist thinking was translated into action on the ground, transcending the response to gendered violence since the 1970s. We have contrasted to the considerable contribution from services such as refuges and RCCs in confronting male violence to the government's commitment to them and their service users. Indeed, we have seen the failure on the part of central and local government to appropriately fund these services. We argue in the following discussion that this failure reflects a much broader failure on the part of the state to confront gendered violence.

State Responses to Gendered Violence

The failure on the part of the state to confront gendered violence has, we argue, occurred at several levels. At one level, there is the failure to confront violence in individual cases. This failure was first revealed in the late 1970s and early 1980s, when feminist researchers started to examine state services' responses to gendered violence. State failures in individual cases have also been seen in more recent times, in several highly publicised cases. At another level is the failure of state services to challenge gender as constructed in issues such as domestic violence, rape and so on, and, indeed, their colluding in gendered assumptions in service provision around these issues. A final level is the state's failure to confront violence *as* gendered. We argue that, even as the government and state services *have* taken these issues on, they have done so in a manner that has denied the issues' gendered nature. We argue that the services have failed to confront violence *as* gendered through substituting gender with other considerations such as crime, health, sexual health and so on.

State services' failure to confront violence in individual cases (then)

In the late 1970s and early 1980s, feminist researchers started to examine state services' responses to gendered violence. The 'knowledge explosion' (Kelly 1988: 43) that followed focused largely on state responses to domestic violence and, increasingly, on criminal justice responses to both domestic violence and rape. Certainly, much research around this time focused on violence in the home, as numerous researchers endeavoured to examine state service provision to women in domestic violence situations. Interviews were conducted with women about the responses they had received and other research was conducted in state services themselves. The extensive literature which developed, based on this research, revealed the gap between the assistance which was, in principle, available to women and their children and that which women received in practice. This gap, it seemed, centred on state services' failure to see domestic violence as something that concerned them.

Doctors did not consider it 'real medicine' to be concerned with how patients received injuries, only with 'treating injuries and illnesses – real medicine' (Smith 1989: 73; Pahl 1978; Dobash and Dobash 1980; Binney et al. 1981; Borkowski et al. 1983). Social workers, it seemed, were not interested in abused women and did not take their situations seriously, often telling women there was nothing they could do to assist them (Dobash and Dobash 1980; Binney et al. 1981; Maynard 1985). Housing departments deemed women 'not homeless' or 'not in priority need' and did not re-house them, contrary to the Housing (Homeless Persons) Act 1977 (Binney et al. 1981, 1985). The police failed to see domestic violence as 'real crime' or 'real police work' – 'every time you get to do some real police work you get stuck with this stuff' (Reiss 1971: 42; see Reiner 1978; Faragher 1985; Southgate 1986; Edwards 1986, 1989; Hanmer 1989; Young 1991) – and were unwilling to intervene in 'domestics'.

Indeed, these police failures around domestic violence attracted increasing attention in the research literature in the 1980s. Researchers found that, even in conditions that supported an arrest, men were seldom arrested (Dobash and Dobash 1980; Binney et al. 1981; Pagelow 1981; Bowker 1982; Faragher 1985; Edwards 1986a, b). In her research, Hanmer (1989) found that the police would arrest only as a 'last resort' and that some officers had *never* made an arrest in a domestic violence case. Other research suggested that the police often made intervention dependent on the likelihood that the victim would carry through with a prosecution (Morley and Mullender 1994) or placed the responsibility for deciding whether charges should be pressed on women themselves. The research literature also revealed that, when men were charged, it was often with a lesser offence – breach of the peace or drunkenness instead of assault (see Edwards 1989).

It seemed in the 1970s and early 1980s, then, that state services were failing to provide an appropriate response to domestic violence. We argue below that these failures were attributable to gendered assumptions that conceptualised women and not their abusers' violence as the problem. Meanwhile, literature in the 1970s and 1980s revealed the same failures in state services on and around rape.

No other service was as open to criticism in this regard as the police. Indeed, most literature on and about state responses to sexual assault around this time focused on the criminal justice response in general and the police response in particular.[3] Interestingly, though, police failings in relation to rape were most markedly revealed, not in the literature, but in a television programme about the Thames Valley Police. In 1982, the criminologist and journalist, Roger Graef, made a fly-on-the-wall documentary about the Thames Valley force. One episode – *A Complaint of Rape* – showed the police questioning a women reporting rape. Alone in a room with three and then two men, the complainant was subjected to brutally insensitive questioning, all the more shocking because the officers knew they were being filmed and were happy to show how they treated rape complainants. An extract from this pioneering programme, which vividly reveals the police's treatment of the woman complainant, can be used as a case-study to explore police response to rape around this time.

Case-study: A Complaint of Rape (Lees 1999; see Adler 1987; Temkin 1987; Lees 1997)

The complainant (C) has described how three men raped her, then gave her 16p for her bus fare.

Police officer Brian Kirk (K): (Shouting) Listen to me. I've been sitting here for 20 minutes, half an hour, listening to you. It's the biggest load of bollocks I've ever heard. I could get very annoyed very shortly ... Stop mucking us all about.

C: I'm not mucking about.

K: I'm not saying you're lying. But get rid of all the fruitiness, get rid of the beauty about it.

(Continued)

(Continued)

C: (Crying) It's not beautiful at all.

K: Some of it is. All this crap about bus stops and tea towels to wipe yourself down with. What the hell's going on? If nothing's going on, let's pack it in and go home ...

Police officer John McIntyre: I would agree that you have had sex this afternoon ... but I think you've been a willing party ... The story you've told us is a fairytale.

C: (Shouting) It happened!

K: I'm not saying it didn't happen. I'm talking about the embroidery ...

M: We know what's happened here. You've had a hard time ... You've had a long, long time of being treated for depression, haven't you? (Shouts) Haven't you?

C: (Nods)

M: You go to the pub, you meet a couple of fellas, they say, let's go back for a coffee and it all goes a bit far.

C: I didn't even know them before!

M: (Incredulous) You got into the car with them. You made no effort to get away from them.

K: I've met some that have been raped and they think their life is crumbling around their ankles like a pair of knickers with the elastic gone. Doesn't hold water this, does it? I'm not saying it's not true ... I'm saying there's a lot more to this. Unfortunately we'll never hear the other side ... All we've got is your side and you're making a fairytale out of it.

C: I'm not.

K: I think you are.

M: Do you realise when we have you examined, it will show whether or not you've had sexual intercourse with three men this afternoon?

C: I know. So it should show ...

M: (Interrupts) It will confirm whether you've had sex with three men. If it does, then I say you went willingly ... You could easily have run away. Easily ... You're not frightened.

C: I was frightened.

M: You weren't. You show no signs of emotion. Every now and then you have a little tear ... I spoke to your boyfriend ... That's how I know all about your periods and when you last had sex ... Why on earth didn't you scream and shout ? ...

K: (Bored) Do you or do you not want to make a complaint of rape?

C: No, I don't.

Importantly, Graef's documentary revealed, as was also revealed in the literature, that police perceptions about rape and rape victims were translated into police *practices*. In other words, not only did the reporting of rape to the police amount in many cases to a second victimisation, replicating the violation felt in the rape itself,[4] but the police's belief that rape was not important, not a criminal justice matter, the woman's fault, and so on, caused many rapes to go no further than the first report to the police. Indeed, numerous studies in the early and mid-1980s showed that the police did not record rape complaints as crimes (Chambers and Millar 1983; Wright 1984; Women's National Commission 1985; Smith 1989; Grace et al. 1992).

A Complaint of Rape caused considerable public concern and can be credited as the impetus (Lees 1997; Gregory and Lees 1999) to far-reaching reforms in the police response to rape in particular (Home Office Circular 25/83; Home Office Circular 69/86) and violence against women more generally (Home Office Circular 60/90). Indeed, the failings in the state response to gendered violence examined in this discussion were first revealed over 30 years ago. Three decades on, has service provision in individual cases improved? We move to explore this question in the following discussion.

State services' failure to confront violence in individual cases (now)

The policy guidance that has abounded in the last decade alone certainly reflects an increasing recognition that domestic violence, rape, etc., are problems that *should* concern state services. Nonetheless, cases continue to appear in the headlines that reveal serious failings in the state response to individual women. Four such cases serve as interesting and important case-studies to examine whether or not service provision around gendered violence has improved in the last 30 years. All concern women who have been murdered by their partners or former partners, following repeated and sustained harassment which services in general and the police in particular failed to take seriously.

Case-study: lessons learnt or lives lost?

In the last five years, several cases have made the headlines, bringing to broader attention the problems in the police response to partner abuse that first appeared in the literature over 30 years ago. Above, we saw that these problems centred on a failure to see domestic violence as a 'police problem' and an associated failure to take seriously the gender and power dynamics therein. In the four cases below, the police again seem to have failed to recognise their responsibilities to protect the women concerned and to prevent the violence, intimidation and threats each was facing. In each case, these police failures proved catastrophic.

Rana Faruqui

In August 2003, Rana Faruqui was murdered by her former partner, Stephen Griffiths. Earlier in 2003, Rana had started a relationship with Griffiths and he had moved into her home. Following several violent episodes, Rana had

(Continued)

(Continued)

ended the relationship and Griffiths had moved out. Soon, his campaign of harassment and threats began. He rummaged through her bins, broke into her home and photographed both her and her house. The police were called several times but did nothing more than warn Griffiths, who, each time, promised not to bother Rana again. Yet, on 21 July 2003, Rana telephoned Thames Valley Police to report that the brake pipes on her car had been cut. Nothing happened, so three days later Rana went in person to the police with the same information. Again, the police took no action. Ten days later, Griffiths stabbed Rana to death. Following his arrest, the police found in Griffiths's car items including a rope, a chisel, a crowbar, rat poison, an axe, a saw, knives, binoculars and a truncheon. In December 2004, Griffiths was jailed for Rana's murder. At the same time, Thames Valley Police issued a statement admitting failures in how they responded to Rana's complaint about the brake-cutting – 'this particular incident should have been dealt with differently and a full internal investigation has been launched' (see *Guardian* 16 April 2005).

Tania Moore

In March 2004, Tania Moore was murdered by her former fiancé Mark Dyche. In 1993, Dyche had been convicted of making threats to kill his former wife and in 1999 had been arrested for and charged with (but not convicted of) harassing his then girlfriend. In February 2003, Tania ended their two-year relationship. Two months later, her harassment by Dyche began. In April 2003, Tania reported to Derbyshire Police that Dyche had abused and assaulted her and damaged her car. The following month, she reported that she had received a threatening telephone call and had suffered further damage to her car – she believed Dyche to be responsible. Also in May 2003, she reported that she was receiving nuisance telephone calls and had again been abused and assaulted by Dyche. Dyche was arrested and bailed. The following month, Tania was attacked in her home by two men. She was repeatedly hit with baseball bats and robbed. Tania believed Dyche to be responsible and there were strong grounds to assume that he had planned and contracted the assault. The police never questioned him about his possible involvement. In March 2004, Tania reported that Dyche was again telephoning her threatening to kill her, and following her, gesturing that he would shoot her. The same month, Dyche drove into Tania's car and shot her in the face as she lay trapped inside. In November 2006, the IPCC concluded that 'simple basic lines of enquiry' that might have prevented Tania's murder had never been pursued and described the police response as 'abysmal' (IPCC 1 November 2006; (see also *Guardian* 2 November 2006).

Hayley Richards

In June 2005, Hayley Richards was murdered by her former partner, Hugo Quintas. One week before she died, Hayley had called 999, reporting that

Quintas had assaulted her and threatened to kill her (Hayley needed hospital treatment following this assault). The police attended Hayley's home but Quintas was no longer present. The following week, Wiltshire Police had opportunities to arrest Quintas but did not do so. On one occasion, Hayley had telephoned the police to inform them of Quintas's whereabouts but at the time officers were dealing with a distressed dog and when they became free did not act on the information about Quintas to arrest him. In addition, on two other occasions, officers unconnected to the case spoke to Quintas about other police matters but, again, did not arrest him for the assault on Hayley. One week after his first assault, Quintas slit Hayley's throat, killing her and her unborn child. In April 2006, the IPCC investigation into the case concluded that Wiltshire Police's handling of Hayley's first report was poor and that 'institutional failings' had caused Quintas to avoid arrest. As the IPCC Commissioner put it, 'Wiltshire Constabulary's response to a woman who had reported a serious assault was not good enough and the force failed to give a victim of domestic violence the priority and protection she deserved' (IPCC 28 April 2006; see also *Guardian* 15 June 2005).

Clare Bernal

In September 2005, Clare Bernal was shot dead by her former boyfriend, Michael Pech, in the Harvey Nichols shop in London. Pech had become obsessed with Clare after briefly dating her in February 2005. Following the end of their relationship, Pech started to harass Clare. He also threatened to kill her. In April 2005, Pech was arrested, charged with harassment and remanded in Belmarsh prison but his case was postponed and he was released on bail. The police did not tell Clare that Pech was free. Pech then travelled to his native Slovakia, where he underwent firearms training and bought a gun. In July 2005, he returned to London, with the gun. On 31 August 2005, he pleaded guilty to harassment but was again given bail. Thirteen days later, he shot Clare four times in the head before turning the gun on himself. In October 2006, *The Times* reported that a confidential internal Metropolitan Police review had found failures in how the police handled Clare's repeated attempts to get assistance (2 October 2006). *The Times* reports, for example, that the review accused officers of not using the latest procedures to assess a stalker's potential threat. In addition, the review found 'internal difficulties' in how the Metropolitan Police record information about the dangers a man such as Pech is thought to present. For example, the lead officer in Clare's case should have undertaken a full assessment of the dangers Pech posed but no record was ever made of such an assessment being conducted (see also *Guardian* 27 February 2006).

Given that two women each week are killed by a current or former partner one has to assume that these four cases represent a small proportion of predictable and preventable domestic killings. Indeed, of greater concern are perhaps those cases that do not attract the attention that these cases have attracted – those ordinary, intimate killings which are not headline grabbers but which are serious and significant nonetheless. Further, as regards other gendered violence, there remain serious failings in the state response. Ian Huntley, for example, had 10 different contacts with the police and social services before he took a job as a school caretaker in Soham and went on to murder local schoolgirls, Holly Wells and Jessica Chapman, in August 2002. He was four times accused of having under-age sex, four times accused of rape, once accused of indecent assault and once accused of burglary. Tellingly, the only accusation to go to court was the burglary. The police once charged Huntley with rape but the Crown Prosecution Service dropped the case. The police and social services took no action against him in any of the under-age sex allegations or the indecent assault allegation.[5]

Thus, although there is an increasing recognition that domestic violence, rape and so on are problems that should concern state services, it appears that state services' failures to confront gendered violence, first revealed in the 1970s and 1980s, continue to be repeated 30 years on. In the 1970s and early 1980s, research suggested that state services were failing to confront both domestic violence and rape, leaving women without protection both individually and more generally. In 2008, this failure to protect remains, causing catastrophic results for individual women and exposing all women to unchallenged and unchecked male violence. In the following discussion, we move to examine how these state failures have been attributable to gendered assumptions and explore how state services have colluded in and perpetuated gendered assumptions in their response to gendered violence.

State services' failure to challenge 'gender'

We saw above that, in the 'knowledge explosion' of the late 1970s and early 1980s, feminist research literature started to reveal the inappropriate response from state services to gendered violence. This literature also revealed that state services' responses to violence were, in numerous cases, determined by *gendered assumptions* that frustrated a positive response to it. On domestic violence, these assumptions were around the family and women's position in it, about the violence and women's connections to it and about women and their proper role. Research found, for example, that social workers sought to reconcile women with their abuser (Binney et al. 1981; Maynard 1985). The Dobashes certainly argued that the response from social service departments was grounded in a 'philosophy which emphasise[d] the maintenance of the traditional position of men and women as husbands and wives' (Dobash and Dobash 1980: 205). Researchers found that children were sometimes used to stop women leaving violent homes – 'social services … said "all we can do if you want to leave is we'll take the children off you and take them into care and we don't want that do we?"' (Binney et al. 1981: 19). Research into the police response also found that, rather than arrest in domestic violence cases, police would endeavour to 'settle the disturbance' (Stanko 1989: 57).

To encourage 'reconciliation' between the parties, it seemed the police sometimes encouraged the woman to change her behaviour (Grace 1995; see also Faragher 1985; Edwards 1986a, b; 1989; Morley and Mullender 1994). Other research also found that services focused on women's behaviour. Researching social service responses, Maynard found an implication that, through domestic and personal failings, women were somehow responsible for the violence. Sometimes social workers were more explicit – 'it seems her nagging is a trigger for the violence' (Maynard 1985: 135).

Likewise, it seemed that assumptions about the 'deserving victim' could explain the police response (see Reiner 1978). Researchers argued that women had to show they did not 'deserve' to be assaulted. Thus Hanmer et al. (1989) argued that the protection the police offered to women was 'conditional upon women meeting police notions of "deservedness"' (1989: 6). Again, these notions were said to be based on misogynistic, racist, classist and heterosexist assumptions about women in general, and wives and mothers in particular. Most obviously, then, it appeared arrest was less likely when women were married to or living with the violent man because the police deferred to the sanctity of the family (Pahl 1985; see Dobash and Dobash 1979; Stanko 1989).

Finally, it was said that the police did not arrest and charge because they assumed that it was almost certain a woman would withdraw charges and not support a prosecution. It appeared that police attitudes were based on perceptions of a 'set pattern' of behaviour – 'you [the police] arrest the husband and suddenly she's in love again' (Stanko 1989: 62; 1985; see Oppenlander 1982; Faragher 1985; Edwards 1986, 1989, 1996; Hanmer 1989; Grace 1995; Walker and McNicol 1994; Clifton et al. 1996). Research also found that some social workers believed that women considered the violence normal so did not respond to reduce it.

State services were, it appeared, failing to challenge gender as constructed in domestic violence. Indeed, the assumptions that appeared to pervade the response from state services in the late 1970s and early 1980s minimised the gendered power relations that are central to domestic violence in particular and gendered violence more broadly. The assumption, for example, that women were sometimes ambivalent to a criminal justice response to violence from their partners because they were 'suddenly in love again' denied the massive power imbalances that characterise violent 'partnerships'. Indeed, in many cases, women's ambivalence to criminal justice interventions is based on *fear* and not on romance or 'love' – 'I hate the bastard but he'd kill me if I got him into trouble with the police' (woman interviewee, quoted in Hoyle 1998: 189). Alongside this, the assumptions that grounded state services' provision around domestic violence maintained traditional stereotypes about men and women and male and female. The assumption, for example, that women should not leave violent homes and that women who did escape violence would have their children removed, reinforced stereotypes about both 'the family' and women's role in it. Again, assumptions about women's 'characteristics' perpetuated stereotypes about, *inter alia*, male rights and female responsibilities.

Literature based on research conducted in the 1970s and 1980s also revealed that state services' responses to sexual violence were determined by gendered assumptions. Largely, these assumptions revolved around women's supposed propensity to lie about rape. Again, no service was more culpable in this regard than the police. The literature suggested that, as in the Graef extract above, the police proceeded from the basis that most rape complaints were false allegations. Indeed, successive research around this time focused on police officers' inclination to disbelieve rape complainants. In their important research in Scotland, for example, Chambers and Miller (1983) found that women were told, 'you haven't got much of a story', 'your statement is likely a fairy tale', 'don't talk rubbish' and 'you're making this up'. Alongside this, the police themselves described the need to 'test' a complainant's 'story' when interviewing complainants and the importance of 'trying to catch her out'. In practice, it seemed these police assumptions could discourage complainants from giving a full account or could even encourage them to distort their account in an effort to be believed (of course, this served only to reinforce police scepticism and confirm police suspicions about women's propensity to make false allegations) (Gregory and Lees 1999).

Associated to findings that the police assumed a complaint/complainant should be 'tested', research also focused on a veracity/violence connection around which police assumptions were said to revolve. The literature repeatedly suggested that the police assumed a complainant was more likely to be lying about the rape when she showed no signs of having suffered violence. The police seemed more convinced about the complainant's veracity in cases ('good' cases or 'real rapes') in which a *stranger* had used *violence* to obtain intercourse (Feldman-Summers and Norris 1984; Koss et al. 1988; Williams 1984). The character of these situations was different, as Chambers and Miller put it, 'for the police placed them beyond the realms of exaggeration and fabrication from the outset' (1983: 87), and so allowed the complainant to avoid suspicion about her truthfulness.

At the same time, though, Chambers and Miller (1983) found that other women were disbelieved because their appearance following a stranger rape was seen as *too* dishevelled. There were other cases in which obvious injuries were nonetheless thought by the police to be questionable. Indeed, of further importance to whether or not a complainant was believed was her character in general and her 'chasteness' in particular.

These assumptions about women's likelihood to falsely allege rape and the associated assumptions about violence/veracity and character/credibility are neatly summarised by a detective sergeant writing in the *Police Review* in the mid-1970s about interviewing rape complainants:

> The offence of rape is extremely unlikely to have been committed against a woman who does not immediately show signs of extreme violence. If a woman walks into a police station and complains of rape with no such signs of violence she must be closely interrogated. Allow her to make her statement to a police-woman and then drive a horse and cart through it ... Watch out for the girl who

is pregnant or late getting home one night; such persons are notorious for alleging rape or indecent assault. Do not give her sympathy. (Firth 1975: 1507)

Finally, the literature revealed that police assumptions about how women *should* behave following a rape were central to how they regarded her complaint and how they responded to it. In Chambers and Miller's research, for example, the police attached considerable importance to the complainant's condition after the attack, whether or not she reported the attack immediately and what she did afterwards – 'does she rush into a nearby house all in tears, or does she quietly get on a bus or a taxi and go home and not think about it until the next again morning [*sic*]' (police officer quoted in Chambers and Miller 1983: 89). On this last point, research repeatedly revealed the police assumption that women who have been raped 'ought' to respond in a hysterical and tearful manner and rush as soon as possible to tell someone, ideally the police, about it, and that women who do not respond in this manner should be regarded with suspicion.

Again, state services appeared to be failing to challenge gender as constructed in sexual violence and, again, the assumptions that appeared to pervade the response in the late 1970s and early 1980s minimised the gendered power relations that are central to rape. Indeed, as we discuss in more detail in Chapter 7, the assumption that women who complain about rape are not to be trusted supports and sustains stereotypes about femininity, female irrationality and female fragility, appealing to assumptions that women are fanciful and frivolous. Assumptions about women's 'proper' responses also rest on stereotypes about femininity (women either cry or are lying). Further, these assumptions fail to recognise the complexity of individual women's reactions to rape (London Rape Crisis Centre 1984; Roberts 1989) and, in doing so, not only fail to recognise but actually reinforce the disempowerment of the rape itself.

Thus, the inappropriate response from state services to gendered violence, first revealed in the 'knowledge explosion' of the late 1970s and early 1980s, appeared grounded in gendered assumptions that frustrated a positive response to it. In the following discussion, we move to examine whether or not there have been challenges to these gendered assumptions, through exploring developments around service provision in the 1990s and 2000s. Central to this examination is our argument that, in these developments, there has been a failure to confront violence as gendered.

Failure to confront violence as gendered

Earlier, we saw that the pioneering responses to domestic violence, rape and so on in the 1970s were grounded in women's liberation and feminism. In contrast, contemporary responses have increasingly centred on the government in general and the Home Office in particular. The state, it seems, has at last taken on gendered violence. Policy guidance that has abounded in the last 15 years, and repeated in government statements is a commitment to the seriousness with which it regards gendered violence:

The Government is determined to prevent domestic violence happening or recurring, to protect and support its victims, and to bring offenders to justice. (http://www.crimereduction.gov.uk/dv/dv01.htm)

Sexual crime and the fear of sexual crime has a profound and damaging effect on individuals and communities. We're determined to reduce this kind of crime. (http://www.homeoffice.gov.uk/crime-victims/reducing-crime/sexual-offences/)

Prostitution blights communities and the lives of those who participate. While kerb-crawlers could choose not to pay for sex, women involved in prostitution often have very limited choices in life. They come from difficult backgrounds, might have drug problems or nowhere safe to live. I want them to have help and support to leave prostitution (http://www.homeoffice.gov.uk/about-us/news/prostitution-strategy).

Sustained interest from the government in gendered violence started properly around 1999, when the Women's Unit published 'Living without fear: an integrated approach to tackling violence against women'. 'Living without fear' certainly heralded a flurry of activity on gendered violence in government circles. There have, for example, been major legislative changes around domestic violence in the Domestic Violence Crime Victims Act 2004, around rape and prostitution in the Sexual Offences Act 2003 and around sex trafficking in the Nationality, Immigration and Asylum Act 2002, the Sexual Offences Act 2003 and the Asylum and Immigration (Treatment of Claimants) Act 2004.[6] There have also been national government strategies on domestic violence in the 2005 National Report on domestic violence (Home Office 2005) and around prostitution in the 2006 Co-Ordinated Prostitution Strategy (Home Office 2006). At the time of writing, a similar strategy on sex trafficking is in preparation.

The purpose of this chapter is not to examine these individual initiatives themselves[7] but is rather to use these initiatives to suggest that, even as the state has taken on gendered violence, it has done so in a manner that has failed to see the violence *as* gendered and that, as such, there has been little challenge to the gendered assumptions that dominated state service provision in the 1970s and 1980s. The suggestion is that the context of these assumptions has clearly changed but the failure to confront *gender* has not.

There are many aspects to state developments since the mid to late 1990s that might be used to suggest that, in these developments, there has been a failure to confront gender. The very point that most developments around gendered violence have taken place, not at a political/philosophical level, but at a policy level is itself an indication that processes and priorities other than the feminist political project of the 1970s have been at play as service provision has developed in the last 10 years or so.

A further point suggesting that factors other than gender have been functioning is that many of these developments since the mid to late 1990s have taken place within the Home Office's agenda on crime and crime reduction. Indeed, in the last 10 years, gendered violence has become a firm fixture in the government's 'fight against crime'. The Home Office certainly took the lead in both the legislative developments and the national strategies on domestic violence and prostitution (and is taking the lead in the strategy on sex trafficking), mentioned a moment ago. Further, domestic violence, rape and prostitution have all been included in one of the government's flag-ship crime reduction initiatives, the Crime Reduction Programme. This inclusion itself is testament to these issues' standing in government discourse as crime problems. The £400 million Crime Reduction Programme (CRP) (which also made funding available to developing crime reduction around burglary and through the use of closed circuit television) saw over £7 million directed into funding action around gendered violence. In February 2000, the CRP's Violence Against Women (VAW) initiative was launched. Local projects were given £6.3 million to devise and develop crime reduction around both domestic violence and rape. Over 30 projects were funded under the VAW initiative. In addition, in December 2000, the Home Office awarded £850,000 to fund 11 projects around prostitution, again within the CRP.

All these CRP projects were evaluated by Home Office appointed researchers and the evaluations were published by the Home Office in possibly the largest contribution to the literature on gendered violence since the 1970s (Douglas et al. 2004; Mullender 2004; Parmar et al. 2005a, b; Taket et al. 2004; Taket 2004; Lovett et al. 2004; Regan et al. 2004a, b; Kelly et al. 2005; Skinner and Taylor 2005; Hester and Westmarland 2005). Indeed, the 'knowledge explosion' of the 1970s and 1980s has been replaced by a similar contemporary explosion. This contemporary knowledge, though, centres very clearly on the Home Office and on the series after series of evaluative research studies it has published since the early 1990s. In the last 10 years, there have been multiple Home Office publications on domestic violence alone.

Our suggestion, based on these and other developments since the 1990s, is that there has been a prioritisation of the *crime* problem in much gendered violence. This prioritisation rests on a failure to confront violence as gendered, since, in placing both domestic violence and rape as crime problems, government developments have denied their standing as *gender* problems. As both become discussed alongside crimes such as burglary, and as responses to them are developed alongside crime reduction measures such as CCTV, their gendering becomes unspoken. Indeed, it is not that domestic violence and rape, or, indeed, violence against prostitute women and other sex workers, etc., should not be regarded and responded to as something other, or less, than a crime. Certainly, as will be discussed in Chapter 7, there remain considerable concerns that men's sexual violence is effectively decriminalised by a law that fails to convict 9 out of 10 men accused of rape. Rather, our suggestion is that, in promoting domestic violence, rape and so on as *crime* problems, there is an inclination to obscure and obviate the empirical evidence that reveals considerable and consistent gendering in relation to them.

In promoting domestic and sexual violence as crime problems, developments since the 1990s have also promoted the *criminal justice* processes and priorities attached to 'crime' in service provision for them, rather than the priorities that are associated with approaching them as *gendered* violence. There have, for example, developed pro-arrest and pro-charge policies in relation to domestic violence (Morley and Mullender 1994), alongside specialist domestic violence courts and so-called Independent Domestic Violence Advisors based in these specialist courts. These developments clearly match police and other criminal justice service priorities (for whom the main considerations are arrest, leading to prosecution and conviction: criminal justice goals) but how do they fit with women's priorities? For most women, their main consideration is immediate protection: past experience might have revealed that this goal is not achieved through criminal justice measures (Hoyle 1998; Hoyle and Sanders 2000). The Home Office has also started to fund the 'Poppy Project' – a research, development and accommodation project that provides services to up to 25 women trafficked into sexual exploitation in the United Kingdom. Importantly, in order to be allowed to use Poppy's service, a woman must fulfil certain Home Office criteria. One requirement is that she must be willing to co-operate with the authorities. So, a woman must be able to give information or evidence that the police judge is likely to be of material value to a prosecution, or to contribute to intelligence information on a trafficking network in order to use the services. Again, though, it is questionable whether and how these criminal justice priorities fit with trafficked women's own priorities.

Clearly, there are tensions that follow as gender problems become (re)defined as crime problems and take on crime-related priorities. The conflict appears to be between the priorities and practices that follow from, on the one hand, promoting the *crime* problem in gendered violence and, on the other hand, promoting the *gendering* in and of this violence (see Welsh 2008).[8] Arguably, in the failure to confront gender, discernible in developments around gendered violence since the mid to late 1990s and documented throughout the present discussion, another set of priorities is also promoted. Through approaching gendered violence in a manner than diminishes and denies its very gendering, attention is turned away from violence as gendered – violence is allowed to be neutralised and the gender politics therein are negated. In the failure to confront violence as gendered, then, *men's* priorities are also promoted.

Conclusion

This chapter began by documenting the 'discovery' of gendered violence and discussing the development of action to confront and challenge men's violence to women. It traced how, in the 1970s, feminist thinking about domestic violence and rape was translated into action on the ground, through the founding of the first refuges and rape crisis centres for survivors of domestic and sexual violence.

Having examined the important role that such organisations assume in challenging and confronting male violence, the role that state agencies have assumed in this regard was examined. The levels of state failures around gendered violence were discussed, including state failures in individual cases in both the 1970s and 1980s, and, 30 years on, the wider associated failure to recognise violence as gendered. Because, as the state has taken on gendered violence, it has done so in a manner that has failed to confront violence *as* gendered, then, in this failure, gendered violence is neutralised, gender politics are negated and, crucially, men go unnoticed.

Yet, it is interesting and important to observe that this last point runs *throughout* the chapter. Men and men's violence have not featured in the discussions. Our focus has been on services for women – men have been hidden. This focus on women, though, is not a construct of *our* choices and concerns. Rather, as has occurred at a philosophical level in criminology in general and, of course, in victimology in particular, at a practical level in provision around gendered violence, there has been an emphatic and enduring failure to tackle men and their violence. Certainly, almost all action has focused on supporting women in domestic violence situations, women who have been raped, women who wish to leave prostitution, etc. Almost no attention has been given to targeting men and male violence. In Sheffield, for example, there is virtually no provision of resources to work with men who abuse their partners and children; nor any to support the boys and teenage men whose model of masculinity, parenting and husbanding is learnt in such families and may well inform future relationships.

Indeed, inevitably, the failure to notice men means that there has also been a failure to turn attention to the sites and locations in which male power is most operationalised and male violence is most routinely exercised – the home and family. As seen in Chapter 4, criminology left to feminism the responsibility to begin to conceptualise this empirical reality. As seen in the present chapter, feminists in particular and women in general have also been left the responsibility to challenge it through the provision of refuges, RCCs and other support to women surviving male violence. In the next chapter, we begin to address the inattention paid to the sites and locations in which male power is exercised, through remembering the empirical evidence presented in Chapter 3 and reflecting in more detail on the spaces and relationships that are most likely to support and sustain sexual violence and abuse, behind the closed doors of the home.

Notes: Issues for Reflection

1 Of course, there were other movements which developed around this time.

What were these other movements? How did they begin and how have they developed since?

2 How do women experience the services of refuges and rape crisis centres?

Try to find studies about women's experiences of these services. What do these studies show?

3 Several studies examined the response women received from medical services (Smith 1980; Chambers and Miller 1983; Davis 1985; Blair 1985; Corbett 1987; Tempkin 1996). Again, though, this examination was in the context of the police response and focused on police medical examinations and the response provided by police surgeons.

What are the main findings revealed in this research? How do those findings compare to the literature on and around doctors' responses to domestic violence?

4 The (potentially shattering) experience of reporting rape was not a phenomenon confined to England and Wales. Research worldwide has highlighted the rough treatment by the police of rape complainants.

Using the references supplied, critically examine the experiences of rape complainants as revealed in research conducted in:

- Scotland: Chambers and Miller (1986); Brown et al. (1992)
- America: Brownmiller (1975)
- Australia: Scutt (1980); Wilson (1978); New South Wales Department for Women (1996); Easteal (1998)
- New Zealand: Young (1983)
- Canada: Clark and Lewis (1977)
- Scandinavia: Snare (1983)

5 Using (i) literature sources and (ii) news/media sources, research and reflect on recent state responses to other cases of gendered violence.

6 What were the main provisions of these legislative developments?

7 Examine these developments. What are their main provisions? What improvements could they bring? Could these developments have gone further? How?

8 Here, we have discussed the substitution of gender with crime but in state and government developments since the mid to late 1990s there has also been the substitution of gender with other considerations, such as, health, sexual health, drugs, etc. Using the information gathered for note 6, critically examine how this has happened.

Complementary Readings

L. Kelly (1988) *Surviving Sexual Violence* (Cambridge: Polity Press) is a seminal text on sexual violence.

T. Gillespie (1994) 'Under pressure: rape crisis centres, multi-agency work and strategies for survival', in C. Lupton and T. Gillespie (eds) *Working With Violence* (Basingstoke: Macmillan) overviews the crisis in organisations supporting women victims of violence.

See also H. Jones and N. Westmarland (2004) 'Remembering the past but looking to the future' (http://www.rapecrisis.org.uk/history.htm).

L. Kelly et al. (2005) *A Gap or a Chasm? Attrition in Reported Rape Cases.* Home Office Research Study 293 (London: Home Office) tracks the continued failure to successfully prosecute rape.

6

THE FAMILY OF MAN

Chapter 6 turns towards the spaces and relationships that are actually most likely to support violence and sexual abuse: the family and close community (McIntosh 1988; Saraga 2001; Grubin 1998). It reviews the history of the family and considers how familial practices not only actively construct gendered subjectivity but also provide the context for much sexual and violent offending. It deconstructs the myth of the dangerous stranger and in its place focuses closely on the extent to which offending between men and women and between adults and children is overwhelmingly found to involve offenders and victims who know each other well and/or live with or close to one another, often in some kind of family unit. Previous examples have shown how much attention to gendered crime has focused on extreme cases of multiple murder, unknown assailants, missing children or celebrity cases, whereas the data shows clearly that most gendered violence happens at home, within families or in intimate interpersonal contexts and is committed by men who are husbands, lovers, friends and fathers. Chapter 4 illustrated the way in which criminology has developed theoretically so as to leave the reasons for men's perpetration of these 'hidden' crimes poorly understood. Such a theoretical shortfall must contribute to a situation where many agencies trying to confront the consequences for women and children of high levels of violence have little chance of prevention or change and are in a situation of perpetual crisis management.

In this chapter the home and family are evaluated as central to sexual reproduction and social reproduction as well as to the construction of subjective and gendered identity. The family, historically and continuously, nurtures high levels of gender-differentiated activity and is also very often a place where gendered crime is violent and/or sexual, so the concept of family certainly has relevance to the nature of gendered crime. Crimes within the family are also overwhelmingly perpetrated by men against women and girls, so looking at the family may help to explain the high volume of male offending and lack of female offending more generally. The level of masculine agency in intra-familial offending counters many preconceptions about family, and this chapter tries to deconstruct some of those and open the closed doors of the home to explore the family and try to relate its role and meanings to the potential *dangerousness* of the men who remain often in fact, and still symbolically, at the head of the household. First, the chapter explores the concept and meaning of family and its place in socio-cultural formations. Second, it considers the relationship between family and subjectivity, particularly in relation to better understanding men and so what it might be about being a man that is apparently criminogenic. It then critically evaluates the idealistic model of the family that is so central, not just to religion and popular culture, but to policy. The chapter concludes by evaluating current debates about families in relation to crime and deviance, but also to gender roles and relations more broadly, to explore the themes of violence, gender and justice.

Family Histories

In 1994, Else wrote: 'Everybody believes in the importance of families – even though no one really knows what it is any more' (1994: 29). Nonetheless most would agree that there is a standard model of the family in Western society which is a married, monogamous heterosexual couple with children, sharing a living space, even if many of us no longer know many (or any) such units. Despite the conceptual centrality of marital family in Western culture, in reality, in England and Wales there were 151,654 divorces in 2005 (http://www.statistics. gov.uk/). Whilst for many, marital relationships are not where family starts, in the US: 'The number of unmarried-couple households with children has been climbing, hitting more than 1.7 million last year, up from under 200,000 in 1970' (Stobbe 2006).

The concept of the nuclear family remains a powerful model of romantic commitment, happy childhood and welcoming hearths, even though the perfect nuclear family is certainly a myth for many of us in the twenty-first century. Indeed, it has arguably always been little more than an ideal, although, nonetheless, an ideal that informs much of Western morality, its sense of stability and value-system. What is perhaps most interesting about the concept of the model family is how persistent and pervasive it is, despite the reality, and how it became such a dominant aspect of social and sexual organisation.

Although the contemporary nuclear family is often attributed to the Victorian period, in practice it was only really an attribute of middle-class life and even then something of a façade rather than a substantial truth. Prostitution was rife in nineteenth-century cities and widely used. Anderson argued that bourgeois morality led to women's *ignorance and prudery*, and to sexual frustrations in many marriages (1983:144) with husbands frequently buying sex from the poor and the children of the poor. Figures for illegitimacy were high in the nineteenth century and alcoholism and violence common amongst working men, whilst the middle-class *pater familias* was a remote, authoritarian figure to his children. Children and wives were usually very dependent on the man with little chance of escaping brutality or infidelity. Further, conventional families did not necessarily last very long: 18% of all households with children were headed by a single parent in 1851, mainly because of early death, compared to 9% in 1981 (Anderson 1983).

Women were subject to their husbands, with few exceptions. Family wealth passed down the male line and any wealth a woman did have automatically went to her husband on marriage. Women were excluded from universities, public life and voting. Women's bodies belonged to their husbands, who had the right to intercourse until as late as 1991 in England, when rape in marriage became a crime. Physical punishment of wives was accepted: 'Common law both north and south of the border, granted husbands the right to "correct" their wives' behaviour and restrict their movements' (Kilday 2003). The term family originates from the Latin *famulus* (servant), and at the end of the nineteenth century one of the first women to qualify in medicine recalled that origin: 'Under exclusively man-made laws women have been reduced to the most abject condition of legal slavery in which it is possible for human beings to be held' (Miller 1890). Although women began to fight for change in the latter part of that century, it was not until the 1970s that legislation genuinely set equality up in the statute books, though not of course in the actuality of many women's lives:

> In 1975 the Equal Pay Act came into force, the Sex Discrimination Act was passed and the Equal Opportunities Commission was established. In the same year the Employment Protection Act 1975 made maternity leave a statutory right. One year later the Sexual Offences Amendment Act was passed. (Fawcett Society 2005)

The ideal Victorian family was somewhat less than ideal for many of its members, yet the construct and concept did consolidate middle-class male power and wealth within the family whilst also promoting that model of family as attractive and morally appropriate for all. Arguably, an institution designed to contain and protect capital within bourgeois families, with the support of the law, was justified on moral grounds, romanticised and so promoted as desirable for all. The growth in literacy, media and libraries publicised a very idealistic model of marriage that disguised its practical role in preserving power and capital:

> 'Romancing' became a synonym for courting, and 'romances' were the first form of literature to reach a mass population. The spread of ideals of romantic love was one factor tending to disentangle the marital bond from wider kinship ties and give it an especial significance. Husbands and wives increasingly became seen as collaborators in a joint emotional enterprise, this having primacy even over their obligations towards their children. The 'home' came into being as a distinct environment set off from work; and, at least in principle, became a place where individuals could expect emotional support, as contrasted with the instrumental character of the work setting. (Giddens 1992: 18–36)

That focus on home and the nuclear family also, of course, served to consolidate patriarchal power over wives and children within the privacy of their four walls.

Prior to the urbanisation and industrialisation of British culture, families had been much larger and looser groupings of extended networks of relatives, either under one roof or in close communal space. Parents and children shared space, including sleeping space, with one another, other relatives and even servants.

Foucault (1978, 1981) argued that the concepts of family and sexual relations barely featured in discourse prior to the eighteenth century but then gradually became a pivotal factor in the reorganisation of popular life that was necessitated by nineteenth-century capitalism. Governments became increasingly conscious of the need to manage the masses to maintain the law and order essential to business; to sustain a productive workforce but also to reproduce that workforce to serve the new economy. 'At the heart of this economic and political problem was sex ... marriage rules and family organisation ... the manner in which each individual made use of his sex' (Foucault 1978: 25–6). The population was both a problem, generating revolution, disease, crime and debauchery, and also essential to produce goods, wealth and orderly workers, with, of course, the former destructive activities inhibiting the latter constructive ones. Social reproduction was key to wealth generation, and sexual reproduction key to producing the next generation of wealth producers. Sex had to be regulated and managed in ways conducive to the needs of state and capital. This involved a dual project of supporting appropriate sexuality and closing down undesirable sexuality. Central to this was the promulgation of the bourgeois model of marriage and family, as these served both capital and patriarchy, whilst simultaneously criminalising, medicalising, imprisoning or concealing other forms of sexuality. For Foucault, making the family the *monogamic conjugal cell* 'defined new rules for the game of powers and pleasures' (1978: 48) that came to define human sexuality in the West and arguably continues to do so.

More than anything, sex was divided into legitimate and illegitimate practices and liaisons and regulated by institutions, particularly the law and medicine but also by education, where children were sex segregated and monitored. Not that unacceptable sexuality disappeared. Rather it was even excited by attempts at repression but its proliferation in a 'visible explosion of unorthodox sexualities' (Foucault 1978: 49) was within a secret, sexual black market, whilst overtly the respectable bourgeois society made anything other than marital, heterosexual, reproductive monogamy taboo for either health or moral reasons. The purity movement of the 1880s acted with *militant middle-class evangelicalism*: 'While the working class was the principal target for purists' interventionary zeal they also provided rank and file recruits for the new movement' (Mort 1987: 88). Central to this was instruction for mothers about home, play and appropriate family arrangements that denounced immorality and used the threat of God's wrath to preach sexual regulation not for health reasons but for religious ones.

Familial morality was seen as essential to a strong nation and educating the working classes was a key part of constructing that *family*, with working-class masculinity seen as particularly in need of containment within the security of the family. The family became the means by which disease could be contained, morality served and the nation thereby strengthened. Women's role and responsibility were highlighted because women were *centrally concerned with sexuality through reproduction* (Foucault 1978: 96) with early feminists calling for united womanhood for the sake of children, family and nation. The family ideal became pervasive through popular culture and moral institutions and was aspired to by the new urban working classes as they sought to emulate bourgeois respectability and thereby acquire its benefits. However, attempts to control male promiscuity were constantly resisted by the overwhelmingly middle-class and male Home Office. It took 20 years of feminist campaigning to force the criminalisation of incest in 1908, but prosecuting the male clients of prostitutes was viewed as unacceptable to the community at large and instead brothels were closed and women were forced on to the streets where prosecutions of women rose dramatically (Mort 1987). This contradiction between the pervading moral discourse and male sexual practice was built on deep class divides around patriarchal power. This was little addressed by the feminists of the early twentieth century who instead, either fought as purists to change male sex obsession to a more spiritual, mystical love, or took on the state in the struggle for suffrage.

Foucault (1978) saw the Victorian process of making family the moral backbone of the nation as the origin of many duplicitous sexual standards, with much sexual life and practice denigrated, obfuscated or unacknowledged within a culture infused with myths of romantic, marital, lifelong bliss. For him such myths ultimately served to reinforce middle-class socio-economic power as part of a technology of control. He rather neglected the fact that the myth of marriage was also quite useful for male power. Mort (1987), however, did not. Rather he recognised clearly the maleness of power in sexual and social structures, however complexly and diversely intersected with class, sexual orientation, race, age, etc. In the conclusion to *Dangerous Sexualities* he wrote:

Discourses of sex have constructed men and women in terms of difference, difference shot through with power relations. That insight must put the issue of male sexuality firmly on the political agenda. Not, let it be clear, men and their desires as the unified, monolithic oppressor, the source of all power, but men as they appear in this history. Men whose constructed sexualities, identities and pleasures have been complexly written into many of the structures of social and political domination. (1987: 171)

Central to that structuration is family, for despite the complexity of defining family, and the tensions between the reality of lived family lives and ideal models, most children's formative experience of self and others is in some kind of *familial* context. However tenuous, unconventional or dangerous, the family is where children first learn to relate to others, gain language and become subjective identities, not least of course gendered identities. Given that family is where men and women take on gendered roles and meanings, is the base of the intimacy of adult gendered relations, is where men abuse women and/or children, and is almost universally supported by authoritative discourses, any effort to understand violence, gender and justice must consider family's place in male power or it will, as Mort argues, *ultimately flounder.*

An Englishman's home is his castle[1]: family stories

From the 1920s through to the 1960s there was a hiatus in feminism until the seismic shifts around civil rights, anti-war and women's issues put sexual politics firmly back on the socio-political agenda. Although that feminist work placed family and intimate violence on the political and criminological agenda, any critique of the family itself is rare today, and earlier challenges, for example by McIntosh (1988), are hardly referred to in contemporary feminist work. Rather the discourses at the end of the twentieth century and beginning of the twenty-first largely mirror those at the end of the nineteenth and beginning of the twentieth. A certain panic about crime still includes the great emphasis on sexual crimes against children that characterised the Victorian period and that has paralleled universal efforts from the main political parties since 1979, in or out of power, to support the family. Strong family units occupy a key discursive space as the means to an orderly public society, whilst family dysfunction, family collapse or single parenting are readily linked to criminalised children in popular and policy discourses. By labelling *abnormal* families as criminogenic the traditional family is immediately posited as a solution to crime, but that also diverts attention from the levels of harm within such families and away from any critical investigation of family *per se*. As a century ago, the common parlance is that 'Restoration of traditional family values will, it is assumed, decrease crime and restore moral/social order' (Saraga 2001: 195). The private domain of the family is shored up by both metaphoric and literal walls, breaching which is hard against a concerted effort to keep the walls in place. One aspect of this effort is a focus on crimes against children by strangers.

An area of male violence within families that is significantly under-represented in recent work is familial child sexual abuse. It took 20 years to force a law against incest in 1908 and it is now 20 years since the furore following the exposure of high levels of incest in families in Cleveland, the Orkneys and Nottinghamshire and the setting up of the *Childline* phone help centre for abused children in the late 1980s. However, initial furore about family abuse soon slid towards disbelief and then to blame and finally to symbolically restoring the credibility of the family. Perhaps in consequence, since the millennium it has been and continues to be the paedophile, often initially preying anonymously in internet chat rooms, who is the bogeyman of this age, not the father, 'uncle' or stepfather. The paedophile is the main focus of much public domain discourse emanating from the government and Home Office. For example, the *cyber-paed* was key to the process of the reform of the Sexual Offences Act as a 'new offence of grooming will, for the first time, protect children from the use of the internet by paedophiles' (BBC News 9 October 2003). This hidden paedophile, now wearing a cloak of invisibility online rather than the dirty mackintosh in the park, is the lead actor in many news accounts of child sexual abuse and perhaps has been since the first case brought against Gary Glitter in 1999, mentioned in Chapter 2.

Despite the furore over the numbers of 'evil beasts' in our midst stirred by the *News of the World* claiming 'There are 110,000 child sex offenders in Britain ... one for every square mile' (*News of the World* 23 July 2000), the programme, *The Hunt for Britain's Paedophiles* (BBC2 June 2002) mainly featured two men, Julian Levene and Mark Hansen. The *Observer* article on the programme is long and pruriently descriptive of their crimes and preferences. It is headlined with the ghastly *double entendre*, 'paedophiles exposed' (26 May 2002). Only half way down the fourth long column do readers learn that Levene began to abuse in his own family: 'Levene seduced his niece, Sarah, now in her early thirties', when she was four. Another niece was also his victim and 'her father was her pimp', who would watch her being abused whilst 'masturbating in a corner'. Nowhere in the paper or on the programme are these offending relationships and the way family structures, secrecy and power enabled them, discussed.

Such journalism matters because most of the public depend on the news for information about such crimes. That public includes the criminologists, criminal justice workers and politicians who respond to crime. So for reasons perhaps not completely disconnected from the agenda set in the factual media, paedophilia, net-crime and child pornography are a major focus in policy and in policing. In the UK, the SSOU Serious Sex Offenders Unit of the Serious Organised Crime Agency (SOCA) has been active since 2000 in the UK and globally – in its focus are net porn, sex tourism and itinerant sex offenders who seek to avoid registration. Yet during this period 'stranger perpetrated physically and or sexually abusive incidents were estimated to comprise 11% of the total incidents of this type of harm' (ESRC 2002: 14). In 2001, of the '9,857 calls to Childline regarding sexual abuse, 90% of the children knew their abuser' (ESRC 2002: 15). Research in the Home Office Police and Reducing Crime Unit found that 'the majority of perpetrators sexually assault children known to them, with 80% of offences taking place in the home of either offender or victim' (Grubin 1998: v). Hood et al. (2002) studied sex offenders and re-offending patterns and found that 60% of their 192 male prisoner sample group had offended against children and of these 'in two thirds of cases, the prisoners victimised solely children within their own family unit' (Hood et al. 2002: 374). Despite this evidence there is no critique of, or suggested intervention in, the role of men in families in their section on 'what might be done to improve knowledge of sexual re-offending?' (Hood et al. 2002: 393).

Mediated Men

Instead, our everyday notion of the family, and perhaps more crucially the role of heterosexual, paternal masculinity within the family, is repeatedly presented in both factual and fictional texts as unproblematic, even when the evidence is to the contrary. Male violence is secure in the family, in the home, behind closed doors, because it is invisible and so symbolically and physically protected and kept secret. If it is exposed and made manifest in ways that make it newsworthy then the familial masculinity at its core is disguised. Blame is regularly shifted from home, husbandry and paternity to attributes such as deviant femininity, psychopathology, beastliness, evil, technology and stranger danger.

This lack of media critique of ordinary masculinity is important because the press can confirm and/or excite the broader explicatory models offered by medicine, the law, social work and fictional culture. These other discourses pick up on the personalisation, rarity and drama central to news values[2] so that violent and/or sexual crime against women and children is often psychopathologised as the exception, leaving the everyday continuity of socio-sexual foundations and accompanying paternal authority intact. The masculine model of home and family is self-perpetuating because it discursively renders alternative models – gay parents; single parents; communal living – denigrated or deviant or disappeared in the 'malestream' discourses of education, law, policy, medicine and the media.

In British newspapers, our everyday notion of the family, and perhaps more crucially the role of heterosexual, paternal masculinity within the family, is seen over and over as unproblematic or rather it is not seen at all, even when the evidence is of systematic human devastation through generations. This lack of critique of ordinary masculinity can confirm the abused woman's self-blame, low esteem and self-loathing, entrapping her and shoring up the traditional family as an ideal place to bring up children. Whilst ordinary violent men remain missing in crime news and other representations, they can also remain hidden, protected and empowered by the aggrandised representations of marriages, homes and families. That imbalanced address informs public opinion, which includes not only the opinion of women, men and children about who should be blamed and held responsible in situations of domestic abuse but also the popular consensus that essentially underwrites political decisions about policy, resourcing and policing. The literal diversion from gendered violence in families to 'cyber-paeds' and pornographers takes not just meanings but resources with it – policing resources, social service resources and research resources – so it is perhaps unsurprising that, as with domestic violence and rape, much familial child abuse falls to the remit of the voluntary sector and charitable support. Meanwhile, the family remains at the heart of the home and the violence therein, and male *sex* remains the secret source of much of that abuse, with the female *sexed body* (whether adult or child) the site on which most abuse is enacted by male *sexed bodies*. This is the structured male sex power that Mort (1987) argued so lucidly must be addressed at the centre of any attempt to change gendered roles and relationships, or perhaps even to begin to understand them in order to find ways of change. There are two key aspects of extremely gendered violence and abuse: it is enacted mostly within families (constituted in myriad ways ranging from ex-couples to generationally and communally extended families) and mostly by individuals with male bodies against those with female bodies.[3] The next section looks at intra-familial explanations for the kind of gendered subjectivities evidenced in such violence.

Power, Place and Psychology

For most of us, it is our family, however far from the *ideal*, that is where the journey to subjective awareness begins and family is more than anything the place of sex: sexual relationships; sexual reproduction (whether biological/adoptive/ IVF/surrogate); and the sexing of its members, adult and child. It is where, through language and interaction, children's biologically sexed embodiment acquires subjectivity and identity, and central to that process is the inscribing of gender on the self. Before the seventeenth century little distinction was made in Britain between the sexual organs of men and women; women's organs were seen as similar to but inverted and inferior to men's and only in the nineteenth century did the profundity of sexual difference become the focus of science and knowledge (Segal 1994: 190–1). Along with other feminists, Segal sees this discursive shift as aligned with broader political and social changes which underwrote a reorganising of power, in that the hystericisation of women rendered them victim to their biology and thus unnatural unless mothering or nurturing. Simultaneously, the essentialness of this role in reproduction explained their attractiveness to men, whilst also making them guardians of reproduction and responsible therefore for all sex.

Sex became subject to the great Victorian scientistic endeavour. Krafft-Ebbing (1886) attempted to classify sex as natural (directed toward procreation) and unnatural (anything else from childhood masturbation to sexual murder). These interjections left a powerful legacy of meanings about familial sexuality between heterosexuals with all else negatively evaluated or denied, including female passion, as respectable wives were passive recipients of their husbands sex-agency, rather than active participants. Moreover, little effort was made to explore heterosexual masculinity which was simply used as the normal model against which everything else was found lesser, wanting or accountable. Efforts, such as those by Havelock Ellis (1897) on same-sex love at the end of the century, to liberate sexuality and alleviate some of the guilt inspired by the prevailing, limiting model of human behaviour were themselves dismissed, by the growing Puritanism, as pornographic and evidence of the author's perversion. Sexual difference was firmly established between men and women but also morally and scientifically evaluated and hierarchised, with anything not initiated by heterosexual men within marriage for the purposes of reproduction rendered valueless at best, perverted, sick or even criminalised at worst. Problematically for dominant discourses of happy marriage, such a model of sexuality did little to ensure happy and satisfied wives (or indeed married men, given the thriving trades in prostitution, pornography and child sex) and initial challenges from another emerging science, psychology, to the biological reductionism of Victorian sexology remain deeply contested in work on sex/gender and self today.

Freud and family

Sexology suggested that physical sexual experience is similar for all. Many were left aspiring, disappointed, frustrated or deluded and in congruence with prevailing knowledge: women blamed themselves and men blamed women for marital unhappiness. This context was one ripe for knowledge intervention and in Vienna at the end of the 1800s a medical doctor named Sigmund Freud began to study the clinical use of cocaine and hypnosis in the treatment of nervous disorders, publishing *Studies in Hysteria* in 1895. His aim was to work out a science of psychology based on neurology, but this rapidly moved towards the concept of psychoanalysis on the death of his father in 1896. This event triggered his self-analysis and the development of controversial ideas about infantile sexuality and the importance of childhood. Although based in Austria until he fled the Nazis for England in 1938, Freud travelled widely to conferences, including to the US, and was published prolifically in translation. His writing bridges the profound disruption and invention of the period from late Victorianism through World War I to the outbreak of World War II. His impact on the way those of us in the Western world see ourselves has been culturally evident ever since, from Hitchcock's film *Spellbound* in 1945 about the unconscious and guilt, to Anthony Storr's (2001) *Freud* on his influence on literature and philosophy as well as psychology and psychiatry.

For Freud (1905) the levels of dissatisfaction that he found evident in his clinics were indicative that sex was not simply physiologically gendered, emergent at puberty and similar for all, but the learnt alignment of *primary erotic narcissism* by the growing child within the family. Freud theorised boy children gravitating towards normal masculinity and girls towards normal femininity unconsciously through both identification with the same-sex parent and awareness of difference from the other parent. The ideal family is therefore central to his model of 'normal' sexual development, thus reasserting the moral and economic construct's validity in yet another knowledge discourse. In Freud's psychology, the family was viewed as the means by which the chaos of infantile libido is nurtured and guided towards adult gender-differentiated sexual propriety and content.

Whilst at least querying the limitations of sexual physical reductionism and its failure to explain the huge range of sexual behaviours and anxieties, Freud still had to explain how the sensual child orients so as to act according to its biological body type. He ascribed this process to psychological rather than physical processes which are nonetheless fundamental and normatively heterosexual and reproductive so long as familial relationships support them. This familial aspect of sexual subjectivity is key to Freudianism, which assumes the presence of the father and mother in a normal family context if normal adult heterosexuals are to emerge from infancy. For boys this process was called the Oedipus phase and centres on both the desire to be sensually close to the mother and the desire for identification with the father, thereby to gain his authority and power. It is resolved when (if) the boy's super-ego develops sufficiently to enable him to ally with the male parent and recoil from sexualised feelings for the mother which would make him a rival to his father and therefore at risk of emasculinisation or castration. For Freud, a failure in this alliance could lead to homosexuality, with feminised men aligning with their mothers and seeking male (father) partners. Dominant (masculine) mothers and weak (feminine) fathers were (and still are) seen as causes of this failure, again reproducing very gender-stereotyped familial ideals. By contrast, proper parenting of boys enables the resolution of fear, prohibition of incest and regulation of desire, which effort produces the adult heterosexual male and his superior intellect.

Alternatively, for girls desire for the father and recognition of their fathers' power (phallic) draws their attention from the mother in the Electra complex, but the taboo of consanguinity diverts the girl from incest and she seeks in adulthood a substitute father figure with whom to have a child, the equivalent for Freud of the female phallus. Lacking a penis herself she is driven to acquire one vicariously and with that acquisition she gains some element of the authority and power conferred on men. This process was not deemed to require much intellectual struggle. Rather, Freud concluded:

> Character traits which critics of every epoch have brought against women – that they show less sense of justice than men, that they are less ready to submit to the great exigencies of life, that they are more often influenced in their judgements by feelings of affection or hostility – all these would be amply accounted for by the modification in the formation of their superego. (Freud 1925: 257–8)

So, theoretically, the savage infant is both socialised to gendered adulthood and directed to heterosexual, monogamous sexuality within the security and nurturance of the normal family and its fathering and mothering. Such a civilising process and control of erotic instinct not only offered support for the rectitude of family but also more broadly complied with the civilising and sexually controlling ideologies of the epoch. So Freud's account of the acquisition of normal gendered sexuality neatly reflected dominant patriarchal, middle-class moralities and interests. By implication, any other child-rearing context might result in sex-role/sexual dysfunction, so women who are not proper wives and mothers are the cause of their own frigidity or hysteria, male infidelity, male abuse towards them and/or children. Further, dominant mothers cause feminised boys with sodomite tendencies whilst the failure to provide a respectable, modest feminine role model for girl children drives daughters to lure their fathers to incestuous acts.

Based almost entirely on case-studies of adult patients, Freud depended on memory and dreams to elicit evidence of childhood experience that might explain mature sexual *abnormality*, theorising not only the developmental stages for successful heterosexual maturation but also the unconscious processes that might cause deviation in relation to subjective, unverified recollections. Although profoundly phallocentric and methodologically limited, Freud nonetheless separated gender from body biology. This somewhat unfixed humans from the physical destiny presumed by early sexology but nonetheless harnessed them to innate unconscious processes with successful sexual maturation dependent on appropriate family roles and relations. Freud sexualised familial places as sites of profound tensions around bodies, gender, desire, identity and power. He theorised the family as a sexual cauldron seething with desires requiring containment and direction. Within that, paternal sexuality was seen as the key. The man of the family is for his wife heterosexual partner, provider, father for her children; for sons, the model of adult manhood (heterosexual sexual partner, provider, father); and, for daughters, the model of a future husband (heterosexual partner, provider, father for her children). So in the Victorian family, the father is the 'member' around whom others' gender identities are formulated.

Arguably, Freud's work on sex does not reveal the basis for gender difference but rather justifies and reproduces the inequality and oppression associated with it. Yet, Freud's ideas remain, despite the lack of a means of proving them and a range of critical onslaughts, deeply embedded in contemporary culture, perhaps not least because they suited the interests of power when formulated and continue to suit them into the twenty-first century. Most of us have *Freudian slips* at some time; advertising is riddled with phallic symbolism; the dysfunctional *family* is blamed over and over for all manner of ills, from criminal youths (Campbell 1991) to anorexic girls (Wykes and Gunter 2005) and popular film is resonant with traditional heterosexual heroes making women respectable through marriage (e.g. *Pretty Woman*, 1990; *An Officer and a Gentleman*, 1982). Nowhere is Freud's dominance of sexual cultural meanings more evident than in news about gendered crime when female failing in the family or marriage is so often blamed for male violence. The diversion towards blaming women was well illustrated by the focus on Maxine Carr in the Soham case, whilst Fred West's murderous sexual behaviour was blamed on women – an abusive mother and sadistic, lesbian wife, with the *Sun* informing us: 'Fred was introduced to sex by his mother' (23 November 1995). In Freudian terms that 'explains' it!

Arguably, Freud, along with Marx and Darwin, was/is one of the key influences from Victorianism on modern culture and thereby on modern identities, including gendered ones. Freud's ideas on family, gendered roles and sexualisation have been systematically reproduced in discourses in education, child-rearing and popular culture, as well as precisely in the one-to-one and utter pervasiveness, in Western society, of counselling and psychoanalysis. Criticisms include Connell (1987), who noted Freud's Eurocentredness and the problem of lack of universality in his theory of culture (family-centred) as taming the nature of the child to produce the civilised adult, whilst feminists during the 1970s were quick to point out that the attainment of gendered identity was perhaps less to do with the essential unconscious than with class and patriarchal power. Yet, despite these relatively recent reservations, Freud's concept of the importance of the unconscious and of gender being achieved through family processes remains a powerful trope for theorising sexuality and identity. More politically problematic is the empirical linking of the unconscious with Freud's specific models of gendered identity – certainly for feminist politics, but also because of the not just patriarchal, but white, middle-class and Christian specificity of what he saw as normal family gender roles and relations. These links and specific models inform much of the English language and other forms of representation, whilst the credence given them within the medical profession, gave/gives them both status and dissemination.

Sex, knowledge and subjectivity

During the upswing of feminist political critique that challenged malestream criminology in the later 1970s there was a corresponding challenge to phallocentricity in both psychology and linguistics in the effort to explain and change the relations between sex, gender and power through a deconstruction of knowledge itself to expose patriarchy. For Moi (1989) feminism was *critical and theoretical practice committed to the struggle against patriarchy and sexism that must include at its heart the meaning of gender*. Moi argued that patriarchy consistently collapses the meaning of female and feminine into one, confusing the denotative dictionary label with the conventionalised social construct of what being female should entail in a patriarchal culture. Female is the biological sex of woman and feminine the socially constructed gender. Femininity is meaningful according to the requirement of dominance, as is masculinity. The pair form binary opposites along the meaning category of gender in a social condition where the male category has power over the female category. As male is socially dominant and female subordinate, so the masculine is associated with positive attributes and the feminine with negative. The connotative value polarities then inform other binary opposites: positive labels are associated with the masculine; negative with the feminine. As we use language we reproduce gendered values about the world we live in and about ourselves as sexual subjects. Cixous (1989) explored such polarities as held in tension by the struggle for meaning with the feminist goal becoming to change knowledge itself in order to re-order value signification in language.

There is a certain irony here in that what was once merely Freudian theory may well be now so deeply part of our meaning systems, and therefore value system, that it is also inevitably part of our unconscious and thereby our sense of self. For in Lacanian 1970s' psychoanalytic theory, as the child gains language, so language enters the child: 'we are possessed and 'spoken' by language we do not own ourselves but are constructed according to the possibilities offered us by words' (Frosh 1987 in Hollway 1989: 82). Phallogocentrism is epitomised by Lacan's (1976) model of a symbolic, social-value fixity, expressed in language into which early psycho-sexual development places each of us appropriately. It is a theorised system which values the visible/masculine/phallic/ penetrative symbol of generative power over the invisible/feminine/ vaginal/uterine enveloping symbols of generative power. Kristeva (1989) took issue with both Freud (whom she dubbed an 'irritating phallocrat') and Lacan. She offered a definition of gender which accepted biological sexual difference but saw the reproductive base reconstructed not in bio-essentialism but in social relations. The *task* for feminists was/is, for Kristeva, to examine the 'terrain of the inseparable conjunction of the sexual and the symbolic' (1989: 200). So although Lacanian theory could offer a means of explaining gender difference, he offered no explanation for how or why that manifests itself in unequal power relations in the social world. Why should the developing human psyche naturally orient sexually around the penis/phallus as desirable, as opposed to the complexity of woman's sexual anatomy? Kristeva (1989) pointed out that acceptance of the castration complex requires the same kind of act of faith as does acceptance the big bang theory of the universe. She saw it as vital to confront the 'system of thought' alongside sexual, social and linguistic systems. Epistemological praxis has developed on masculinist structures of explanation which legitimate and reproduce male power over women often by simply not recognising patriarchy, as in Freudian psychoanalysis and Marxism. As capitalism developed, buoyed by and driving colonialism, male social domination gradually became, also, middle-class and white, so the epistemological model adapted by integrating patriarchy, capitalism and racism in an ideological symbiosis that remains substantially intact despite significant critical challenges.

Deconstructing the family of man

Hollway's (1989) critique was of psychology as knowledge. She saw that subjectivity is a constant process of negotiation of power relations according to the various discourses encountered during human life, in order to arrive at a sense of self appropriate to the context – a process deriving not from the Oedipal but from the inevitable anxiety of the infant's realised dependence on the adult. This anxiety is cultural, according to the child's, and adult's, place in social discourses, not natural. Hollway's focus was gender difference as a social construct. So studies of women which leave men out of the account 'cannot produce a theory of how women are produced' because 'gender is produced through difference, in relations' (1989: 106). For feminists, in order to understand how they come to be feminine, women must also concern themselves with the construction of men as masculine, and Hollway argued that women are likely to more easily address such concerns than men. This is because women (and other subordinated groups) incorporate greater multiplicity into their subjective identification than men (and other dominant groups) in that they relate meaningfully both to dominance and within subordinance. Through their creation of systems of denigration and negation of subjectivity and experience different from their own, men have left themselves with 'the ideal of the unitary, rationalised, subject to which they are more or less rigidly bound by what are in effect cultural systems of defence' (Hollway 1989: 131). They have thereby legitimated and, by psychologising the process, naturalised the oppression of *others* on the grounds of them being lesser. Non-compliance, therefore, to a dominant masculine agenda is in practice *against* the norm, deviant and punishable whether in public (by the power of law) or in private (by power that is supported by law – lack of or failings in – should it become public). Men are both bound by this male ideal because their power depends on it and also disempowered by those bonds, as women's greater potential for multiplicity (at the cost of power) has increasingly allowed women to adapt to a rapidly changing post-industrial/ post-national and, perhaps consequently, less gendered world. Such theory may well have implications for understanding the relations between gender, violence and justice.

For the subject, family is both the starting place of engenderment and, perhaps more and more, the site where gender is at its most vulnerable and variable. The language the infant enters drags with it clouds of patriarchal glory that often conflict with the growing sexed child's experience of relations and perception of lived gender in a world of massive change. The confusion of perception, experience and representation is, and has been, the stuff of Western culture perhaps since that shift in the decade from the mid-1960s to the mid-1970s[4] that witnessed the overt demise of industrialisation combined with the liberation of women from reproductive slavery, and as a consequence of both had an enforced impact on men that has never been properly acknowledged, theorised or embraced. Ordinary men have been hidden, secured by economic and sexual power, and shored up by the institution of family which, however idealised and mythologised, has underwritten Western social and sexual organisation. But foundations and boundaries have been shaken and transformed by technological advance and political disturbance leaving cracks, or what Husband (1984) called tears in the ideological umbrella, that reveal the mechanisms of family structure, composition and meaning and show them as wanting, unjust and damaging. Arguably, the family has been over-invested as a technology of power leaving us with a false consciousness of what it is and therefore what we should be as men and women. It has been, for patriarchy and capital, an ideological mechanism of meaning *par excellence*, reproduced discursively and pervasively not least through the phallogocentric psychoanalytic work of Freud and Lacan, the authority of their acolytes and the impact of that *knowledge* on discourses spanning the length and breadth of the twentieth century. The family provides an excellent component of that ideological mechanism because it is the site where most children enter into language and identity.

Absent Fathers, Feminists and Broken Families

Despite such critical commentaries, or perhaps because of them, in this time of struggle, difference and change, family remains symbolic of security, stability and the known. It is represented as such throughout Western culture and therefore internally in the way we see ourselves. Family also has been and remains a central tenet of explanation for all manner of social problems with its assumption that the ideal nuclear family is the solution. In terms of criminology, offending is very often explored in terms of family, and as offending is predominantly male a relationship between family and masculinity as criminogenic is central. What is taken for granted is the premise that ideal nuclear family relationships produce normal girls and boys and consequently men and women, so deviance must indicate dysfunctional family life.

Perhaps most contentious is that, given the well-documented major collapse of the traditional family, the numbers of criminal men seems surprisingly low if there is a causal relationship, just as hormonal changes as an explanation for female crime might presuppose rampaging hordes of pre-menstrual, post-partum and menopausal women on a global scale. Moreover, if Freudian theory is to be accepted, non-ideal families would generate roughly equal numbers of deviant women to men, given the close to equal numbers of male to female in the population. Curiously, even when statistics relating to family dysfunction are brought to bear on male crime they are often contradictory. For example the 2007 Social Trends Survey showed 37% of households as conventional (legally married or not), i.e., two parents and child/ren, a fairly significant drop from 1991 at 53% (Social Trends 37, 2007: 15). Yet the same survey showed recorded crime as consistently falling since 1995, when it peaked at 18 million offences, to 12 million offences in 2006/07 (Social Trends 37, 2007: 114). Further, the fall in violent crime is even more dramatic with a fall of 43% from 1995 to 2005/06 (2007:116). Arguably this suggests that increases in single-parent families might correlate with reductions in violent crime. Yet, the leader of the Conservative Party in Britain still insisted on the reverse interpretation: 'Mr Cameron also said the three "horrific" killings in a fortnight represented a "broken society". He said: "We urgently need to reform the law, and the rules around child maintenance, to compel men to stand by their families"' (*Independent* 17 February 2007). Yet, despite this, 'the Social Exclusion Task Force says government agencies have failed to help the 140,000 most "at risk" families in the UK, whose lives are blighted by a dangerous combination of poverty, poor housing, drug abuse and criminality' (*Independent* 17 June 2007). Nonetheless, 'family' dysfunction, not poverty, poor housing, drug abuse and masculinity, is the continuing trope of explanation for youth crime, which is crime in the public space, rarely interpersonally violent, most frequently involving some form of theft, and committed by young men. The murder of three youths on the streets in the UK in a fortnight in 2007 was rare, in fact it may be an unprecedented event in criminological records. So it gained much attention from politicians and the press. In contradiction, violence against women inflicted by men they know within intimate relationships is common: 'One incident of domestic violence is reported to the police every minute' (Women and Equality Unit 2004 website). The *shock/horror* that such violence occurs in close familial relationships often within the home is not deemed newsworthy. Similarly, when it comes to the sexual abuse of children it is the dangerous stranger on the street or cyber-highway who provides the news story rather than the systematic rape of children by fathers, stepfathers and *family friends*, as studied by Grubin (1998). An unusual and welcome address to parliament in 2002 revealed that: '1 per cent of all our young people have been sexually abused by a parent and 3 per cent have been sexually abused by another relative' (Allen 2002).

Yet even that unusual incidence of concern in parliament failed to focus on the fact that nearly all such abuse is perpetrated by a male relative, that most victims are little girls, and that the *normal* heterosexual family is more immediately a potential focus of explanation for private violence than the *abnormal* family might be for the street violence of youths. The explanation may simply be that the public nature of street violence heightens its visibility, whilst domestic violence and familial child sex abuse are metaphorically and physically hidden behind closed doors,[5] but making spurious connections between criminal youths and single mothers maintains the myth of the ideal heterosexual family (whilst domestic violence against women and the rape of children by fathers destroy it).

Criticism of that ideal family is made even more unlikely while it remains central to British government discourses, as it has since the early 1990s when the press claimed: 'For communities to function successfully they need families with fathers' (*Sunday Times* 28 February 1993). While more recently the Conservative Leader in Opposition argued: 'If we get the family right, we can fix our broken society ... we have the highest rate of family breakdown in Europe.

And we have the worst social problems in Europe. Don't tell me these things aren't connected' (BBC News 10 July 2007). Such adherence to the myth of the ideal family is not just a Conservative ideology but key also to New Labour. Prime Minister Gordon Brown stated: 'We need to mobilise all of our energies and commitment to support children and families – to help parents as they do the most difficult job in the world, raising a child' (Helm 2007). He did, however, at least acknowledge that not just family but the media, teachers and peer groups have a significant impact on children. Crucially, the constant adherence to family in such discourse, faithfully reproduced as news because of the value of the elite utterances of senior politicians, 'frame the problem of violence in a manner that renders the perpetrator invisible' (Mckie 2005: 157) so masculinity remains unaddressed.

The upswing of that family ideology in political discourse in the early 1990s can be traced to the neo-conservatism of the US and particularly to the work of Charles Murray. In many ways it mirrors the Puritanism of the 1890s that arguably underpinned the patriarchal and bourgeois investment in family. Illegitimacy and unemployment were Murray's key explanations for *barbarian boys*, with marriage seen as the 'deeply civilising force' (1990: 23) necessary for their salvation, first as sons and then as husbands. The emergence of an *underclass* in America was a result, Murray claimed, of behaviours that caused a deterioration of the lower class, central to which was change in family organisation and stability. In the UK he claimed that Middlesbrough in the north-east of England was an example of such deterioration with the attitudes of the *new rabble* justifying their welfare dependency. In Murray's thesis, both the state and women are blamed for emasculating men, with unemployment reducing their attractiveness as husbands and benefits making fatherless families tenable. His resolution was partly to counter such attitudes through the removal of state support, forcing men into their proper role as breadwinners and providers for the family whilst withdrawing benefit to illegitimate children and their mothers, even threatening the removal of illegitimate children for adoption by proper families. The meaning of masculinity is thus irrevocably linked to 'providing for and teaching children' (*New York Times* 19 June 1994), much as in the Victorian *pater familias* model.

Conclusion

Although deeply criticised for his lack of attention to socio-economic issues and his overt sexism (Lister 1996) Murray's thesis clearly fitted with a powerful and popular moral agenda reminiscent of a century previously whereby the traditional ideal family and commensurate gender roles are viewed as vital for stable sexual roles and relationships, and hence a stable society. *Ipso facto*, crime is caused disproportionately by males because their sexual and socio-economic roles have been eroded though liberalism, welfarism and feminism, which have allowed men's natural proclivity to wildness to be unchecked.

Freud's influence is so pervasive throughout history and culture that the social psyche readily recognises such claims as true – they fit our cognitive templates that are informed by the meanings in discourse. We anticipate them as true just as we anticipate a happy ending when we encounter a reformulation of the story of Cinderella, for example in the film *Pretty Woman*.[6] Implicit in that 'truth' is that women are responsible for men's behaviour and the arena for the enactment of that is the ideal family, where men are divested of their social and sexual dangerousness by appropriate femininity to become role models for their sons. Rather than discover through scientific rigour some truth, Freud instead took for granted as truth the commonplace ideologies of the late nineteenth century – patriarchal authority, marital heterosex and bourgeois values – and assumed individual crises must indicate ideological non-compliance. Within the new application of a scientistic paradigm to human experience this generated knowledge powerfully reinforced political and economic interests and secured them within the concept of family.

That security depends on power and its operation, public and personal: publicly, control over and perpetuation of the myth and reality of family through law and policy for socio-economic reasons; and personally, within the privacy of family, battles for gendered identity that range from the trivial to the murderous. In the early twenty-first century, the family as a space is a site for struggle and control where ultimately the very privacy engendered by its place in public and political discourses enables that struggle finally to be between bodies themselves. Campbell identified a millennial struggle between the sexes over space – 'from the region of the body to the neighbourhood to the space of society' (Campbell 1993: 317–18). Just as the street and the football terraces are spaces where men jostle men for identity and control over space, so the family is clearly a space wherein 'men's movement emphasises exclusiveness, restrictions, symbolic ordering and control over access' (1993: 318), but it is also a place where resistance and challenges come not from other men but from women and children. Ultimately such conflict is all too often resolved by the power of the male body operationalised sexually and/or physically against weaker bodies and it is this bodification of violence and gender and the implications for justice, that the theoretical discussion returns to in Chapter 8. First, Chapter 7 considers how and with what implications the law operates in gendered space, whether the street, the family or the body.

Notes: Issues for Reflection

1 Attributed to William Pitt, Earl of Chatham (1708–78). The concept of the Englishman's home as his castle remains buoyant. In his judgement in Southam v Smout, Lord Denning cited William Pitt the Elder's famous saying: 'The poorest man may in his cottage bid defiance to all the forces of the Crown. It may be frail – its roof may shake the wind may blow through it, the storm may enter, the rain may enter – but the King of England cannot enter all his force dares not cross the threshold of the ruined tenement'(Hansard 2007).

Under what circumstances can forced entry be gained to a family home? Do these circumstances protect women and children?

2 See Galtung and Ruge (1965) for the seminal and still valid account of news values. They are also featured in Chibnall (1977), Wykes (2001) and Jewkes (2004).

How might such values work against the process of justice for women?

How might they serve to promote violence against women?

3 Critically evaluate research on violence against male bodies in familial and intimate contexts.

What happens to men and boys who have been victims of abusive relationships and with what consequences?

4 At the outset of the 21st century those representations of women are discontinuous – frail but fertile; sexual and maternal; career-girl and geisha; independent but arm-candy; flirtatious but faithful. With the demise of a feminist critique during the Thatcher/Reagan years in the 1980s, it is unsurprising that some, perhaps in some ways most, women simply try to comply until they die – sometimes early and tragically when the effort ends in self-harm and disease – whilst others reach the threshold of womanhood, say 'no' to what is on offer and simply self-starve themselves back to childhood. (Wykes and Gunter 2005:208)

Look at self-harm as a gendered phenomenon and think about why and how that might inform the relationship between crime and gender.

Try to explain the rise in suicide amongst young men in the UK.

5 There is just one chapter on the family in Maguire et al. (eds) 2007. Farrington in that volume (pp. 602–40) deals entirely with risk factors in childhood leading to offending. One further chapter on violent crime mentions family twice (Levi et al., pp. 687–732).

How would you explain this lack of attention to family violences?

What if any model of family do the chapters present?

Do these two issues matter?

6 This is an example of a myth. Myths are analogous to stereotypes in that they offer a pre-ordained account of events/people. News about gendered crime frequently uses myths and stereotype to provide readers with short-cuts to explanations.

Try to identify some of these in the press and consider their implications for violence, gender and justice.

Complementary Readings

M. Foucault (1978, 1981) *The History of Sexuality, Vol. 1: An Introduction* (Harmondsworth: Penguin) historically analyses the relationship between sexuality and power.

D. Grubin (1998) *Sex Offending against Children: Understanding the Risk*, Police Research series, paper 99 (London: Home Office) http://www.homeoffice.gov.uk/rds/prgpdfs/fprs99.pdf is one of the few pieces of research to highlight the familial context of child sexual abuse.

E. Saraga (2001) 'Dangerous places: family as a site of crime', in J. Muncie and E. Mclaughlin (eds) *The Problem of Crime* (London: Sage, pp. 191–239) overviews the relationship of the 'family' to crime.

L. Mckie (2005) *Families, Violence and Social Change* (Maidenhead: Open University Press) focuses on adults and offers an account of the contemporary family and the agencies that work with family violence, with some global contextualisation.

W. Hollway (2006) 'Three family figures in 20th century British 'psy' discourses', *Theory and Psychology*, 16 (4): 443–64 considers the role of the family in subjectivity.

7

THE LAW, THE COURTS AND CONVICTION

Chapter 7 examines violence and the law and explores the deeply gendered assumptions about female and male sexuality that have characterised the law's approach. The focus here is *rape*, since it is arguable that this, more than any other issue, encapsulates the sheer inadequacy of the law in relation to gendered violence and the deeply gendered assumptions that surround legal responses to it.* As seen in Chapter 3, sexual abuse and sexual violence also feature strongly in much 'domestic' violence and, as seen in the previous chapter, most child sexual abuse takes place in families, committed by fathers or other male carers on their or their partners' daughters. In some form, then, sexual violence in general and rape in particular features in much violence against women.

Of course, there are many other issues on which we could have chosen to focus in this chapter. Obvious issues around which the law plays on and perpetuates deeply gendered stereotypes about female and male sexuality and female and male roles in relation to both sex and violence, include the law around: provocation as used by women who kill their abusive partners; prostitution;[1] pornography; domestic violence; stalking; trafficking;[2] genital mutilation; sadomasochism; homosexuality and so on. Our focus on rape is not to suggest that it is somehow more important that these others, though rape is, of course, a serious issue. It can be a shattering experience for victims (London Rape Crisis Centre 1984; Lees 1996, 2002; Myhill and Allen 2002; Walby and Allen 2004) and is one of the few offences that can attract a life sentence. Indeed, rape is an interesting issue because of the very disjuncture between the seriousness the law and legal institutions purport to attach to it and the indifference it attracts in practice. Nonetheless, our choice to focus on rape is not to suggest its importance over other issues but rather is based on the law's especial enduring failures in relation to this issue and the endemic fascination with assumptions about female and the male sexuality in responses to it.

Our decision to focus on *the law* on rape rather than, for example, the prosecution process is also to present to readers without past experience in the law the opportunity to examine issues that they might otherwise not have had the

---

*As this chapter deals with the law in considerable detail legal style footnotes are used to direct readers to the relevant legislation and cases.

opportunity to encounter. A further point is that a discussion about the law involves an unavoidable use of legal language. Readers will have noticed already that the tone of this chapter is rather different from that assumed in other chapters in the book, as the law and its language have come to prevail over the discussions. This, though, is just the process that occurs as a woman reports that she has been raped. Throughout the process that follows, *her* experiences are (re)defined and (re)conceptualised to fit into *the law* and its categories. Her experiences are generally denied as legal discourse prevails. In this sense, then, the chapter provides a metaphorical experience. The language is, indeed, different and the tone sometimes difficult but, in so being, is a metaphor for the law and its response to rape and sexual violence.

Rape: the Law, the Courts and Conviction

A man who is convicted of rape in 2008 must consider himself particularly unlucky. His chances of being convicted are certainly astonishingly low. Research suggests that an average accused's chances of being convicted of rape are currently between 1 in 20 and 1 in 12 (Lea et al. 2003; Kelly et al. 2005; see also Harris and Grace 1999) – this compares to a 1 in 9 chance in the 1980s (Wright 1984). Home Office statistics are even more staggering. These statistics suggest that rape convictions range from 1% to 14% over England and Wales – just 0.86% of all rapes reported to the police in Gloucestershire end in a conviction. Put another way, between 92% and 99% of rape cases reported to the police do not end in a conviction for the offence.

The purpose in this chapter is to discuss those aspects of the law and its implementation that explain why such a staggering proportion of men appear to be getting away with rape. Central to this discussion are the assumptions about female and male sexuality that pervade the approach of the law and legal institutions to rape and other sexual offences. Understanding these deeply gendered assumptions is crucial to explaining how the law has conceptualised sex, sexuality, power and violence and, in turn, how it has contextualised rape and the response to it. Arguably, these assumptions reveal themselves most clearly in relation to the continuing focus on penile penetration in the definition of the offence, the centrality of 'consent' to this definition, the 'rapists' charter', created in the case of *DPP* v. *Morgan* [1976] AC 182, and, finally, the preoccupation with a complainant's sexual experience in rape trials. These are discussed in turn but first the legal definition of rape is addressed, although it isn't possible here to cover each aspect of the law and its implementation in comprehensive detail.

The legal definition of rape

Rape originated as an offence at common law.[*] A statutory definition of the offence was not given until 1976. The most recent definition of the offence is

---

[*] Common law is law that is created through court decisions, not legislation.

contained in the Sexual Offences Act 2003. To prove rape, the prosecution must prove beyond all reasonable doubt:

(1) that the accused (A) intentionally penetrated the vagina, anus or mouth of the complainant (B) with his penis
(2) that B did not consent to the penetration, and
(3) that A did not reasonably believe that B consented.[*]

The Sexual Offences Act 2003 represents the most comprehensive and coherent redefinition of the law on rape and other sexual offences ever undertaken in England and Wales. It followed an extensive review of the law on rape and other sexual offences (the sexual offences review). Nonetheless, it has attracted criticism (Lacey 2001; Rumney 2001; Temkin and Ashworth 2004; Finch and Munro 2006). Criticism here is focused on the Act as a missed opportunity to reconceptualise the law in relation to sex and violence. The concern is that, notwithstanding its ambitious aims, the Sexual Offences Act 2003 has failed to challenge or change the law's fundamental framework.

Penile penetration

The *actus reus* of rape centres on *penile penetration*. For many years, rape was limited to penetration of the vagina. This meant, of course, that rape could only be committed against a woman. The Criminal Justice and Public Order Act 1994 changed the law in this regard, establishing that rape included both vaginal or anal penetration and thus that a woman or a man could be raped. The 1994 change was followed in the Sexual Offences Act 2003 by a further change to include penetration of the mouth by the penis. Thus, a man who forces fellatio on his victim can now be convicted of rape and receive a maximum life sentence. However, penetration of the vagina, anus or mouth by other body parts or by objects remains outside the definition of rape set out in the Sexual Offences Act 2003 and falls, instead, under the offence, created by the 2003 Act, of 'sexual assault by penetration', which carries a maximum life sentence.

Because rape centres on penile penetration, it follows that only men can rape, although a post-operative transsexual can also, since the 2003 Act, commit rape by penetration with a reconstructed penis. However, women cannot commit rape. Women are sometimes described as 'rapists' but can be no more than an accomplice to rape. A woman who forces a man to penetrate her can also not rape. Since the Sexual Offences Act 2003, a woman in such circumstances could be liable for the new offence of 'causing a person to engage in sexual activity without consent' and could receive a maximum life sentence. Under the law that

---

[*] In general, a person cannot be found guilty of a criminal offence unless two elements are present – an *actus reus* (guilty act) and *mens rea* (guilty mind). The *actus reus* of rape is penile penetration, of the vagina, anus or mouth, without consent. The *mens rea* of rape is intentional penetration and without reasonable belief in B's consent.

preceded the 2003 Act, those accused in these circumstances could only have been convicted of indecent assault (an offence which also covered less serious offences, such as unwanted touching of a person's clothes, and which attracted a much lower sentence). It is to be welcomed, then, that a man (or woman) who subjects his (or her) victim to a serious penetrative assault can now receive a sentence of life imprisonment, as can a woman who has intercourse with a man without his consent. However, are these people really less abusive than men who penetrate the victim's vagina, anus or mouth with their penis? It is right that they are not classed as 'rapists' and that many humiliating, harmful and horrifying behaviours continue to fall outside the most serious sexual offence, 'rape'?

At a fundamental level, sexual assault is wrong because it gains without consent that which should be shared consensually (Lacey 1998). Its wrongfulness is that it is 'the sheer use…[and]…objectification of a person' (Gardner and Shute 2000: 205). The wrongfulness of both rape and other serious penetrative assaults is in the challenge to sexual choice. We would argue that *all* serious penetrative assaults (as a man penetrates a woman with his penis, a person penetrates another with objects, or as a woman forces a man to penetrate her) threaten sexual autonomy and, therefore, that there is little justification for distinguishing between different penetrative abuse (see also Hall 1988; Bridgeman and Millns 1998). Indeed, research in New Zealand highlighted that female survivors 'saw *all* acts of penetration (vaginal, oral and anal) as a fundamental attack on their body and integrity' (Barrington 1984: 316).

Anyway, it may be misleading to talk of penile penetrative assaults as against non-penile assaults. Research certainly suggests that many forced vaginal penetrations are accompanied by other forced penetrations or sexual acts. In their pioneering research in the 1970s with rape victims, Holmstrom and Burgess (1980) certainly found that vaginal penetration by the penis had been accompanied by forced fellatio in 22% of cases, forced cunnilingus in 5%, forced anal intercourse in 5%, urination on the victim in 4% and insertion into the vagina of an object in 1% of cases (see also Wright and West 1981; Smith 1989). The broad abuse that characterises many sexual assaults appears inconsistent with the law's narrow differentiation between different sexual acts.

Largely, this differentiation is attributable to the early origins of the law on rape, which, as we discuss below, was concerned particularly with the theft of virginity (Temkin 2002). The more recently rehearsed reasoning for excluding from the definition of rape penetration other than by the penis includes the argument that such penetration does not carry with it the risk of pregnancy and/or the risk of disease (CLRC 1980; Home Office 2000). The sexual offences review, which led to the Sexual Offences Act 2003, also 'felt [that] rape was clearly understood by the public as an offence that was committed by men on women' (Home Office 2000: para. 2.8.4).

As regards the risk of pregnancy, the fact that pre-pubescent, post-menopausal, sterilised and infertile women can all be raped rather undermines this reasoning, as of course does the fact that men can also be raped. In addition, the sexual intercourse in the *actus reus* of rape is completed upon penetration 'without the emission of seed' (Ormerod 2005: 617). The slightest penetration will suffice. Again, these rules rather undermine the significance accorded to pregnancy as stated above. Undoubtedly, though, pregnancy[3] and the fear of pregnancy will serve to exacerbate the trauma of rape for some women, as, indeed, will the risk of sexually transmitted disease.

The argument that if the public assumes that a particular law covers particular behaviour the law should continue to cover that behaviour is unconvincing, not least because of the limits such an argument places on law and legal reform (Temkin 2002) and the educative function of such reform (Rumney 2001). Regardless, the review team did not question the public about its understanding, relying, instead, on how legal practitioners thought the public understood rape. Also, this argument about public understanding did not feature in the review discussions about the decision to extend the definition of rape to forced oral sex – would these circumstances be clearly understood by the public as rape?

It is this last point that demands the greatest examination as the most sustainable problematic in the differentiation between penile penetration and penetration by other body parts or by objects. A move from a focus on penile penetration to include in the definition of rape other penetrative assaults would appear to necessitate that the law on rape would become gender-neutral. In deciding to preserve the differentiation between penile and non-penile penetration, however, the sexual offences review rejected such an approach, recommending that rape should continue to cover only the former and, thus, remain a gender-specific offence, despite one of the overall aims of the sexual offences review and resulting Sexual Offences Act 2003 being to gender-neutralise the law around sexual violence (Home Office 2000).

Yet, why is there this reluctance to include women within the definition of the most serious sexual offence, rape? The obvious argument is, of course, that sexual abuse is predominantly perpetrated by men and therefore the law should reflect this and allow for rape to be an offence that can only be committed by men (Temkin 2000, 2002). Naffine expresses this argument thus: 'it is still men who are raping and women who are being raped ... Rape [is] a crime of men against women' (1994: 24).

This is, of course, true. Rape is perhaps *the* gendered crime. It is certainly in relation to sex crimes that the gendered nature of violence is most seen. Indeed, as we have explained, this empirical reality has largely determined our focus on the extremes of interpersonal violence as the topics of discussion in this and other chapters in the book. Yet, is this reason alone to exclude women from the definition of the offence? Just because a group infrequently engages in certain activities should not mean that the law fails to recognise that they *might*. More challenging is the argument, developed since the 1970s, that rape and sexual violence is about men's power and domination over women and that to remove this gendering from the definition of the offence would be to 'render invisible the gendered power relations between men and women expressed through men's sexual violence to women' (Gillespie 1994: 151). Again, though, can the law not recognise these gendered power relations but also recognise women's capacity for violence in general and for sexual violence in particular? At a practical level, 'it seems unfair that a woman should not be labelled a rapist for coercing a man, another woman or a child into a penetrative sex act when a man would be convicted of rape in very similar circumstances' (Rumney 2001: 896). At a conceptual level, the 2003 Sexual Offences Act's maintaining of gender-specificity in relation to rape in the face of its otherwise concerted move to gender-neutrality, serves simply to sustain stereotypes about women and their relation to violence and about women and their relation to *sex*. On this last point, these stereotypes were made explicit in the White Paper that preceded the 2003 Act, in which it was claimed that: 'The anatomical differences between men and women must sensibly direct that the offence of Rape [sic] should remain an offence that can only be physically performed by a man' (Home Office 2002: para. 42). This statement is grounded not in anatomy but in deeply gendered assumptions about male and female sexuality. Most obviously, it is premised on the assumption that a man cannot engage in sexual intercourse unless he is sexually aroused – unless *he* wants it – and, if he is aroused, he is consenting to intercourse. Not only does this assumption sustain stereotypes which emphasise men as active and women as passive in sexual relations, it is also inconsistent with research into male survivors' experiences of rape. The statement is also premised on the assumption that physical attributes and, in particular, physical strength determine the ways in which people can be coerced into unwanted sexual activity. Physical strength may be important but there are many other ways that this coercion can occur – some of which may involve a man being 'genuinely' aroused but not, in a legal sense, genuinely consenting to intercourse.

On one level, the 2003 Sexual Offences Act's providing for circumstances of serious penetrative sexual abuse and, indeed, for women who commit serious sexual abuse is to be applauded. Whether or not abusers in these circumstances will receive comparable sentences to those who 'rape' will remain to be seen, but the Act does at least make provision for serious assaults to be treated accordingly. On another level, though, the Act's provisions have been added on to the framework in which phallocentricity continues to prevail. The law has clearly moved from its fascination with one object and one opening (Walklate 2004) but it continues to focus on the penis as the object of penetration. In doing so, it sustains the focus on penile penetration as *the* instance of sexual intercourse and *the* instance of sexual violation. As we have discussed, this focus is inconsistent with principles of sexual autonomy, with the violation that characterises non-penile penetration and with survivors' lived experiences of sexual violation. At the same time, the focus appeals to highly traditional attitudes about women and violence and deeply gendered assumptions about female and male sexuality.

Consent

Rape is sexual intercourse which takes place without consent – the offence turns on consent. The case of *Camplin* (1945) 1 Cox CC 220 first established that rape could take place even though there was no force threatened or used, provided that the victim did not consent to the intercourse. The case, though, offered no definition of consent. Thirty years later, the Sexual Offences (Amendment) Act 1976 defined rape as sexual intercourse with a woman without her consent. Again, it did not define 'without consent'. The nearest to clarification the law came on the meaning of consent was in the case of *R v. Olugboja* [1981] 3 All ER 443, which established that a distinction should be made between a mere submission on the one hand and consent on the other – that a complainant had submitted did not mean she had consented.

Improving the law through clarifying the meaning of consent was one of the most important parts of the sexual offences review, which led to the Sexual Offences Act 2003. Repeatedly during this review, the government emphasised the need for clarity in the meaning of consent so that 'the boundaries of what is acceptable, and of criminally culpable behaviour, are well understood' (Home Office 2000: para 2. 7. 3). To this end, three sections in the Sexual Offences Act 2003 seek to clarify the meaning of consent. Section 74 provides a general legislative definition of consent. It provides that 'a person consents if he [*sic*] agrees by choice, and has the freedom and capacity to make that choice'.

Whether or not the meaning of consent has been clarified since 2003 (see Temkin and Ashworth 2004; Finch and Munro 2006; Ashworth 2006) the centrality of the concept to the definition of rape has not been challenged. This, in itself, remains a deeply problematic feature of the law and its response to sexual violence. In the same way that the 2003 Act has failed to challenge the law's fundamental framework in relation to penile penetration, so it has failed to change or reconceptualise this framework in relation to consent. The problem is that the concept of consent focuses on the *victim's* state of mind rather than on the *defendant's* state of mind (Hall 1988). The law requires the prosecution to prove the absence of consent rather than requiring the defendant to prove that he had taken steps to ascertain consent. As Westmarland (2004) points out, this approach is exclusive to rape. The focus on the victim's state of mind, not to mention her or his demeanour, words and actions, means that, in rape cases, it can sometimes seem that the *victim* rather than the *defendant* is the person on trial.

This shifting of responsibility on to the victim from the defendant in individual cases reflects the shifting of responsibility that occurs much more generally in relation to sexual violence. Throughout both lay and legal opinion, women are held responsible for controlling male sexuality in general and for controlling male sexual violence in particular. A recent survey has revealed the astonishing views the public hold about women and rape – 34% of people surveyed believed that a woman was partially or totally responsible for being raped if she behaved in a flirtatious manner, 30% believed the same if she was drunk, 26% if she was wearing sexy or revealing clothes and 22% if she had had many sexual partners (ICM 2005). Meanwhile, men have been allowed to abdicate responsibility. As the stereotype goes, men 'just can't help themselves' – male sexuality is conceptualised as uncontrollable, unavoidable and inevitable. These stereotypes are central to the concept of consent, as the law again appeals specifically and sustainedly to assumptions about female and male sexuality.

Of course, though not challenging the centrality of the concept of consent to the definition of rape and thus not *removing* the focus on the complainant, the 2003 Act does at least move to *reduce* this focus through introducing notions such as agreement, choice, freedom and capacity to the section 74 general definition. The sexual offences review team chose these words because it intended this definition to revolve around 'an agreement between two people to engage in sex' (Home Office 2000: para. 2.10.4). The review intended that 'consent' should mean a negotiation between equal partners: 'each must respect the right of the other to say "no" – and mean it' (Home Office 2000: para. 2.10.4).

In this sense, the focus on the complainant's actions, resistance, etc., is reduced as attention turns to the context in which agreement to intercourse is given or not given (Finch and Munro 2006). The court's attention is also directed to what the *accused* did or did not do to establish whether or not there was free agreement to sexual intercourse. The sexual offences review team certainly had this change in focus in mind as it talked about 'shift[ing] the consideration away from what was in the victim's mind, in order to focus attention on what the accused *did* to ascertain whether there was free agreement' (Home Office 2000: para. 2.11.4). Reflecting in 2002 on the government's proposals, Sue Lees appeared optimistic about their move to change the focus in rape trials. As she put it:

> Under these proposals a defendant would need to show that a complainant's consent had been 'freely agreed'. This would at least put some pressure on the defendant to explain what led him to consider that the woman freely agreed. (2002: xliii; see also Lacey 2001)

It was astonishing, then, that in November 2005, just 16 months after these provisions came into operation, the case of *R v. Dougal* (2005 Swansea Crown Court) made the headlines, suggesting that, far from 'putting pressure' on men to demonstrate *communication* between the parties, the law would continue to centre on assumptions about women, their appropriate conduct and their proper responsibilities.

Case-study: R v. Dougal

The case concerned a 22-year-old student who, during a University party, had become heavily intoxicated. A fellow student, Ryairi Dougal, who was working as a University security guard, had been appointed to walk her home. The woman admits that she does not remember the walk home. On the corridor floor outside her room the two had sex. She claimed that she was drifting in and out of consciousness. In her words:

the next thing I know, I'm outside my flat door on the floor ... I see a dark figure at my feet and then I think I must have fallen unconscious again. When I wake up again, he's still standing over me. Again I can't see his face or anything like that, and he ejaculates on me, which horrifies me but I don't understand what's happening. (*Observer* 25 June 2006)

The next day, as details about the previous evening gradually returned to her, the woman went to the police. Following a forensic examination, she was told that someone had had sexual intercourse with her. Dougal claimed the intercourse was consensual. The woman insisted, though, that she would not have agreed to have sex with Dougal, saying: 'If I had wanted to sleep with him I would have taken the few steps to my bedroom.' Dougal was charged with rape. At his trial at Swansea Crown Court, the woman told the jury that she had no recollection of the events but that she was certain she had not consented. Following intense questioning from the defence, however, she was forced to admit that she could not remember whether or not she had consented. This admission caused the prosecution to abandon its case. The prosecution barrister said, 'drunken consent is still consent. She said she could not remember giving consent and that is fatal for the prosecution's case.' The judge agreed that the prosecution could not go on and threw the case out.

Unsurprisingly, the case caused outrage amongst women's rights campaigners. Many questioned how intoxication to the point of partial or periodic consciousness could relate to a woman 'agreeing by choice' and having 'the freedom and capacity' to choose whether or not to have sex. How could a woman who was too intoxicated to even get home be free to choose or agree to take part in sexual interaction? But these questions were not put to the jury.[4] Neither, of course, was the jury allowed to examine Dougal's actions. Indeed, although the defence suggested that the woman had seduced Dougal – 'The defence said it was steamy and passionate sex, that I had grabbed the man's crotch and seduced him' (*Observer* 25 June 2006) – the jury was not allowed to explore how a woman almost unable to stand could have been such a determined seducer. Rather, the case rested on the woman's actions. The case turned on the complainant – everything revolved around whether or not she could remember having said no. Again, responsibility was shifted from the man. Far from promoting a model in which sexual interaction is negotiated, the *Dougal* case retained the focus on the complainant and released the accused from all his responsibilities.

Of course, in cases such as this, the centrality of consent to the definition of rape appeals to assumptions about women's responsibilities for men's violence but also appeals to assumptions about women's responsibilities more generally. The barely concealed message of the *Dougal* case is clearly that women should not drink to excess and that women who *do* drink excessively really only have themselves to blame for whatever happens to them whilst in an intoxicated state. The implication is clearly that women should conduct themselves in a certain manner and that women who do not cannot complain, and certainly cannot turn to the courts, should a man take their intoxication to be an opportunity to have sex. Again, the problem is presented as women who are intoxicated almost to unconsciousness rather than as men who choose to have sex with unconscious, unaware and unresponsive women.

Having preserved the centrality of consent to the definition of rape, the sexual offences review set out to clarify its meaning so that 'the boundaries of what is acceptable, and of criminally culpable behaviour, are well understood' (Home Office 2000: para 2.7.3). In turn, the provisions that followed this review set out to advance communicative sexuality. Though it did not remove the focus on the complainant's consent, it reduced this focus through directing examination to the accused's communication and conduct in establishing the woman's agreement to sex. Nonetheless, these provisions appear to have done little to promote acceptable, and even less to punish unacceptable, sexual conduct. Rather, as some predicted (see Rumney 2001), the old assumptions about women and their responsibilities *versus* men and their responsibilities persist. As women, our responsibilities are limitless – women should not drink, dress in certain clothes, agree to be escorted home following a night out, lose composure. Men, on the other hand, will be men. Of course, not all men would have sex without having established 'free agreement' or would choose to have sex with a woman who was intoxicated to incapacitation. The question, though, is whether the law and those charged with implementing it will punish him should he do so. At the moment, it seems improbable that it will.

Inexorable logic or inexcusable law?

The 1976 case of *DPP v. Morgan* established that an accused could not be guilty of rape if he *honestly* believed that the victim had consented, no matter how *unreasonable* his belief might have been. Here, a husband, Morgan, had been drinking with three junior colleagues. He invited the men to come back to his house to have sex with his wife, telling them that his wife might appear to protest but that they should ignore her protests since protesting was her way of increasing her sexual pleasure. The three men accepted his invitation. On arriving in the house, Morgan woke his wife, who was asleep in their child's bedroom, and dragged her into another room. The men then forced her to have sexual intercourse with them. She struggled and protested throughout. The three men were charged with rape but they argued that Morgan's comments had led them to believe that his wife was consenting, notwithstanding her protests. The House of Lords accepted that, had this been the case, they would not have been liable – their mistake did not need to be reasonable it had only to be genuine (their convictions were upheld on the grounds that a jury would not have accepted that the men honestly believed Mrs Morgan was consenting). To one Law Lord hearing the case, Lord Hailsham, the decision in *Morgan* was one of 'inexorable logic' ([1976]

AC 182 at 214). An accused who made an *honest* mistake had no *mens rea* and could not be convicted. Nonetheless, the case caused considerable public concern and attracted sustained criticism from feminist researchers and activists. One author even suggested that, rather than '*mens rea*', a more appropriate term to use in relation to rape might be 'men's rea' (Cousins 1980). Described as 'the rapists' charter' (Temkin 1987), the decision certainly seemed to mean that a rapist who could create a convincing story, demonstrating that he thought the victim was consenting, would be able to escape a rape conviction, even in circumstances in which the woman was shouting 'no' and struggling to escape.

Central to the decision is the popular but deeply problematic assumption that women who say 'no' do not always mean 'no'. This idea reflects the general situation in which 'what [women] have to say is for many purposes discounted or reinterpreted for them' (Temkin 2002: 122), but the situation in which women who state that they do not consent to intercourse but are nevertheless considered to consent to it reflects a particularly astonishing denial of women's autonomy and agency.

Temkin has argued that, to justify this denial: 'Resort has been had to a ragbag of ideas about female and male sexuality, varying from the bogus to the irrelevant' (2002: 122). The assumption that women who say 'no' do not mean 'no' is certainly based on stereotypes about the sexual games that women are supposed to play. In Clarke et al.'s (2002) research, these stereotypes were commonplace in men's discussions about women and sex. Some were sure that 'no' did not mean 'no': 'When a woman says "no" she means "yes" (male respondent) ... when she says "no" she means "maybe"...when she says "maybe" it means "yes" and when she says "yes" she's no lady (male respondent)' (Clarke et al. 2002: 27–8). Other men in this research took 'no' to be about women's 'teasing' – a sexual game in which "no" actually meant 'not here', 'not yet', 'not now' and would eventually become 'yes' (Clarke et al. 2002).

Other ideas about female sexuality include the view that women are masochistic, deriving pleasure from pain in sexual encounters, and/or that women fantasise about rape (Temkin 2002). At the same time, many (men) have sought to rely on the 'passion of the moment' (HC Deb., vol. 905, col. 833) or the 'natural spontaneity of the action' (HC Deb., vol. 905, col. 826) to suggest that men may genuinely and honestly be mistaken about a woman's consent.

Other ideas about male sexuality are that men are entitled to use proactive strategies to secure intercourse (Finch and Munro 2003). The assumption that men have a right to 'loosen women up' with alcohol is certainly commonplace. Research in the 1980s found that 75% of men were prepared to admit that they had used alcohol to increase the likelihood of intercourse with an initially reluctant woman (Masher and Anderson 1986). *Morgan* appeals to the further assumption that this right extends to overcoming women's 'coy', 'teasing', 'tokenistic' (Williams 1978) resistance.

Since there has been no research into how the *Morgan* ruling operated in individual cases (and thus how many men succeeded in claiming an honest but unreasonable belief in consent), the case might have been a problem in principle rather than in practice. We argue that it was both. Whatever the Lords' reasoning and the jurisprudential support *Morgan* attracted, the principles around which the case revolved were, indeed, problematic. Ultimately, the case established that the law would afford protection to the man who acted upon an unreasonably held assumption about consent rather than to the woman about whose consent the unreasonable assumption had been made. Yet, many have contrasted the relative costs to the man and woman in situations such as this (Law Commission 2000; Ashworth 2006; Lacey 2001). For the woman, the price paid is potentially devastating and catastrophic. For the man, the costs are small in comparison. How would it burden him to establish whether or not the woman is consenting – to find out the true position? She is, after all, there next to him – all he needs to do is pose the question. As regards *Morgan's* operation in practice, a claim of honest but unreasonable belief in consent was a very easy claim to make but a very difficult, if not impossible, one to disprove (Westmarland 2004). In addition, the case encouraged those accused in individual cases to appeal to assumptions about female and male sexuality in court proceedings. As the law reform body, the Law Commission, put it, 'the more stupid and sexist the man and his attitudes, the better the chance he ha[d] of being acquitted on this basis' (2000: para. 7.20(2)).

The *Morgan* decision was finally overturned by the Sexual Offences Act 2003, which demands that a defendant's belief in consent be both honest *and* reasonable. How this change will operate in practice is uncertain. It was clearly intended to hold men to a higher standard in rape cases but whether or not it will succeed in this regard remains to be seen. Paradoxically, the supposed panacea – the reasonable standard – could prove the greatest problem. Certainly, popular but problematic opinions about appropriate – *reasonable* – sexual behaviour pervade the public consciousness. The difficulty, of course, is that the public sit on juries and there is nothing to prevent these opinions about appropriate/reasonable conduct finding their way into the jury room. An accused who, for example, thinks that women who say 'no' really mean 'yes' might find these views concord with a jury of his peer who thinks the same. His belief in consent would be both honest and reasonable – he would not under *Morgan* and would not now be convicted of rape. Even if the jury do not agree, the Act does not prevent the accused from running such a plea and thus the complainant from being questioned about it (Ormerod 2005).

Indeed, the 2003 Act does not talk of a 'reasonable person' standard[*] but instead sets out a general test of what is reasonable *in all the circumstances*. So, those accused are not to be measured against what would be reasonable to the normal person in the situation – what a reasonable person would have done. Rather, the standard is much less demanding. The provisions allow for the personal characteristics of the defendant to be considered when assessing the reasonableness of his conduct. Though clearly intended to protect young defendants or those

---

[*] Often explained to Criminal Law students as 'the man on the Clapham Omnibus'.

with learning difficulties, the Act does not state which circumstances and characteristics should be considered. Ministerial statements suggest that the expression
'all the circumstances' will allow for consideration of all *relevant* characteristics
of the defendant (HC Deb, col. 1073; HC Deb, col. 674) and that it will be for
judge and jury to decide on relevancy for this purpose (HL Deb, col. 1073).
Relevancy will probably extend beyond age and intelligence to the defendant's
sexual experience, generally or with the particular complainant (Ormerod 2005),
but what about a defendant's sexism or misogyny? Ministers have said that these
characteristics will not be considered but the concern is clear:

> What if the accused has led an especially sheltered life, in a rural place, within
> a sexist family, has not been schooled in the shifting gender power relations
> of the 21st century, and believes a sexual partner may be consenting despite
> her protestations: will it be reasonable for him to think she is consenting?
> (Cowan 2007).

Ultimately, because the 2003 Act does not provide a 'reasonable person' standard but a general test of what is reasonable in all the circumstances there is a
good chance that the more objective standard it purports to impose may, in practice, again become a subjective test, focused on the accused's mind and centred
on his 'stupidity' and 'sexism'. The 2003 Act's failure to use the reasonable person against whom to measure the accused means it is likely that the law will continue in its leniency to men who did not but *should have*, by most normal
people's standards, taken greater care to establish consent.

Of equal concern is that the term 'all the circumstances' might be taken by
jurors to mean just that – to mean *all* the circumstances, even those unconnected
in time to the intercourse or those unconnected to the decision (or otherwise)
about consent between the parties themselves. 'All the circumstances' could be
taken to mean, as one 'juror' in Finch and Munro's research based on fictional
juror deliberations in fictional rape trials put it: 'The whole situation, the party,
the drinking and so on' (2006: 318; see Temkin and Ashworth 2006). Of course,
this might lead jurors to examine the *complainant's* conduct – her sexual experience generally and with the accused in particular, whether she had been drinking with him or flirting with him, whether she had invited him into her home,
and so on – in order to assess the reasonableness of the *accused's* conduct
(Temkin and Ashworth 2004; Finch and Munro 2006). In practice, jurors in
rape trials may be just as reliant on assumptions about women, their appropriate conduct in social settings and their appropriate sexual conduct under the
new provisions as they were under the old. Far from solving the problems in the
previous law, the operation of the concept of reasonableness under the 2003 Act
could serve to sustain the centrality of highly questionable attitudes in the law's
response to sexual violence.[5]

Thus, to some legal minds, the decision in the case of *Morgan* that a man who
had an honest but unreasonable belief in consent could not be guilty of rape was
one of 'inexorable logic'. For others, the decision was inexcusable, creating a

'rapists' charter' and colluding in the assumption that 'no' does not mean 'no'. The 2003 Sexual Offences Act purports to have turned the law to a more objective position but, again, this legislation appears to have missed the chance to truly hold men to a higher standard. Only time will tell whether the 'reasonable in all the circumstances' test it introduces will place greater responsibility on men, but the prospects of this look far from hopeful.

Sexual experience and rape

Historically, the law on rape was concerned with the theft of virginity. Indeed, in the twelfth and thirteenth centuries, the law was restricted to the rape of virginity (see Temkin 2002). The following discussion focuses on the use in rape trials of evidence about the complainant's sexual history in order to argue that the law has not fully disabused itself of the assumption that only virginal women deserve protection from rape.

Evidence about the complainant's sexual history has been routinely used in court during rape trials. Until the late 1970s, the admissibility of such evidence was governed by nineteenth-century common law rules. Against a background of concern about the use of sexual history evidence in rape trials, section 2 of the Sexual Offences (Amendment) Act 1976 was passed. Under this section, past sexual experience with the particular defendant was always admissible and evidence of such experience with someone else would also be admissible if the judge concluded that 'it would be unfair to that defendant to refuse to allow the evidence to be adduced or the question to be asked'. Though rather unambitious (see Temkin 1984), the legislation was intended to limit the use of sexual history evidence in rape trials. Unfortunately, the courts gave section 2 a very broad interpretation. In practice, it seemed that judges were easily persuaded to admit sexual history evidence – some judges themselves even questioned complainants about their sex lives, without the defence having applied to do so (Adler 1982; Brown et al. 1983; Temkin 1984; Chambers and Miller 1986; Adler 1987; Temkin 1993; McColgan 1996a; Temkin 2000).

Increasing concern that rape victims were not being protected in court proceedings culminated in the publication of *Speaking up for Justice* (Home Office 1998), the report of a Home Office Working Group, established to examine the treatment of vulnerable or intimidated witnesses in the criminal justice system. Following this report, the Youth Justice and Criminal Evidence Act (YJCEA) 1999 was passed. Sections 41 to 43 replace section 2 of the 1976 Act. Section 41 sets out a rule of exclusion so that evidence of the complainant's past sexual behaviour, including with the present accused, cannot be used in rape trials. Section 41 also sets out four exceptions to this general exclusionary rule, detailing when evidence of the complainant's previous sexual behaviour *can* be allowed.

There is no exception which specifically permits evidence of previous sexual behaviour with the particular accused where this is relevant to this issue of consent.

In the case of *R v. A* [2001] 3 All ER 1, the House of Lords considered that this omission was in conflict with Article 6 of the European Convention on Human Rights, which guarantees the right to a fair trial. The Lords used the Human Rights Act to hold that evidence of a complainant's previous sexual behaviour with the particular accused could be admitted when it was 'so relevant to the issue of consent that to exclude it would endanger the fairness of the trial'.[6]

Following the decision in *R v. A*, there had been concern that the Lords' ruling would be used to permit sexual behaviour evidence in *any* case where the judge considered that to exclude it would contravene the defendant's right to a fair trial. The Court of Appeal has, however, resisted such a move and has emphasised that the decision is restricted to evidence about a previous sexual relationship with the particular accused. In other cases, though, defence teams have used the Human Rights Act to frustrate the YJCEA's efforts to restrict the use of past sexual history evidence in rape trials. In general, the Court of Appeal has resisted this defence manoeuvring but it is clear that 'sexual history remains on the agenda as part of the strategy for defending in sexual assault cases' (Kelly et al. 2006: 21). Indeed, Kelly and colleagues' research confirms the extensive use of sexual history evidence in rape trials.

Why are defence teams so keen to use evidence of a woman's sexual history in court? Well, such evidence is clearly used to discredit the victim in the eyes of the jury – to suggest that a woman who has had an active sex life with men other than a husband cannot be trusted and is thus not a good witness, or to imply that if a woman has consented to sex with various men in the past, she would probably consent to sex with anyone, including the present accused. Sexual history evidence is used 'to discredit and demean the complainant's evidence and thereby influence the jury's perception of its veracity' (Chambers and Miller 1986: 126). As one barrister, interviewed by Temkin in research with ten experienced barristers about prosecuting and defending rape cases, put it, 'juries [are] not very good [at convicting] when somebody can be depicted as a slut' (2000: 225).

More broadly, discrediting the victim is, it seems, a primary defence tactic in rape cases. As one barrister in Harris and Grace's research said: 'The defence has little choice but to seek to undermine the credibility of the complainant' (1999: 36). In addition to introducing evidence about her sexual past, other means to discredit a victim include questioning her about her clothes, including the clothes she wears in court. One barrister in Temkin's research mentioned a case in which 'the girl was basically just cross-examined because she had a miniskirt with a zip in it' (2000: 234). Questions also focus on complainants' mental health (Harris and Grace 1999) or their lifestyles. In their Scottish research, Chambers and Millar (1986) found numerous examples of defence questions about women's lifestyles, which were often loaded with strong moral overtones and were clearly designed to discredit the complainant's character. Similarly, Sue Lees found in her research that defence questioning routinely focused on a complainant's lifestyle and morality:

Whether she was a single mother; whether the man she was living with was the father of her children; the colour of her present and past boyfriends ... who looked after her children while she was at work; whether she was in the habit of going to nightclubs on her own late at night; whether she smoked cannabis and drank alcohol ... what underwear she had on; whether she wore false eyelashes and red lipstick'. (Lees, 2002: 134)

The impact on complainants of this game-playing by the defence can be cata-strophic and can mean their experience in court amounts to a second victimisa-tion. Certainly, in research by Victim Support (1996), complainants described their experiences in the witness box as 'patronising', 'humiliating' and 'worse than the rape'. Numerous women questioned said that they had been asked intrusive and inappropriate questions. Similarly, 72% of women in Lees's (1996, 2002) research said that they had been asked irrelevant and unfair questions during cross-examination. Eighty-three% said that they felt *they* were on trial and not the defendant. In 2002, the case of a 17-year-old Scottish girl who had been raped made the headlines, demonstrating the devastation that can follow a woman's appearance in court. The young girl gave evidence against her attacker at his trial for rape. During this evidence, defence counsel twice told her to hold up the underpants she was wearing on the night of the attack and to read out in court what was written on them – 'Little Devil'. The defence's obvious appeal-ing here to assumptions about her sexual morality 'mortified' and 'horrified' the girl. Four weeks after her appearance in the witness box, she committed suicide (*Guardian* 2 August 2002).

Ostensibly, the treatment to which women are exposed in rape trials takes place in the name of justice, the suggestion being that evidence about a woman's sexual history should be admitted in rape trials in order to preserve the balance between the accused's interests and those of the complainant. The question, of course, is whether justice is really served by demeaning a complainant to such an extent that her account is discredited and disbelieved by the jury. Research certainly suggests that juries are not keen to convict when presented with evi-dence about the complainant's sexual experience. As such, McColgan has argued that 'sexual history is improperly employed to secure acquittals for men who have been guilty of rape' (1996: 275). Whose justice is served in these situ-ations? At the other end of the process, research repeatedly suggests that victims are deterred from reporting rape or supporting a rape complaint because they fear questioning in court, particularly about their sexual history (Kelly et al. 2005; see also Home Office 1998). Not only does the use of sexual history evi-dence allow men to escape responsibility for their sexual violence, then, but its use also acts as an informal control over women and their sexual interactions. Clearly, here, the criminal justice system is sustaining the interests of patriarchy rather than delivering justice.

Indeed, far from being about justice in rape cases, it seems that sexual history and other such evidence is used to undermine the 'unchaste' woman's right to the law's protection. Certainly, the processes described here play on the thinking that only 'good' (virginal/virtuous) women deserve protection from rape. Juries are being asked to decide, not whether a woman was raped, but whether she is entitled to the protection of the law – not whether she was raped in this instance but whether she is a 'rapeable' woman (McColgan 1996a).

Clearly, the chastity/credibility/deservedness connection rests on the traditional distinction between 'good' (asexual) and 'bad' (sexual) women. As Lees (2002) notes, a woman's sexual reputation is central to her reputation more generally. Female sexual agency and autonomy is seen as indicating low morals and 'promiscuity', attracting pejorative descriptions such as 'slag', 'slut' and 'whore'. Male sexual agency, on the other hand, is seen as signifying health and virility and attracts much more positive denotations such as 'stud' and 'stallion'. The use of sexual history evidence and other evidence about a woman's appearance, etc., appeals to this good/bad (madonna/whore) nexus. Perhaps more than any other aspect of the law and its implementation, then, the admissibility in a rape trial of evidence about a woman's past sexual experience plays on and perpetuates the assumptions about female sexuality that pervade the approach of the law and legal institutions to rape and rape complainants.

Conclusion

We chose rape as the focus of this chapter about violence, gender and justice because on no other issue does the law and its application fail so crassly and consistently to administer justice. It does so largely by focusing closely on assumptions about female and male sexuality and in so doing it also reproduces and legitimates assumptions about female/male sexuality. So the law as applied to rape doubly damns women both inside and outside of the courtroom despite their role in rape as victims of male violence.

The focus on penile penetration in the definition of the offence appeals to assumptions that penile penetration is *the* sexual action and *the* sexual abuse. The centrality of consent to the definition of rape is grounded in ideas about female/male responsibility/irresponsibility in sexual relations in general and sexual violence in particular. The *Morgan* ruling has allowed men who did not but should have, by most normal people's standards, taken greater care to establish consent, to escape a rape conviction. Finally, the law has been fixated on a complainant's past sexual experience in rape trials. This fixation rests on assumptions about female chastity, female credibility and women's right to the law's protection. At each turn, the law and its implementation plays on and perpetuates very particular stereotypes about female and male sexuality.

Yet, underpinning these very particular stereotypes about female and male sexual relations is one much more general stereotype. Arguably, *all* aspects of the law on rape and its implementation in rape trials appeal to one abiding assumption – that women who complain about rape are not to be trusted. Almost *every* aspect of the law is grounded in the general stereotype that women are inclined to 'cry rape' following regrettable sexual encounters. As such, the law's response to sexual violence supports and sustains stereotypes about female sexuality on the one hand, but it also appeals to assumptions about femininity, female irrationality and female fragility on the other. Women, the law assumes, are liars, prone to fanciful, frivolous and even vindictive allegations against men. Men, the law thus assumes further, need protection against these falsehoods. As the legal expert Hale put it in 1734, rape 'is an accusation easily to be made and hard to be proved, and harder to be defended by the party accused, tho [sic] never so innocent' (quoted in McColgan 1996: 280).

At one level, the suggestion that a rape complaint is an easy claim to make but a hard one to counter is unhelpful. The suggestion certainly overlooks the demands that can be involved in reporting a rape to the police, involvement in the police investigation, supporting the complaint through court and so on. It also overlooks the evidence that most men who are accused of rape find such a charge far from difficult to disprove – rather, the massive majority are not convicted. At another level, though, Hale's suggestion *is* helpful in explaining why so many men are getting away with rape. In his remark, the fear that pervades the law and legal institutions is revealed. This fear – that men will face false accusations – is helpful in exploring why, in the law and its implementation, male interests are promoted and preserved.

It appears that the law has developed to protect male interests against 'false' accusations. To this end, the (male-dominated) law and legal institutions have organised around disbelieving complainants and denying the male role in the offence through appealing to popular but profoundly problematic assumptions about female and male roles and sexuality. The legal response to rape has taken place within a 'hermeneutics of suspicion' (Denike 2000, quoted in Kelly et al. 2006). As seen in Chapter 5, this suspicion begins in the police station and it continues throughout the criminal justice process, bolstered by legal provisions that allow the complainant's account to be actively challenged or her very right to complain compromised. Indeed, until 1994, the judge in a rape trial always had to warn the jury that it was unwise to convict on the complainant's evidence alone. This did not mean that there could be no conviction without evidence corroborating what the woman said, but clearly the warning could have raised doubts in jurors' minds where none would have existed without it. The warning also demonstrated the assumption that women were liable to falsehood and fantasy. The corroboration rested on the notion, as some formulations of that warning put it, that 'women in particular and small boys are liable to be untruthful and invent stories ...' and that 'in sex cases women sometimes imagine things which various ingredients in their make-up tend to make them imagine' (McColgan 1996a: 277).

As regards those legal provisions discussed above, the concept of consent clearly appeals to the assumption that women in general, and in rape cases in particular, cannot be trusted, as does the investigation into the accused's belief in consent (whether under the *Morgan* law or under the current reasonableness standard). Another aspect appealing to that assumption is the law's fascination with force and violence to prove rape and the implication therein that women's evidence alone is not enough and that 'extra' evidence is needed to establish that the complainant did not consent. Kelly et al. certainly found in their research into over 2,000 reported rape cases that, 'whilst injury alone had little impact, cases involving the use of a weapon and resulting external injuries were twice as likely to result in conviction compared with those where neither was present' (2005: 72; see also Chambers and Miller 1983; Temkin 1997, 1999; Adler 1987; Harris and Grace 1999).

Criminal justice is about balancing competing and contrasting rights and interests but it appears that the law on rape has gone further than this, in practice promoting the 'notion that there could be two contradictory, mutually exclusive understandings of a singular event' (Phoenix and Oerton 2005: 35). Moreover, the law has prioritised the male understanding in such circumstances of contradiction, through appealing to gendered assumptions about female sexuality on the one hand and femininity on the other. At both an individual and general level, the law has thus left the dangerous body literally free to act again whilst also metaphorically shoring up very traditional meanings about sexual bodies that have implications beyond the courtroom for gender identity and subjectivity. Rape law is itself heavily focused on the body – the focus on *penile* penetration, the significance accorded to female failures to control their bodies in 'drink', the attachment to evidence of violence on the body, and so on. In trying to understand violence, gender and justice, then, there is perhaps a need to review the 'body'. Chapter 8 explores this relationship between bodies, meanings and behaviour in relation to gender, justice and violence.

Notes: Issues for Reflection

1 What does prostitution tell us about (a) gender (b) law?

2 Many would argue that trafficking is, in fact, about 'rape'. As will be seen, 'consent' is central to the definition of rape. In turn, consent requires 'freedom and capacity' to choose.

Can trafficked women give consent, so defined, when many are kidnapped, drugged, addicted, dependent or poverty stricken?

3 In her pioneering research into rape, Ruth Hall found that 5% of the women surveyed had become pregnant through the rape (Hall 1985; see also Lees 2002).

The 2001 BCS found that, of women who had been raped, 4% had had to deal with an unwanted pregnancy following the assault (Walby and Allen 2004).

How many different kinds of impact may rape have?

4 Interestingly, though, research suggests that, even *had* these questions been put to the jury, the outcome might have been the same.

Finch and Munro (2006) conducted fictional rape trails in order to examine jurors' deliberations.

Read this research. What are its main findings?

5 Would it be right to suggest that, whatever changes are introduced to improve the law around rape and sexual violence, whilst social attitudes remain unchanged there is little hope of expecting justice for complainants in rape cases or accountability from men in their sexual relations?

6 What does the law's approach to the use of sexual history evidence in particular reveal about the law's approach to acquaintance rape?

Complementary Readings

A. McColgan (1996b) *The Case for Taking the Date out of Rape* (London: Pandora) considers the importance of the language used to describe rape.

E. Finch and V.E. Munro (2006) 'Breaking boundaries? Sexual consent in the jury room', *Legal Studies*, 26(3): 303–20, is an interesting piece of research where participants were asked, having observed a mock rape trial reconstruction, to apply the tests set out in the Sexual Offences Act 2003 in order to reach a verdict.

J. Phoenix (2006) 'Regulating prostitution: controlling women's lives', in F. Heidensohn (ed.) (2006) *Gender and Justice* (Cullompton: Willan) explores the exploitatation faced by women selling sex.

8

EMBODYING VIOLENCE

Masculinity, Culture and Crime

This chapter returns to theory to re-evaluate some of the evidence of the relationship between gender and crime. There are many variables that intersect with crime so as to exacerbate or mollify offending or victimisation, for example, age, race, economic status, marital status, geography and mental health. Each of these offers a continuum along which the relation to crime varies in the reported/recorded data and each therefore requires the development of theoretical interstices between identity and crime and justice – identity which may be clearly demarcated by bodily representations of racial identity, sexuality, wealth, age, domicile or well-being. Yet in each case, however demonstrable the variations are along these specific variables, what is invariable is that in each case the gender of the crime/agent/patient nexus is overwhelmingly constant. What is shared across other identity variables relating to crime is the 'body' as sexually differentiated and the represented values and roles attached to that 'body' through the cultural construction of gender. The reasons for writing *Violence, Gender and Justice* are manifold. This data on domestic violence, from research funded by the Northern Rock Foundation at Bristol University, alone indicates the problem of both injustice and violence:

- Out of a total of 2,402 domestic violence incidents, perpetrators were arrested, charged and convicted in only 120 incidents (5%).
- Nearly one in five (18%) perpetrators who re-offended did so against a different partner from the one they were originally reported for.
- The highest number of domestic violence incidents involving one perpetrator over the three-year follow-up period was 44. Twenty-nine perpetrators were involved in ten or more incidents.
- Previous domestic violence offending was the strongest predictor of further domestic violence offending (Hester and Westmarland 2006: 3).

But the way the data is represented in this report also illustrates perfectly the obfuscation of the masculinity at the heart of these crimes, their gendered nature and the masculinism in the Criminal Justice System that fails to deliver justice.

Masculinity is attributively missing: 'masculinity' is not used in the report, 'male' occurs several times but as an adjective, and 'man' appears just twice.

A second piece of research highlights other obfuscations of the violence of masculinity. Dobash et al. (2002) studied 786 males convicted of homicide. Of these, 41% killed women or children they knew; 'victims and offenders are unlikely to be strangers but are much more likely to be known to one another either as acquaintances, friends, family or intimate partners' (2002). Explanations were sought across a range of variables:

> Before the age of sixteen: 61% had problems in school; 48% had at least one conviction; 39% were from broken homes; 24% had a father who was violent to their mother; 26% had been in care; 24% had multiple carers; 25% had problems with alcohol and 17% had abused drugs. (Dobash et al. 2002)

At first reading this seems shocking, but on reflection the data means that of these violent men: 52% had no previous conviction; 61% were from 'whole' homes; 76% saw no domestic violence; 74% hadn't been in care; 76% hadn't had multiple carers; 75% had no problem with alcohol and 83% hadn't abused drugs. They had been, in the majority of measured sectors, normal young men – even sharing 'problems at school'. What seemed to mark them out more than anything was just that *ordinary* maleness.

Gender has been somewhat diluted by genuine and very pertinent criminological work on other identity variables. This chapter explores the lack of work on masculinity *per se* as opposed to black masculinity, working-class masculinity or homosexual masculinity, let alone the work on areas such as youth, terrorism, white-collar crime, state crime, gangs, street violence and drugs that doesn't discuss masculinity or often even acknowledge that this is men's crime. This chapter brings the boys back to that work: not boys diluted to be 'other' through alignment with various distancing variables, but mainstream male bodies who commit over 90% of all known crime; even more violent crime and virtually all sexually violent crime. It asks what it is that aligns differently sexed bodies so differently but so discretely to different crime roles, queries the efficacy of any concern with crime that negates, obfuscates or denigrates the sex variable and asks why it is so difficult to blame *men* for crime when they commit so much of it.

Identity Intersections

Poverty

Even when crime is non-violent it is deeply gender differentiated and this is true regardless of the presence of other identity variables. When poverty is a key variable men commit very different offences from women, more serious offences and many more of them. When asked about crimes women commit, TV licence evasion, prostitution (and non-payment of fines for it) and shoplifting are the offences undergraduate students new to criminology can readily name. All of these do relate to poverty but also to feminine gender roles. It is women who tend to run the household, offer sexual services as part of a heterosexual relationship, often in return for security, identity and/or material support, and women do most shopping. Davies challenged gendered explanations for such crime as repeating stereotypes of women's irrationality:

> The classic explanations throughout criminology; anomie, sub-culture, differential association, rational choice all draw upon examples using men and/or boys either explicitly or implicitly as illustrations. In contrast women and girls who shoplift can be much more easily explained. It is their sexuality rooted in their biological make up and psychiatric characteristics that are the root cause of their criminal tendencies (Carlen, 1985; Allen, 1987; Heidensohn, 1994). As in any other area of crime or social life women have never been deemed to act rationally, not even when in dire material need. (Davies 1999: 5)

There seems to be no irrationality in aligning these women's crimes with sex difference. What would be irrational would be for a poor woman, with sole responsibility for a young child or two, to attempt to hijack an expensive car from a large man or burgle a house in a wealthy suburb in the small hours of the morning. Davies argues that some such crimes are purely financially motivated and highly rational but she still implies some diminishment of women by not acknowledging positively that they are also committing the kind of crimes they can (and can hope to get away with) because they are women. That still maintains a discursive devaluation of women for using their sexed identity and bodies practically and profitably and continues a double standard that is never applied to men.

By contrast, with male crime accounts readily condemn the crime and perhaps the poverty or unemployment but rarely address the masculinity of the offender. A BBC report on a Sheffield University study in 2005[1] illustrated this:

> Professor Danny Dorling found a link between rising murder rates and the number of young men leaving school at a time of mass unemployment. Feelings of hopelessness and a lack of opportunity 'bred fear, violence and murder', Prof Dorling concluded. (BBC News 17 October 2005)

Nowhere in the article or report is there any criticism of men who turn to violence and murder, nor does the term masculinity appear in the article, despite the litany of economically and politically culpable *men* listed:

> Behind the man with the knife is the man who sold him the knife, the man who did not give him a job, the man who decided that his school did not need funding, the man who closed down the branch plant where he could have worked, the man who decided to reduce benefit levels so that a black economy grew. (BBC News 17 October 2005)

There is almost sympathy for violent men, and impoverishment is viewed as causal, implying that somehow economic power is a male norm and right. Nor is it asked why equal poverty clearly didn't turn women murderous and indeed why everyone concerned looks everywhere, except at men, for explanations.

Youth

Goliath (1993) was written by Beatrix Campbell as a response to the distur-bances on many of Britain's large social housing estates in the early 1990s, which included arson, joy-riding, vandalism and intimidation. This was youth crime that was community based and poor. In Cardiff and Oxford TWOCing (taking without owner's consent) of the fast and powerful cars that symbolised the suc-cessful man of Thatcherite Britain became commonplace. The cars were driven recklessly in front of, and egged on by, admiring audiences, including journalists eager for a story. Joy-riders were often chased by police (sometimes resulting in accidents) and the stolen cars were frequently wrecked or torched. Campbell commented: 'All these boys becoming men, stealing and steering an object impregnated with fantasies ... There is something ultimately transgressive in their culture because, of course, they are connoisseurs of cars – but they can't keep them' (*Marxism Today,* December 1991). Youths, often the second gener-ation excluded from work and certainly from the rampant entrepreneurialism of the Thatcherite economic model, took the trappings of masculine power they couldn't earn and briefly did *being a man.*

That process of doing masculinity is relatively easy to recognise in joy-riding, less obvious perhaps in other youth crime. Noisily, perhaps drunkenly, occupying public space, desecrating or taking property they cannot own, marking with graffiti their identity as if claiming ownership, and competing with other youths as gangs and as individuals are all deviant emulations of dominant masculinity – the other side of the coin. Just as lads doing handbrake turns in stolen sports cars are the illegitimate equivalent of mature police offi-cers breaking the speed limit in fast chase vehicles to stop them. Crime offers the heads and tails of masculinity, and it is masculinity, not femininity – it would be difficult even to understand the term youth as feminine. Moreover the data tells the same old story: 'In April 2004, there were over 2,800 young people in custody. Of these only 138 were female' (ESRC 2007). Yet the press[2] constantly refers to youth crime or juvenile delinquency not male crime: 'The youth crime statistics...within Ministry of Justice reports, relate to offenders aged 10 to 17 who were either convicted in court or issued with a police cau-tion' (Leapman 2008).

Policy papers, politicians and academics use much the same language with the neat effect that the gendered aspect of much offending by young people is disappeared by not labelling the offenders as overwhelmingly young men. The Nuffield Foundation rightly criticized the media for focusing on extremes: 'Media representations of youth crime focus on violent crimes, and report specific examples of the worst kinds of juvenile offenders. But these are not the cases that appear in youth courts on a daily basis' (Hough and Roberts 2003: 4). But the remainder of the website summary of this report then de-sexes the boys. The Home Office does no better, recognising just about everything but masculinity as relevant:

These are some of the major risk factors that increase the chances of young people committing crimes:

- troubled home life
- poor attainment at school, truancy and school exclusion
- drug or alcohol misuse and mental illness
- deprivation such as poor housing or homelessness
- peer group pressure. (Home Office 1998–99)

This obfuscation of the masculinity of youth crime sets the pattern for accounts of criminal careers generally but is particularly puzzling as early sociological accounts of crime, such as Parsons (1937) and Cohen (1955) did discuss delinquency as male, albeit by accepting as non-problematic 'the biological basis of sex-role theory' (Walklate 2004: 59). Ironically, it seems gender was thrown out with biology in the subsequent years, whilst biology in terms of racial identity remains firmly in place.

Race

When race is the variable focus of choice, similar patterns of missing masculinity emerge. A racialisation of crime in the UK can perhaps be traced to the use of the term 'mugging' to report the killing of an elderly man on Waterloo Bridge during a street robbery in August 1972. With the election of Margaret Thatcher's government in 1979, on a law and order mandate, street crimes became the target of a series of aggressive police operations. From 1981 to 1985 the response to increased 'stop and search' tactics by police was violence in the inner cities, driven by what Hall et al. called 'proto-political criminalised consciousness' (1978: 397) amongst second-generation black youths. The excuse for the policing offensive was to control mugging, drugs and illicit drinking clubs, but the use of 'stop and search on suspicion' or SUS had 'the effect of defining the entire African diaspora as criminal. Its use meant all blacks could be arrested on suspicion of being about to commit a crime' (Cumberbatch 1998: 17). Drugs and violence have since remained closely allied to young black street culture. Lee Jasper, a leading black Briton, 'blamed London's upsurge in shootings and carjackings on a moral vacuum inhabited by many black people' (Summerskill 2002).

SUS 'stop and account or search' has also remained focused on black citizens as Ministry of Justice data shows:

For every 1,000 black people in England and Wales, there was an average of 102 stops and searches in 2005/6. This is almost seven times greater than the average of 15 per 1,000 people within the white population. The Metropolitan Police conducted 75% of all searches on black people in England and Wales. (BBC News 30 October 2007)

Yet these much higher levels of stops for black people are not justified by significantly higher arrest rates: 'Of those black people stopped, 13% were subsequently arrested. This compares to 12% of stops leading to arrest across all ethnic groups' (BBC News 30 October 2007). This indicates a second major intersection of race and crime which is the institutionalised racism of the criminal justice system that was revealed by the 1999 Mcpherson report on the murder of Stephen Lawrence, commissioned by the Labour government soon after its landslide victory in May 1997.

Case-study: Stephen Lawrence

Four years previously, an 18-year-old black student, Stephen Lawrence had been knifed to death at a London bus stop. Metropolitan police were slow in making arrests of three white teenagers and then charges were dropped in September 1995. When the family's private prosecution against five white youths collapsed, despite the inquest's finding that Stephen had been unlawfully killed, the *Daily Mail* named the five, under the huge headline MURDERERS and calls went up for an inquiry. The Lawrences claimed that racism was both the motive for the crime and the reason for the failure to prosecute successfully. The report recognised and emphasised precisely institutionalised racism and made 70 recommendations, including applying the Race Relations Act to the police, dismissal of officers for racist behaviour, anti-racist training and higher levels of freedom of information on policing processes. Moreover, the white suspects came from a London council estate rife with unemployment, vandalism and racist graffiti and they were filmed being overtly racist and threatening violence.

The racism of the murder, the police and the criminal justice processes also obliterated the fact that again this was men; physically aggrandising themselves through the violent subordination of an 'other' man on a public street, but also legitimately protecting dominant white masculinity through cop culture and the legal system.

It is extremely difficult to find any gender breakdown for racist offences and even more so for race-motivated violence. Studies such as Larrson (2002) on Swedish race crime note, in the section on perpetrators, that these are working- or lower middle-class youngsters influenced by white power music, but does not mention gender. Scotland has data for the age and gender of racist incidents for 2005–2006 that confirms that youth is significant and indicates 3,150 male perpetrators and 870 female (75% male) but does not break the data down to show gender and violence associations (Scottish Government 2007) nor is comment made on the gendered profile. The Home Office website refers to the report, as 'Ethnicity and victimisation: findings from the 1996 British Crime Survey' (HOSB 6/98) that apparently included 'nature of the offences' and the 'age, ethnic origin and gender' of perpetrators, but it is not available on the website and is 11 years old. Ray et al. (2003, 2004) interviewed 64 racist offenders of whom just 5 were women. Their explanation for racist offending includes a mention of unemployment as eroding masculine roles and focuses on shame, but it does not directly interrogate the massive gender disparity found. The full report by the European Monitoring Centre on Racism and Xenophobia (now European Union Agency for Fundamental Rights, the EUMC) for European racist crime alludes to the perpetrators being young males but has no data to demonstrate this (though it does have gender data for victims). Yet, though the findings allude to culture they do not mention cultures of masculinity as needing attention. This even though they refer to Ray et al. (2004) to acknowledge that the profile of racist offenders is similar to the profile for other public crime: white, male, ill-educated, unemployed, young and with a previous history of offending and little political motivation.

As with highlighting poverty in relation to crime, when race is the key variable gender again seems to get disregarded, or at least masculinity does. The Metropolitan Police 'SUS' records for Westminster show 2,529 male stops and 279 female for the period April–August 2007 under the 2000 Terrorism Act, close to 10:1. Ethnically 1,549 were white; 1,077 black/Asian and 213 other. (Metropolitan Police 2007). Significantly, regardless of ethnicity, the gender of those stopped is still the clearest demarcation line of suspects and way out of proportion to the 50/50 approximate split of men and women in the general population.

Nor does the news, or the sources it uses, do anything to redress the lack in academic and Criminal Justice System research and data on masculinity. When violence erupted on the streets of Bradford in 2001, the efforts to account for these events focused on everything but 'young men'. Political conflict was highlighted (despite the findings of the EUMC and Ray et al. 2003, 2004) as was immigration. At the time the then Home Secretary David Blunkett was 'considering making citizenship classes a condition of citizenship for new immigrants' (BBC News 26 October 2001) to improve integration. Similar events in Burnley led to a report calling for 'local and government action to tackle the deprivation and "disillusionment" of young people … [and which] made 67 recommendations covering areas such as housing, political leadership, education, youth and leisure facilities and regeneration' (BBC News 11 December 2001), reminiscent of the Scarman Report after the inner-city disturbances of the 1980s. Though nowhere in the news were there images of rioting women, nobody discussing the events, whether politicians or journalists, seemed to have noticed this, even though: 'The summer's disturbances were some of the worst seen in the UK, with the Bradford violence alone causing damage estimated at £10m, and injuring 300 police officers' (BBC News 11 December 2001). Indeed policing itself, despite issuing policies to tackle its institutionalised racism, has barely addressed its macho profile and aggressive approach to public disorder. 'Within the total of the 43 forces, 22,784 [officers] were female … [which] represents 18 per cent of the total' (Smith et al. 2002: 3), against 51% of women in the general UK population.

Violence between men on the streets (police and perpetrators) is carried out by men not ethnic minorities, youths or the poor as suggested by the accounting discourses. When violence is not public but private, sexual or intimate the difference in gender is most profound and highlights the role of men as perpetrators,[3] yet even here men's actions are often obfuscated as we have discussed throughout this book, either by focusing on their female victims as responsible for what happens to them or by re-labelling men as beasts, strangers, perverts and evil. If race is a relevant variable this too offers a diversionary mechanism from the masculinity of the crime.[4] Current concerns around honour killing and forced marriage focus on Asian cultural practices and religious customs rather than entering into a debate about male sexual and economic power over women and children. Even the United Nations is reluctant to deal with these crimes as misogyny:

> In 1994 the UN's Commission on Human Rights appointed a special rapporteur on violence against women ... Last year the special rapporteur on extrajudicial, summary or arbitrary executions was criticized by a coalition of member countries for including honor killings in her report, and a resolution condemning honor killings failed to pass. (Mayell 2002)

CNN news in 2007, rather than address the patriarchy at the root of honour killings, reported:

> A 17-year-old Kurdish girl whose religion is Yazidi, was dragged into a crowd in a headlock with police looking on and kicked, beaten and stoned to death last month. Authorities believe she was killed for being seen with a Sunni Muslim man ... The Yazidis, who observe an ancient Middle Eastern religion, look down on mixing with people of another faith. Each year, dozens of honor killings are reported in Iraq and thousands are reported worldwide, said the United Nations. (CNN 2007)

The report hence finds another justification of the US/UK invasion of Iraq and damns Islam but does not criticise the male perpetrators or male police onlookers who failed to intervene. In the UK, *Southall Black Sisters* has been working since 1979 on behalf of black and Asian women victims of domestic violence, forced marriage and honour killing. Rahila Gupta has exposed the use of the race(ist) agenda to deflect from the truth of the violence:

> The killing of women as the ultimate method of exerting control over them is not the preserve of any one class, community, race or religion ... Crime of passion? Jealousy? Honour? Different labels, but they are all about the control of a woman's body and mind ... The debate on honour killings occupies that slippery ground between race and gender – a no-man's-land, so to speak. (Gupta 2003)

Though of course a 'no-man's land' is exactly what violence against women (or any violence) is not. Exactly the sensibility that Gupta identified featured in the furore over the documentary *Edge of the City* (Channel 4, 26 August 2004) that included an account of Asian men in Bradford grooming young white girls into drugs, sex and prostitution. Media-reported fears that the programme would exacerbate racial and religious tension in the city led to a deferral of the screening rather than a furious outcry about male sexual abuse and the prostituting of under-age girls.

Sexuality

Sexuality is a further variable that deflects from masculinity in issues of violence, gender and justice, with male sexual crime being associated wherever possible with either paedophilia or homosexuality or blamed on women's sexuality rather than on heterosexual masculinity. Sexual crime, sex and sexuality also have news value as discussed in Chapter 2, and the British press report on them in abundance aligned with such deflections.

The paedophile diversion featured in many of the cases discussed in Chapter 2, and indeed in the Soham case, that inspired this book. The accounts of Ian Huntley neglected the fact that he was in a live-in heterosexual relationship with an adult woman, Maxine Carr, unless she could be implicated in his crime, as when the *Sun* reported: 'It is believed the very image of Carr going out on her own may have pushed Huntley over the edge' (18 December 2007: 8), but regard for his status also retarded the search. Similarly, in the case of missing Shannon Matthews, aged 9, in Dewsbury (February/March 2008) the immediate assumption was of a paedophile kidnapping and instant comparisons were made with the case of missing 4-year-old Madeleine McCann in Portugal (see Chapter 2): 'Police became increasingly convinced they would not find her alive. Every house on her usual route home was searched and known paedophiles in the area were all visited' (Stewart-Robertson 2008). After 24 days Shannon was found in an uncle's house and by 7 April 2008 five members of her extended family were under arrest including her step-father, mother and grandmother. As in Soham and Portugal much time and money was lost chasing 'dangerous strangers' through ineffective policing, but also this is indicative of the continued reification of the family as discussed in Chapter 6.

Homosexuality works differently to deflect from the dangerousness of mainstream masculinity by presenting a deviant alternative beset with disease and perversion, that by default constructs its 'opposite', heterosexual masculinity, as healthy and 'straight'. During Thatcherism, homosexuality was subjected to a real and symbolic attempt to drive it back into the closet in the ideological struggle to secure traditional family values complicit with patriarchy and conservatism and discussed in Chapter 6. Two assaults illustrate the process, with homosexuality being associated with disease and as corrupting of children. HIV/AIDS legitimated an assault on both promiscuity and homosexuality, which reasserted repeatedly that safe sex was monogamous heterosex. Disease was used, as it had been a century previously, to divide sexuality into good and bad – the Contagious Diseases Act of 1864 divided sex into monogamous-good/promiscuous-bad and a century later AIDS discourses divided heterosexual/homosexual sexual practice along the same divide. Secondly, in 1988, section 28 of the Local Government Act was explicitly anti-queer and a response to Labour-controlled councils anti-homophobic strategies and information. Department of Education circulars stressed the importance of stable married life and the responsibilities of parenthood and banned the publicizing of a gay lifestyle. The idea that gayness could be learnt shored up legislative debates that retained the age of homosexual consent at 21 and underwrote the concept that gay men seduce 'under-age' boys, feeding into the paedophile 'fear', whilst mature heterosexual men were left free to bed 16-year-old girls.[5] Through AIDS and Clause 28, in the late 1980s heterosexuality shored up its 'ontological boundaries, by protecting itself from what it sees as the continual, predatory encroachment of its contaminated other, homosexuality' (Fuss 1991: 3).

Curiously, the one 'crime' that involves heterosexual men spreading disease, being promiscuous and perhaps seeking perversion (the negative associations with homosexuality) is constructed as a woman's crime: prostitution. In Britain, the law means a prostitute cannot live with another woman which might constitute a brothel, nor with a man, who would then run the risk of being charged with living off immoral earnings (Macleod 1982). So prostitutes are isolated and men have stepped into the space to exploit and control prostitution by acting as pimps and punters – men sell women to other men with neither kind of man particularly inhibited by the law (Kennedy 1992). Women's bodies are commodities in prostitution and in the UK they are not commodities that women can safely sell themselves. Because brothels remain illegal in Britain any attempt, such as the 1985 Sexual Offences Act, to criminalise men who solicit (effectively bribe women for sex) has made prostitution more secretive as men avoid public spaces where they may be policed, making women more vulnerable. Illegal trafficking of women has added to that vulnerability and dependence by removing for them what little recourse to law prostitutes have anyway and any potential to earn legal money. Since 1997 kerb-crawling has been a recordable offence and section 4 of the Criminal Evidence Amendment Act allows the taking of DNA from any man charged, but this has little deterred the purchasing process: 'The National Survey of Sexual Attitudes and Lifestyles found that 8.9% of men in London aged 16–44 reported having paid for sex in the past 5 years' (Home Office 2004).

Prostitution grounds violence and gender with injustice in a way that can't happen in any 'discussion of other categories of inequality less subject to taboo, such as those of power and gender. Men's sex-right is central to contracts, from marriage to prostitution' (Holland 1998: 26). The current 'legal construction and signification of both the "prostitute" body and that of her client' (Brooks-Gordon and Gelsthorpe 2002) reinforces that male bodily right. Yet prostitution is arguably rape, as the potential for poor, trafficked, and/or drug-addicted women to freely consent (see Chapter 7) must be questionable. It is legalised rape in which the law criminalises the victim and so legitimates male sexual abuse because of her criminality. It symbolically suggests that when women's sexuality *deviates* from respectable, private, monogamous heterosex it deserves to be assaulted – that symbolism spreads beyond the prostitute to other non-conforming women, especially rape victims who are readily blamed in court or the press for what they wore, where they were and how they behaved. What should be an area of significant male crime against women is simply not seen as such because of the law and perhaps because 'men as males have not been the objects of the criminological gaze' (Cain 1989: 4). Fifteen years later Walklate was still calling for 'foregrounding men as "the problem" in relation to the question of crime' (2004: 53).

Regardless of all the diversions and mitigations of identity variables that constitute the complexity of masculinities, and there are many more than can be addressed here, the constant is 'masculinity', and that constant more than any other intersects with crime despite being subsumed by work on the range of identities that intersect with it. The next section considers if it is possible to discover what it is about masculinity that makes it criminogenic.

The Boys are Back in Town: Gendering Criminology

'What is it about men not as working class, not as migrants, not as underprivileged individuals but as men that induces them to commit crime?' (Grosz 1987, quoted by Walklate 2001: 53). Masculinity was pretty much absent from mainstream academic research prior to the 1980s, with men taken as the normative standard, their subjectivity taken as objective knowledge and patriarchy universal. From the late 1970s, feminist work on women both within and without criminology named men as a problem, but solving that problem was less the feminist impetus than dealing with the effects of it on women and children (see Chapter 4). Moreover, men reacted quickly, not least in the academies, to resist any unitary term that condemned them all as misogynistic and masculinity rapidly devolved into masculinities. Any lingering biologism that reduced male behaviour to testosterone was excised swiftly from theory as too universalising. Gender was no longer seen as natural but cultural, constructed socially, historically and politically and incorporated into the sexed body. So the question became: male bodies commit most crime so what is it about the way masculinity is constructed that is criminogenic? Three broad frameworks offer accounts that have been brought to bear on men and crime.

Psychologising gender

Early psychologists were particularly interested in inherited traits to explain deviant behaviour as criminogenic (for example, Lombroso (1835–1909) and Goring (1870–1919)) but the eugenics associated with it brought any focus on biological characteristics into disfavour. However, Freud's work, developing in parallel, became popular in the study of delinquency (Aichorn 1955; Bowlby 1951), despite Freud's lack of focus on crime *per se*. Freud's work on the family as the site of the acquisition of masculine identity that is at once heterosexual and civilised is discussed in Chapter 6 but crucially depends on the infant experiencing ideal familial conditions, based on his theories of appropriate Victorian patriarchal, bourgeois families which he in turn never examined. Male children, he theorised, not experiencing such role models might fail to negotiate the Oedipus complex where the boy strives to sexually possess the opposite-sex parent by usurping the same-sex paren's position (Freud 1905). Such failure might cause psychic splitting with women and a never-ending striving for one-upmanship with other men. His influence has been profound. For Chodorow (1978) excessive masculinity was linked to *fear of 'regression' to the female* and a resulting over-compensation of male traits, particularly violence and sexual aggression. Or, according to Frachel and Kimmel (1995), Oedipal problems exacerbate intra-male relations resulting in excessive *'homosocial' enactment (scrutiny of other men)* and competitiveness or/and *homophobia (men's fear of men)* with likely criminal outcomes. For Hollway (1989) men's struggle for mastery over self and the feminine 'other' is not a 'stage' of development in childhood but a constant process. So masculine subjectivity/practice keeps adapting in order to gain/keep power, whether over women or other men, by whatever means possible. Hollway's theory would allow male crime to be seen as a method of gaining power for powerless men (however briefly as in a rape or a joy-ride), and therefore crime is an essential aspect of *excluded* masculinities but also a marker of those included who are by comparison *legitimately* powerful – crime as a coin of two sides. According to the psychoanalytic framework, the resolution of this [Oedipal] complex is the cornerstone upon which a man's sense of masculinity is built (Kupfersmid 1995). With the failure of its resolution, potential deviancy as in any or all of misogyny, homosexuality, aggression or hedonistic infantilism may result.

The Oedipal myth remains influential within psychoanalysis and central to Western culture but it is and was a myth. Problematically, psychoanalysis has become popularised, commercialised and somewhat devalued, with childhood emotional trauma regularly cited by offenders as the reason for their adult male crimes such as domestic violence and child sexual abuse. For example, actor Chris Langham downloaded child pornography but 'did not want to be called a paedophile' ... he himself had been abused as an eight-year-old and was therefore looking at these issues 'to resolve a longstanding psychological problem' (Wilson 2007). Wilson continued: 'Over the years, I have got used to paedophiles doing this – in other words, trying to see themselves as the victim and not the victimiser.' Such claims may relate to the popularisation of mythically based Freudian models of explanation but also to the growth of victimism, discussed in Chapter 4, each attributing responsibility for the crime outside of the offender. Psycho-analysis is inherently biographical. It can perhaps help to explain the individual actions of individual men after the act – it may even over time and alongside other therapy interrupt a criminal career and is currently part of rehabilitation programmes for sex offenders in some prison units. But it offers no means of explaining the wholesale phenomenon of the place of men in offending. Recent work has tried to address some of those limitations of the approach for criminology.

Gadd and Jefferson's psycho-social approach retained the Freudian 'attention to detail of complex case studies' (2007: 184) and a focus on the unconscious but embedded those in a careful account of motive that relates to the criminological subject's phenomenological sense of themselves in the social world. Crime may be a means of countering profoundly sensed weakness, conscious or unconscious, that is briefly ameliorated by seizing power (see Hollway 1989, 2001). Like Ray et al. (2004), Gadd and Jefferson identify shame as arising from the fear and weakness associated with powerlessness, aligning the offender with victimhood. That shame they theorise erupts as 'hateful actions' towards others but they don't explain why this should occur instead of, for example, self-harm. Further, it is hard to see what power is gained or shame ameliorated by many crimes, and to claim that those who act callously cannot 'identify with the suffering of others '(Gadd and Jefferson 2007: 186) returns too cleanly to a model of individual psychological damage as unconsciously causal of crime and sidesteps masculinity. Gadd and Jefferson identify acquisitiveness, envy, sexuality, will to power, celebrity and status as discursively entrenched in our *social* world but stop short of exploring those to think 'psychosocially at the level of the group and beyond that the level of society' (2007: 188) in order to try to explain men's affinity to crime.

Sociology and gender

At its crudest, sociology's intervention into gender saw social roles determined by biology, reproductive and physiological, that placed women as child bearers/carers and men as protectors/providers. The heterosexual family and man's place at its head represents the natural gender order. This essential nucleus of human reproduction not only biologically underwrites gender roles and relations but informs evolving social organisations to support those. Society thus becomes a function of reproductive biology, as argued by Talcott Parsons (1937), and within society sex-role behaviour conducive to reproductive biology is learned particularly through the family. This is the natural order of things and if flouted then social and personal chaos is the presumed outcome including deviance and crime. Moreover, that natural order places men in situations (public space, work, darkness, leisure) where they can commit crime more readily than women. It also means crime may offer advantages to their masculine status in ways not applicable to women (competitiveness, material power, sexual potency). Male delinquency is viewed as a rite of passage to manhood, with clearly Freudian influences. It is a means of learning the aggression, competitiveness, cunning and ambition of mature masculinity and negotiating the Oedipal phase. Cohen, one of the first to align masculinity with crime, argued that, for a delinquent, crime does 'not threaten his identification of himself as a male' (1955: 140). The emergence of such sociological perspectives from the phallocentric scientism of biology and psychology meant that the masculinity envisaged and the family that engenders it were taken for granted. Any difference was readily rendered deviant from what was normal, though that male norm was largely unexplored except in terms of what it was not: not feminine, not homosexual, not dependent, not emotional, not barbarian, not deranged – therefore a man. Mature male criminality 'simply' became aligned with such not 'normal' male characteristic/s and therefore a matter of individual aberrance until in the 1970s it was explained politically as a means for subordinate males to 'take' dominant male roles.

Even during those shifts of the 1970s, the new criminology and feminist criminology did not turn precisely to the male 'sex' and crime, focusing instead on class, youth and race and crime on the one hand and women, precisely 'sexed', and their place in crime on the other, as discussed in Chapter 4. For Tolson (1978) male competitiveness was less to do with sexual reproduction and more to do with the functional requirements of capital. Deeply influenced by Marx, the model of masculinity posited aligned sexual reproductive interests with social reproductive interests with the relations of both productions understood in class terms. Marx also influenced 1970s criminologists (Cohen 1972; Murdoch 1973) to provide politicised explanations for crime, without, though, acknowledging masculinity as a key variable, as also discussed in Chapter 4. Problematically for class-based models of gender, 'The subordination of women began long before capitalism, occurs in all classes under capitalism and has continued in countries where capitalism has ceased to exist' (Connell 1987: 42). All feminisms of the 1970s – radical, socialist, liberal – viewed gender inequality as allied to sexual reproductive roles and relations, even if they differently theorised the reasons why and the means of change. But although feminism in other disciplines continued to develop concepts of the problem of men, within criminology feminists focused on women as missing, as victims, as offenders, as prisoners, as suffering injustice and as criminal justice system workers. Perhaps because men in criminology were already 'bifurcated', as (Collier 1998), the project of men was less clear than elsewhere. So although feminist criminologists gendered criminology they never engaged with the task of changing men in relation to crime in the way that, for example, feminist sociologists tackled sex discrimination in the workplace. It did not have the same kind of singular target of all men because quite clearly all men are not overtly or practically criminal in ways that damage women, in the way that all men in the 1970s experienced better employment rights than women.

Despite that dearth of work on masculinity in criminology, the concept was developed elsewhere and interrogated to the point where 'in the wider world of the social sciences the concept is in trouble' (Hood-Williams 2001: 39). Perhaps the most significant conceptualisation of masculinity to emerge in the post-feminist period of the later 1980s was that of hegemonic masculinity, which challenged the idea that men were uniformly powerful by applying a Gramscian critique to masculinity as intersected by race, class and age (Connell 1987) as well as relating to femininity. Masculinity thus became 'masculinities' differently oriented to power at different stages of life, or according to race or economic power or myriad other variables. At the top of this hierarchy of power is dominant masculinity which integrates the most authoritative markers on each composing variable's continuum – simplistically: whiteness; wealth; heterosexuality; potency; maturity; logic; able-bodiedness, and so forth. Powerful status, though, is not fixed but won, over time; originally perhaps based on biology but reworked through capital, colonialism, patriarchy, religion, politics and the construction of laws to shore up and legitimate its authority in these institutions and discursive practices. As social, emotional and symbolic practices evolve and change, so hegemonic masculinity must redo the ideological work necessary to reproduce and legitimate its power. Not that *all* men need to act powerfully, as the representation of the actions of those that do ultimately benefits all men by reproducing masculinist power discursively. Connell's concept of hegemonic masculinity was arguably first applied to crime by Messerschmidt (1993). Hegemonic masculinity seems to explain the sexism, racism and intense machismo of London's East End gangs, such as the one implicated in Stephen Lawence's murder in 1993, but also problematically for attempts to explain crime, it also illuminates the sexism and racism and intense machismo of cop culture (Fielding 1994). In the end it helps explain crime less than it isolates certain traits of masculine identities as potentially both powerful and/or problematic.

Post-modernism, masculinities and subjectivity

In 2005, Connell and Messerschmidt reworked the concept of hegemonic masculinity, with some address of crime. They agreed its association

> [s]olely with negative characteristics that depict men as unemotional, independent, non-nurturing, aggressive, and dispassionate – which are seen as the causes of criminal behaviour – becomes the explanation (and the excuse) for the behaviour hegemonic masculinity. (2005: 840)

Their review included Whitehead's point that the concept results 'in obfuscation, in the conflation of fluid masculinities with overarching structure and, ultimately, in "abstract structural dynamics"' (Whitehead in Connell and Messerschmidt 2005: 842), and accepted Jefferson's point that it offers an 'over-socialized view of the male subject' that ignores how men actually relate psychologically to hegemonic masculinity. They take on such criticism to argue:

> Men can adopt hegemonic masculinity when it is desirable; but the same men can distance themselves strategically from hegemonic masculinity at other moments. Consequently, 'masculinity' represents not a certain type of man but, rather, a way that men position themselves through discursive practices. (2005: 842)

This, though, is to separate the sexed male body from gendered discourses of masculinity and place the investigation of masculinity firmly in the realm of the symbolic and mythic so that whereas once the bio/psychology of the body explained men's criminality, the body is now merely a function of discourse. For Butler, hegemonic masculinity and the heterosex at its core are just the naturalised effect of the historically and politically constituted and contextualised repeated performances that construct *gender ontologies*. The unitary knowable subject of the modernist project is shattered into reflective shards each showing different dimensions of identity depending on orientation to surrounding representations. 'There is no gender identity behind the expressions of gender ... identity is performatively constituted by the very "expressions" that are said to be its results' (Butler 1990: 25). Gender is a performance; what you *do* not *who you are*.

Post-modern men mirror masculinities actively in as much as each subject may find differing dimensions of being male available/valuable according to time and place, but do they act consciously? It is possible to consciously act the gender that does not correspond to the sexed body – do we also consciously choose how we interpellate ourselves into the gendered discourses that do match our sexed bodies? If men do choose, do they do so always, is it sometimes deliberately, sometimes by accident, and why? All of which relates back to Gadd and Jefferson's psycho-social point about men acting as most extremely masculine when feeling most powerless (2007: 185). If discourse is key to men's violence then two simultaneous projects are needed to disrupt the masculinity/crime nexus in relation to violence and justice: one is for men themselves to engage with consciousness-raising, their own and other men's in relation to men's lives and actions and their responsibilities for those, and the other is to change the masculine gendered discursive frameworks available, perhaps to dismantle the hegemonic heterosex that underpins them. Moreover, if criminality and violence are discursively reproductive of male power then all men are implicated, not just the actualised criminals, and all men must engage in change and self-critique. Both projects parallel the kinds of work on language and consciousness that are now barely acknowledged but so characterised the collectivism of 1960s and 1970s feminism.

Culture, Violation and Post-modern Bodies

The problem is that until and unless such projects succeed, attributing discourse with the violences running through our culture raises representation to extraordinary significance in this mediatised age (see Chapter 2) and obfuscates the reality that 'bodies' act out and receive crime. The idea that words can hurt is endemic: incitement to racial hatred; hate texts; pornography; cyber-stalking; bullying; Islamic radicalisation; e-libel and many other forms are powerful post-modern tropes that attract attention away from real harm. This is perhaps nowhere more evident than in the case of online paedophile activity, where grooming, 'chat' or exchange of pornographic images seem to be treated more seriously in policing, policy and media than real abuse of children.

Obviously it is important to close down many deeply unpleasant and illegal representations and their markets, but it is perhaps naïve to claim such closure would significantly stop real violence and it is downright complicit with the perpetrators of that violence to divert resources and concern away from its real incarnation. This is a major problem with the turn to representation in our culture and, not disconnectedly, to discourse in theory – it distances the act from the actor. So the effort to separate the male sexed body away from hegemonic masculinity with its crimino-legal, hetero-sexual, logical-emotive continua of power contributes to the erosion of responsibility of men for their acts – they are no longer rational actors on a criminal stage but emotional victims of a discursive drama. If the latter is so then they must realise and rewrite the *male violence* that represents their sexed bodies just as women, for so long oppressed, are realising and rewriting *herstory*.

Men's bodies may not determine crime in any unitarily attributive way but men cannot deny their bodies. The body is both agent and symbol; its sexed flesh is the surface that gender is projected on to but to move from arguing that women are at the mercy of their sex to saying they are at the mercy of gendered discourses is just another kind of attribution of responsibility and changes nothing. It may be useful to think of crime inscribed on the sexed body through gendered discourses – with different discourses informing different bodily acts and responses – but it is not useful to think that individuals are powerless over those released bodily acts and responses, as then change is not possible:

> For Foucault (1977), the body has been seen as the site where discursive power, mediated through disciplinary practices, inscribes certain forms of subjectivity. The gaze, the look, enables power to define and control ... on the other hand, the 'naturalistic' approach suggests that the body provides the basis for agency and self-articulation ... Elias (1978) charted the body historically as the site of the 'civilizing process'. (Langman and Cangemi (n.d.))

Meanings and acts work in tandem, the one informing the other, and change requires conscious engagement with both.

However, modern and post-modern criminology has tended to focus on the crime, the context, the victim (including the perpetrator as *victim*) and discursive meaning rather than on the agency. One exception is within constitutive criminology, which although broadly post-modern seeks to change, rather than just deconstruct, discourses. Problematically, the effort seems to marry a kind of chaotic anarchism with action to bring about instability (Cowling 2006). However, two key aspects help illuminate the apparent criminogenisis of masculinity:

> Crime is a socially constructed and discursively constituted legal category. It is a violent categorization of the diversity of human conflicts and transgressions into a single category 'crime.' It melts differences reflecting the multitude of variously motivated harms into a single entity or series of legal abstractions, such as 'violent crime' or 'property crime.' As such the conventional and legalistic conceptions of crime are celebrations of homogeneity that sustain and perpetuate the violence of crime's power relations.
>
> Whether one is referring to victims experiencing harm, or to offenders experiencing ennui, rage, rationalization, seduction, or dehumanization, constitutive criminology argues that unequal power relations, built on the construction of difference, provide the conditions that define crime as harm ... People in relations taken to be 'crimes,' are in relations of inequality ... Thus we define crime as 'the expression of some agency's energy to make a difference on others, and it is the exclusion of those others, who in the instant are rendered powerless to maintain or express their humanity' (Henry and Milovanovic, 1996: 116). This agency may be comprised and energized by people, social identities (men, women, etc.), groups, parties, institutions, the state or even constitutive interrelational-sets ... 'Crime then is the power to deny others their ability to make a difference' (Henry and Milovanovic, 1996: 116). (Barak et al. 1997)

Crime is thus the 'exercise' of 'power' so it is both agency and a trope of inequality, a position reminiscent of the arguments of the Marxists scholars of the 1960s and 1970s

Law designed to uphold power differentials cannot protect against harm; it frames its construction (Young and Rush 1994 in Barak et al. 1997). Crime is operationalised through law which disseminates discourses of citizenship through myriad mechanisms (including the family, discussed in Chapter 6) contributing to the gendering of our sexed bodies. It may therefore, developing from Barak et al., be more useful think of crime as masculinist rather than masculinity as criminogenic. Crime serves the interests of 'legitimate' men twice: by constructing their authority through the state and securing challenges to that authority (by subordinate men or women) through the courts (including protecting 'legitimate' male offenders[6] from criminalisation). The media are complicit with both processes not least because of the news value of crime, as discussed in Chapter 2, and the masculine profile of journalism.

Conclusion

At the outset of this chapter the data offered on the gender of offenders could suggest that the relationship between crime and masculinity is straightforward; men are more likely to commit crimes, therefore crime is related to masculinity (Croall 1998). This leaves two problems: the first is that despite the high rate of offending there is very little focus in criminology, policy or the media on men *per se*. Men as agents and objects of study barely feature in accounts of crime and if they do they are rarely critically addressed as men. In crimes against women and children, husbands, lovers, fathers, friends are not the offenders but beasts, evil-doers, madmen, strangers or perverts, or the focus is on unfaithful wives or scantily dressed girls as causal. Even when male crime is against property or other men, the maleness of the event is discursively disguised by emphasis on other variables such as poverty, youth and race. Sexuality as a variable also obfuscates men's agency in prostitution by criminalising women, whilst demonising homosexuals leaves male heterosex uncriticised. This may well be evidence of the bifurcation of men around the pivot of crime (Collier 1998) which allows the 'good' men to make the 'bad' men 'other' through discourse. Crime thus is a constituent of masculinities rather than masculinity being a constituent of crime. Crime is also an exercise of power and power remains patriarchal.

Second and consequently, if masculinity causes crime then how is it that not all men commit crimes becomes redundant, if crime is in fact constitutive of masculinities, 'good' and 'bad'. Crime is an act of power as Barak et al. (1997) describe, and requires an agent, an acting body which is 'normally' an acting male body. Gadd and Jefferson (2007) identify shame related to disempowerment as a powerful psychological constituent of hateful actions towards others but don't engage with why men act hatefully against others significantly more than women do, even though their book relates mostly male-stories. Transgressing criminology to consider gender and subjectivity in relation to hateful agency helps with this. Women too act hatefully and violently, and perhaps out of shame and despair, but often they strike out at themselves:

> Body shaping even to starvation is arguably an expression of violence – that young women express violence against their own bodies whereas young men express it against each other or against property or, as they mature, against women and children they have power over, has much to tell us about gendered norms and roles and how discourse constructs subjectivity accordingly. (Abridged from Wykes 2003)

Crime discourses legitimate the acts and interests of some masculinities through the rule and application of law whilst simultaneously making illegitimate 'other' masculinities that might challenge or threaten. Women barely featured in criminological discourses prior to second-wave feminism because they barely featured as a threat to power. When they did, and do, they are readily represented as 'other' women, explaining both their offending and punishment and maintaining as 'legitimate' femininities that are complicit with male heterosex. Because crime is discursively structuring and constructing, actors may move across its stage in different ways, at different times and playing different roles but because historically those roles (legitimate or criminal) are masculinist it is easier and more usual for male bodies to occupy them – they are roles constructed around men's physical strength, patriarchal authority, occupation of public space, competitiveness and materialism.

That crime serves powerful masculinities might also help explain masculinity's obfuscation in authoritative discourses: law, the academy, journalism and politics remain in the twenty-first century male dominated and it would not be in their interest to expose or deconstruct a significant constituent of that domination. Not that this is conspiratorial (though of course it may be for some), rather it would be unlikely that authoritative men could be critical without significant self-reflection, unless subject to *injustice* which can tear holes in hegemony by revealing its power-investing processes and demarcations. Just that sense of injustice is what impelled women's consciousness-raising and action for change in the 1970s. Initially this was collective but soon devolved down to differentiated struggles informed by other variables, such as race, sexuality and class, until it became possible to write: 'There is nothing about being female that naturally binds women. There is not even such a state as "being" female, itself a highly complex category constructed in contested social-scientific discourses and other social practices' (Haraway in Keen n.d.: 1). The legacy of this deconstruction of collective sensibility was indicated in a letter to the *Guardian* about the current sexualisation of young girls. The retiring head of a sixth-form college noted the arguments that 'girlification' is just fun and reminded readers:

> But this is among the girls destined for professional careers, and, yes, they will still hit glass ceilings … they will not notice their less privileged sisters with their

feet stuck firmly to the floor. No one collectively fights for them – there is no consciousness-raising movement outside of the huge efforts of education – and aspirations and chances need nurturing throughout society. The girls who become the influential and powerful women have not been brought up to fight for women as a whole. They honestly see the battle as won. It isn't. (Robinson 2008)

When it comes to men any potential for collectivity is not only devolved along class/race/age/sexuality identity lines but also by criminal/not criminal identity. Power needs crime, so whilst men have power they too must orient about crime – they must construct crime in order to develop the law to control it and in both processes continually reconstitute power. When Brownmiller (1975) wrote that all men are rapists she was not being literal but metaphoric in that rape symbolically serves masculinity whosoever commits it. It maintains male power over women (and in the case of male rape, over some kinds of 'other' men), promotes male heterosex and legitimates traditional, marital, patriarchy by criminalising men who 'take' women outside of hegemonic models of sex. It is possible to see all crime in the same way as a trope of masculinity. It is not so much that men cause crime but crime is both an act and discourse of power – it constructs, separates, labels and contains – and historically, and many would argue contemporarily, power remains patriarchal and perhaps the evidence is crime. Historically also things change, and in the contemporary world

[a] renovated analysis of hegemonic masculinities … has a growing relevance in the present moment of gender politics. In the rich countries of the global metropole, the shift from neoliberalism (the radical market agenda formulated in the 1970s) to neoconservatism (adding populist appeals to religion, ethnocentrism, and security) has made gender reaction an important political and cultural issue. In the developing countries, the processes of globalization have opened regional and local gender orders to new pressures for transformation and have also opened the way to new coalitions among groups of powerful men. In the global arenas of transnational corporations, media, and security systems, new patterns of hegemony are being forged.[7] (Connell and Messerschmidt 2005: 854)

Such patterns are supported by law which operationalises crime and constructs legal and illegal citizens, and still, in the twenty-first century, does so phallogo-centrically. It may be that there is no one clear model of masculinity that can be singled out to explain crime but not recognising the alternative significance of crime for masculinity may have cost dearly. The final chapter reviews the material covered in this book and summarises it in terms of 'costs'.

Notes: Issues for Reflection

1 Dorling is a contributor to the report 'Criminal obsessions: why harm matters more than crime' (2004) which is at http://news.bbc.co.uk/1/shared/bsp/hi/pdfs/17_10_05_murder_report.pdf.

Try to explain why a search of the report for 'masculinity' came up with zero hits.

2 Imagine the outcry if the article read: *The young women's crime statistics ... relate to girls aged 10 to 17 who were either convicted in court or issued with a police caution. Total offences by girls climbed steadily from 184,474 in 2003 to 222,750 in 2006 ... But the increase in violent teenage girl offending was steeper...43%.*

What empirical evidence is there of girls' crimes?

How are they described in the media and literature and with what possible implications?

3 Offending policemen (serving and ex) have featured in several high-profile gendered crimes, such as the Sara Thornton case (Chapters 2 and 4) and Soham (Chapter 2).

Look up the cases of Gary Weddell 2007, and Karl Bluestone 2001. Is cop-culture (Fielding 1994) implicated?

4 Do some research on honour killing and dowry deaths. Open Democracy's 50/50 section has many articles from different cultures across the world on violences against women (http://www.opendemocracy.net/editorial_tags/16_days).

What other cultural 'defences' of male violence against women are there?

Why and with what implications for violence, gender and justice?

5 The logic Section 28 offered was that access to positive representations of gayness in childhood might increase the numbers of practising homosexuals (Local Government Act 1988 Section 28).

What are the prevailing images of homosexuality today? Do they relate to the family and/or to crime and if so how and with what implications?

6 Consider the kinds of cases that this statement might apply to – in other words where would convicting have implications for masculine power more broadly?

How might the idea that crime is doubly masculinist help explain injustice for women?

How might it explain injustice for some men?

7 Consider what might constitute hegemonic masculinity in a global context and how/if that is different from Connells's 'white, mature, heterosexual, employed' model of 1987.

How might global law and crime be constitutive of twenty-first century masculinities?

Complementary Readings

G. Barak et al. (1997) 'Constitutive criminology: an overview of an emerging postmodernist school', in *Vol. 1, Introduction to Postmodern Criminology* (http://critcrim.org/redfeather/journal-pomocrim/vol-1-intro/001overview.html) offers a revised model of the relationship between power and crime.

R. Collier (1998) *Masculinities, Crime and Criminology* (London: Sage) is a theoretical review of the Connell (1987) concept of hegemonic masculinity.

R. Connell and M. Messerschmidt (2005) 'Hegemonic masculinity: rethinking the concept', *Gender and Society*, 19(6): 829–59, reworks hegemonic masculinity for the twenty-first century.

M. Kimmel et al. (eds) (2004) *Handbook of Studies on Men and Masculinities* (London: Sage) collates readings on masculinity and theory, institutions, globalism, the body and politcs.

D. Gadd and T. Jefferson (2007) *Psycho-social Criminology* (London: Sage) offers case-studies to explore the psychological state of several male offenders in relation to social conditions.

9

CONCLUSIONS

The Cost of Gendered Crime

In conclusion, this chapter considers the costs of gendered crime in terms of money, resources, justice, harm and knowledge in the light of the key discussions and arguments from each chapter. It begins by looking briefly at the financial burden of gendered violence and the level and range of harms caused before considering in turn: the role of the media; methods and data; feminist theory; statuary and voluntary agencies; the family; the law and courts; and masculinity, and then reviews and concludes *Violence, Gender and Justice*.

Counting the Costs: Crime

Domestic abuses

Domestic abuse covers many cruelties that remain secret but domestic violence injuries alone have serious financial implications, as well as the damage done to women's bodies (including foetal morbidity) and mental health. 'According to Home Office figures, physical injuries caused by domestic abuse cost the NHS £1.2 billion a year' (Derbyshire Police 2006). A further knock-on cost is the process of rehousing both in short-term refuges but then often in social housing. Other costs are incurred around social services, legal advice, policing, courts, child welfare, counselling and to family and friends. Figures for the UK put the costs at over £5.7 bn annually including £2.7 bn lost 'economic output' as the greatest economic burden of the crime (Women & Equality Unit 2004). Moreover, the problem is global. In Australia: 'Domestic violence was the main reason homeless people sought out crisis accommodation' (*The Age* 11 February 2005) and the misogyny is not always recognised:

- More than 60 million women are 'missing' from the world today as a result of sex-selective abortions and female infanticide.
- The Russian Government estimates that 14,000 women were killed by their partners or relatives in 1999, yet the country still has no law specifically addressing domestic violence. (Amnesty International 2007)

The United Nations launched a campaign directed towards its member states in 2008 focusing directly on men's role:

> Violence against women is linked to gender inequalities. By intention or effect, it serves to perpetuate male power and control ... Men and boys can make a tremendous contribution by using their power for positive change ... Together, we can change deeply rooted attitudes and practices that discriminate against women and girls. We can ensure that all those who respond to violence against women – whether they are police officers, judges, lawyers, immigration officials, health personnel, or social workers – are sensitized and trained to provide a response that is compassionate, comprehensive and effective. (Obaid 2008)

Obaid's speech focuses on exactly the issues so often missing in Western criminological, political and media accounts: men, power, structural inequity, agency and change.

Rape

Rape occurs within domestic abuse contexts and these are often multiple attacks. As this book was being finished a case in Austria demonstrated incestuous rape, domestic violence and child abuse in a well-to-do suburb. Hans Fritzl imprisoned his daughter Elizabeth in a series of low cellars for 24 years, where she gave birth to seven of his children with no medical aid: one died; three were moved upstairs to live with his wife/their grandmother and three were kept imprisoned without ever seeing daylight until they were released. Despite the actions of this father and husband even the liberal *Independent* journalists seemed unable to question the family, paternalism or masculinity, but instead the comment was similar to coverage of the Cleveland case 20 years previously:

> The Amstetten scandal is certain to raise further questions about the conduct of Austrian police in cases involving missing persons. Above all, why police, social services, doctors and teachers at the schools attended by the Fritzl children failed to detect than anything was amiss for nearly a quarter of a century. (Paterson 2008).

Fritzl himself blamed the women in his life and Hitler:

> Fritzl also admitted incestuous feelings for his mother – who he described as 'the greatest woman in the world'. In a bizarre attempt to defend his conduct he said Hitler's Germany had instilled 'a high regard for decency and uprightness' in him. He claimed he had 'rescued' Elisabeth, who was then 18, to keep her from 'going out to seedy bars' and 'drinking and smoking'. (Andreas 2008)

This case is the apex of a continuum of universal profound violence against girls and women. Only between 8% and 17% of rapes are stranger attacks (Myhill and Allen 2002; Walby and Allen 2004) yet our media and politicians are unable or unwilling to deal with what men do to women and children they are supposed to love and protect. Rape in marriage, let alone rape of children, disturbs the myth of family and intimacy, as well as damaging the body. Clarke et al.'s (2002) report to the Sentencing Guidelines Panel was that any preceding relationship should not be a mitigating factor in sentencing. 'The overwhelming message is that 'rape is rape' (2002: 4). The report refers not just to rape as forced intercourse but to many other indignities that often accompany that: it refers to violence, fear and shame, to possible pregnancy, sexually transmitted disease and psychological damage. It also mentions the trauma for victims of the policing process, forensics and courts. Since the report, little, if anything, has improved. The press and politicians continue to minimize rape by a partner: 'A senior Tory party adviser suggested rape accusations made by women against their partners should be treated as "disagreements" between lovers' (Martin 2007), whilst 'the police significantly over-estimate false reporting in rape cases' (Dustin 2006: 8). In 2008 the Lilith Project reported in Mahria (2008) that Home Office figures for 2006–07 showed a half to two-thirds of all cases never proceeding beyond investigation (HM CPS 2007: 8) and conviction rates dropping from 32% (Kelly 2001) to 5.29% in 2005 (see Mahria 2008: 11). The cost in pain and suffering for women is uncountable but also rape is the most economically costly violent crime. The overall economic cost of one sexual offence averages at £31,438 (Crime Reduction 2005). The same is true in the US: 'Rape and other sexual assaults of adults cause an annual minimum loss of 127 billion dollars, or about $508 per U.S. resident. This figure makes sexual assault the costliest crime; even higher than murder' (US Department of Justice 1996).

Also in the US rape resulted in an estimated 32,000 rape-related pregnancies a year among adult women (Holmes et al. 1996). In many African countries there is a further indirect economic cost:

> Women in rural Uganda who reported having been forced to have sex against their will had eight times the risk of becoming infected with HIV ... Sub-Saharan Africa's economic growth rate has fallen approximately 4 percent because of Aids. Labour productivity has been cut by 50 percent in the hardest-hit countries. (Walsh 2006)

Sexual violence against children

Rape is also a crime against children, committed by men, except in that context it is rarely called rape but the euphemistic child sexual abuse. Just as the familial context of child rape is overlooked in the British press so it is globally with online media sites much preferring the problem of cyber-child pornography. The British press even try to deflect that from the UK: 'Hardly any of the sites traced are based in Britain, with most located in the United States and Russia ... About 80% are thought to be commercial operations with the remainder made up of offenders using message boards to share abusive images' (Travis 2008). This article also emphasised that sexually violent crime is big business. In its represented form it is highly profitable for those who produce representations, both legally in the film and gaming industries, and illegally where the market value of real and represented sexual violation is unmeasurable.

The emotional and physical costs to child victims are unimaginable but there are other costs as well and the likely numbers of victims are huge. In the US:

> Estimates of the incidence of abuse in the United States range from 100,000 to 500,000 cases a year ... 88 percent is not reported to authorities. Most such offenses occur in the homes and neighborhoods of the children. (Rosenberg 2004)

Rosenberg identified many costs to these victims as adults, including: increased health risks for alcoholism, drug abuse, depression and suicide attempts; increase in smoking and poor self-rated health; promiscuity and sexually transmitted disease; and physical inactivity and severe obesity (2004). In the US the 'estimated annual cost of child abuse and neglect is $103.8 billion in 2007 value. This figure represents a conservative estimate' (Wang and Holton 2007: 2). Cost was a contributing factor to the passing of the Sexual Offences Act 2003 in Britain, where: 'The current cost of child abuse to statutory and voluntary organisations is £1 billion a year' (Child abuse http://www.politics.co.uk). The General Assembly of the United Nations recognised sexual abuse and violence against children and 'the exploitation of children under 18 in prostitution, child pornography and similar' (Pinheiro 2006: 58) as a global problem as well as highlighting the levels occurring in the family, but added further kinds of abuse that the West is less familiar with:

- Unregulated employment and exploitation and sometimes servitude or slavery.
- Eighty-two million girls are estimated to marry before age ... frequently coercively, and face a high risk of violence, including forced sex.
- Female genital mutilation, which, according to WHO, is carried out on increasingly younger girls, is prevalent in Africa, and also occurs in some parts of Asia and within immigrant communities.
- Harmful traditional practices affecting children include binding, scarring, burning, branding, violent initiation rites, fattening, forced marriage, so called 'honour' crimes and abuse and dowry-related violence, exorcism, or 'witchcraft'. (Pinheiro 2006: 53–60)

The report also documents crimes more familiar in the Western world:

> The exploitation of children under 18 in prostitution, child pornography and similar activities ... It is estimated that 1 million children enter these sectors every year. Many are coerced, kidnapped, sold and deceived into these activities, or are victims of trafficking. (Pinheiro 2006: 58).

So a link is made between the sexual violation of children and the wholesale trade of (mostly female) bodies in prostitution.

Prostitution

Evident in the UK is that link where many prostitutes are effectively victims of men who either abused them, prostituted them or paid for sex (now a crime in Sweden). Yet they are not victims who get much care, sympathy or voice, nor is there much idea of the costs to them of what they do:

> Up to 5,000 young people (under 18) may be involved in prostitution at any one time ... It is increasingly recognised that those involved in street prostitution exercise little choice ... prostitution is more of a survival activity ... as many as 85% report having experienced physical abuse in the family, with 45% reporting familial sexual abuse. As many as 75% of women in prostitution were under 18 when they were originally coerced into prostitution. (Home Office 2004: 1–2)

'Controlling prostitution is currently estimated to cost in the region of £176m – additional costs of responding to reports of anti-social behaviour linked to prostitution are estimated at around £42m' (Home Office 2004: 1–2). Moreover, the UK and US invasion of Iraq has led to further injustice for women. Britain has increased contributions to 'UNHCR to £7.75 million' to help resolve the problem of 'Iraqi girls and women who have turned to prostitution in Syria' (*Hansard* April 2008). The costs are not just financial and in degradation, but in health, with prostitution accelerating the spread of HIV/AIDs particularly in Russia, China and India, yet the US congress passing a global AIDS package worth $15 billion 'voted for an amendment requiring one third of the funding to go to "*abstinence-until-marriage programs*"' (POST 12/2003). However, whatever the costs to state and prostitute there is huge profit in prostitution. *The Global Sex Trade: The Industrial Vagina* (Jeffreys 2008) sees it as integrated into the international political economy.

The concept of in/justice impelled this book. The concern is not justice merely in the legal framework but in all aspects of women's lives. We focused here on interpersonal violence but there are many other gendered behaviours, some criminal, some deviant, harassing, oppressive, denigrating and negating. They are part of the continuum of gender relations of which violent crime is the most negative apex and equally, romantic love is perhaps the most positive, yet of course the two also occur in the same 'place' of family and/or intimacy. Gendering occurs in contexts other than family and intimacy: it is in discourses like politics, representation, law, religion, education and knowledge, and in contexts such as work, friendship, and leisure, but one reason for focusing on interpersonal violence was that it is hard enough to get accurate evidence of the extreme material we have looked at, let alone the everyday violences of harassment, degradation, offence and negation (Stanko 1990; Carter 1998) that are women's ordinary experience. We started looking at the 'evidence' for this book with news about violence, gender and justice.

Counting the Costs: Power and Knowledge

Mediated crime

Sex 'n violence are newsworthy and even more so if they involve celebrities, which leaves many everyday injustices without news value, unreported, unacknowledged and unaddressed. The media is complicit in this injustice. Journalism focuses on rarity, extremes and titillation in news about real crime whilst fictional media repeat the focus in television, film and games. The power to harm is made *other* in such accounts: not ordinary, not familial, not marital, and not male. Even when the violence is male versus male, *men* are missing with causes attributed to youth, 'class', race or sexuality. When women transgress and commit violent crime all women are taught a moral lesson about what happens when women do not conform. And when there is no clear diversionary discursive route and the news has to deal with male violence against women or children it blames the woman victim (again offering a morality play about women's behaviour, dress and role) or turns men into beasts and strangers (creating a fiction about the sanctity of home and promoting fear and dependency). When this is difficult to achieve the news media often end up blaming the entertainment media, as happened with the Bulger case and most recently with the killing of Lindsay Ann Hawker, in Japan:

> 'Detectives are probing the possibility that comic book fan Tatsuya Ichihashi had played out a sick fantasy from one of the stories in hentai manga … the adult comics are extremely popular in Japan and often contain scenes of girls and women being raped and tortured.' So we have our prime suspect: comics did it. Case closed. Good work, gentlemen. (Beauman 2007)

To give Beauman his due, the piece is titled 'Men don't kill women, Manga does', though neither it nor the comments following do actually discuss the fact that a man did kill this woman.

In media accounts of violence, gender and justice the relation between the real exercise of power and the representational exercise is potent; so potent that whether men or women kill, the discourses of law and gender resolve the contradictions on behalf of the state and patriarchy. McGuigan's (1993) assertion that if we cannot say that the *Sun* has told lies on behalf of oppressive power then we are in trouble, still applies, and lying by omitting masculinity as violent is still lying. The press offer ideological resolutions to gender crises on behalf of male power, and men violating women intimately is certainly a crisis of gender ideals; journalists offer knowledge about the world and such representations help constitute us as social subjects but they reproduce injustice and this is wrong.

Statistics and secrets

Much of our knowledge about violence, gender and justice comes from the media but the media *represent* for audiences data from official sources, both statutory and, to a much lesser extent, academic and voluntary. Those data also inform policy making, legislative change and political action. Chapter 3 reviewed those data to expose even more clearly the gap between what we know about gendered crime from mediated sources and what we know from research and records. Further, it revealed that even 'real' data are limited and compromised because the intimacy of much gendered crime inhibits victims from reporting it whilst myths about family hide, metaphorically and literally, male offenders from public view. Alternatively, discourse devolves masculinity into masculinities so divesting it of blame, whilst the law operates with definitions, for example of violence and rape, that exclude many harmful behaviours and/or problematise victims' self-perceptions and/or compromise court cases. Measurement is therefore at best partial and at worst downright inadequate, with significant implications for resourcing partly explaining the dependence of many victims of domestic violence, rape, paternal sexual abuse on the voluntary sector, whilst prostitutes have little support bar the distribution of condoms and clean needles and are rarely seen as victims despite being trafficked, abused as children, made drug dependent, traded and bought by men. That current measures probably miss much gendered violence makes popular accounts that focus on only the extreme and rare instances of stranger attacks especially troubling, when even the available evidence shows women and children to be at greater risk at home and from men they know, not just in the UK but in the US, Canada and Australia. In 2005 a World Health Organisation study collected the first global dataset that illuminated just these problems of measurement. Researchers interviewed 24,000 women of childbearing age from Bangladesh, Brazil, Ethiopia, Japan, Peru, Namibia, Samoa, Serbia and Montenegro, Thailand and the United Republic of Tanzania 'using state-of-the-art methods to enhance disclosure and ensure women's safety' (London School of Hygiene and Tropical Medicine 2005) The range of results shows not only previously unrealised levels of violence but also wide variations that may indicate methodological problems despite cautionary strategies. Between 15% to 71% of ever-partnered women have been physically or sexually abused by intimate partners … The study also shows the remarkable degree to which women in some settings internalize social norms that justify abuse … In all the sites, between one-fifth to two-thirds (21% to 66%) of women reported that they had never told anyone else about the partner abuse … 55% to 95% said they had never gone to the police, health service or other agency to seek help (abridged from London School of Hygiene and Tropical Medicine 2005).

Finding ways to address such harm, also likely to be barely a fraction of the real violence, 'remains open to accusations of western interference' (Phillips 2006: 243) and resistance on national cultural grounds, but also the very pervasiveness of abuse places women's 'rights' on a universal agenda and exposes male violence as endemic regardless of colour, race or creed.

None of this is to argue that all men abuse nor that some men aren't also victims of violence, some of female violence, but even in this latter case men's physical strength and generally better economic situation and lesser role in child care means their experience is likely to be different as well as much rarer, as discussed in Chapter 3 (also see Gadd et al. 2003). What it does show is that what we do know about gender and violence is probably a significant underestimate and that myths, secrecy, culture and power continue to obscure much male violence which is either not defined as such or disappeared in due process. Perhaps one of the biggest problems with statistics, and part of this problem of definition and disappearance, is the focus on victims when the problem is male offending. Feminist anthropologist Heinonen expressed this neatly in a talk in 2006 about her work in Africa when she recalled being admonished by an 'Ethiopian woman peasant farmer, being empowered from domestic violence, who said: "stop telling me where it pinches, I am wearing the shoes. Go and talk to the men instead"' (2006: 1), which neatly links to some criticisms of the feminist impetus in violence and gender.

Gendering criminology: feminism

A contribution of feminism to understanding meaning and the construction of gendered identity recognises that such an exercise of power has also constituted the very knowledge we deem valid and the research that produces it. The traditional dynamic of western social research readily structures such investigation so as to reproduce dominant social relations. Outgroups such as criminals, women, black people and psychotics become the focus of interest in that they present a problem for dominance and so work gets funding. Focus on the separate membership groups of the oppressed and disadvantaged too easily becomes victim study and the most cynical might say provides dominance with all the information required to maintain and legitimate its power. Such research is resourced, its methods validated and its findings disseminated, but alongside 'the noise of criminology – the ceaseless chatter advocating the extension of criminal justice practices and "solutions" – there stands a series of telling, sustained silences' (Hillyard et al. 2004 in Silvestri 2006: 223), including the 'absence about questions of power' (Silvestri 2006: 223). Yet it is so often power that is the problem: racism is a white problem which affects black people; industrial unrest may owe much to inadequate management of production let alone exploitative pay and conditions; domestic violence is largely a male problem that affects women and children. Yet in each case it is the subjects of the *violations of rights* who are the objects of knowledge, not the one unifying factor of the majority of perpetrators according to crime statistics, maleness.

Maleness is only made subject to study when qualified by some factor removing it from dominance: race; religion; youth; homosexuality; immigrant status and more. The concept of masculinities itself is diversionary, not wrong but rarely inclusive of middle-class, western, mature, white masculinity, or even just one of those, as a problematic category. By self-consciously inverting the research focus towards dominant discourse as actively reproducing subjective social inequality, and including men in any inquiry into gendered relations and roles, the task becomes immediately more politically subversive and encompassing. When the context of those gendered roles and relations is crime then men feature both as dominating offending, and dominating the construction and processing of crime and criminals through state power operationalised as law. Mainstream criminology seems to have ignored masculinity as a problem whilst feminist criminology has preferred, and rightly so, women's place in crime (although knowing about men's crime against women and naming it crime has come from feminism). But women, even feminist women, are entangled in what Cain (1990) calls a hegemonic web of taken for granted ideologies of family life and commensurate gendered subjectivy, making it hard enough to deconstruct their own experience let alone address men's. But to develop Cain's *strategy of reconstruction* in order to benefit women we have to take on and seek to change the problem of masculinity – the shared sexed body masculinity – not the *othered masculinities* that are so often the object of studies of crime in criminology and that do not name the subjects, men.

People, policies and agencies

Processing gendered crime integrates masculinist state power with what are very often feminist initiatives, in a rather uncomfortable alliance, not least in that the state focuses on everything related to it as a problem – mental health, financial costs, injury, sexual disease – except gender, yet feminist initiatives focus/ed on women and their children. Both miss out men. Refuges and rape crisis centres provide safe havens, information and empowerment but also spend much of their time raising funds to keep going, inhibiting development and service provision. State services, on the other hand, were and remain slow to deal with either the crime or the gendered nature of it. Until the 2002 Housing Act, 'fleeing violence' did not enable women to be prioritised for rehousing by local councils. Even with that provision, English councils very often refer women to Domestic Abuse Projects for support, for example, 'If you would like advice or help with fleeing violence or going in to a refuge, you can call Domestic Violence Matters [an Islington based charity]' (Islington Borough Council 2008). Women's fear that children would be taken into care if they approached statutory agencies like social services for help, either for their own sake or because of abuse of the children, has also left them and their children vulnerable and has impacted on the voluntary sector.

Cop culture (Fielding 1994) meant/means the police viewed 'domestics' as largely private and certainly unglamorous, unlike public appearances such as driving fast cars and brandishing 'stun-guns' in riot gear. Moreover, the difficulty of gaining convictions means 'domestics' remain unattractive to officers working in a results-based, performance-related-pay context. Rape cases too are often handled on the assumption that the victim is either mad or bad, as discussed in Chapter 5, with judges doing little to redress this if the case reaches court. The greatest injustice for women has been done to those left unprotected from male violence by the police and courts: 'Clare Bernal, 22, was shot by her ex-boyfriend

Michael Pech ... while he was on bail after admitting harassing her' (*BBC News*, 7 October 2005). Agencies dealing with women forced into prostitution barely exist and the state's only real involvement is in fining them, and occasionally finding and convicting their killers as happened in the 1980s with the Yorkshire Ripper and in Ipswich in 2006/07.

Chapter 5 discussed how pressure, mostly from feminists in the justice system, academia and the voluntary sector, has seen state intervention in the development of law and policy around crimes such as domestic abuse, child sex abuse, rape and trafficking. The Home Office has funded and published prolifically in something of a 'knowledge explosion' in these crime areas but not generally done the same around the gender relations they reveal. The concern for state and feminists alike in these new initiatives is to stop the crime rather than recognise its place in gender relations, which makes 'stopping the crime' something of a conundrum because, of course, it renders the violence of men invisible, not least in the family where they become men.

Family

Familial ideals include privacy and sanctity, real and metaphoric, inhibiting efforts, real or represented, to access and change family, let alone deal with men's violences therein. Moreover, the promotion of family ideals, and the gender models they require, serve/d and reproduce/d patriarchal power but do so by damaging and denigrating women to construct a false premise of the essential superiority of men. The concept of family is therefore a trope of knowledge about gender that naturalises patriarchal power as well as a site where gender identity is assumed. The centrality of family in sexual and social reproduction requires that the state manage it in the interests of the continuance of the state, which, since the Victorian period, has been a capitalist state in the UK and its colonies, based on Judaeo-Christian values and patriarchal authority. That state hegemony was overtly regulated through formal institutions of control but also covertly regulated through more subtle discourses of morality and scientific knowledge, both of which engaged with the family. The ideal family was purveyed as the site of moral sex and healthy bodies and minds but was actually a construction site, as Mort (1987) described, for gender difference shot through with power relations. Its vital place in power has ensured its consistent conceptual reinforcement from the law to popular culture via policy, education and the news as discussed in Chapter 6, part of which has also been a deflection from discussions of its potential as a dangerous place for women and children, apart from within feminism. That critique, since the 1970s, has resulted in the intervention on behalf of damaged women and children, described in Chapter 5, but still leaves intact the ideal family and masculinity's symbolic/men's real place within it perhaps because the practical need to support victims was not informed by well-developed *criminological* theory, and other interests buoyed up the myth through policy, resourcing and diversions. Family is a technology of power with sex at its centre. It operates to support and legitimate hegemonic masculinity by appropriately placing women and children in relation to that and calling all men to comply. That process is underwritten by the state because the family is also a mechanism of social control and ordering. Its role in maintaining both power domains, state and patriarchy, protect it not least through the reproduction of discursive accounts that maintain it externally. These are often infused by the authority of the law but also work much more covertly, for example, 'continued calls for a specific form of privacy for families present barriers to achieving respect and equity' (Mckie 2005: 158). Calls made, not least, by the famous (and sometimes infamous) – including the British royal family – and therefore regularly aired in the media. Also, for each of us the intra-familial is the site of the acquisition of our subjectivity, problematising the potential for critical distance even for criminologists.

Law

Violence acts to support male power because it is institutionalised and represented conducive to the broader long-term interest of men. The law supports such interests. Through its apparent equity it ignores the real and systematic disadvantage commonly experienced by women and in ignoring that leaves no productive space for feminist work. Reforming the law to recognise women's disadvantage would do little to address the way ideas about women's violence are continuous with their other lived experience. To change the way society treats women's crime means a whole change in social attitudes to women. Chapter 7's focus on rape explored these issues from a more critical legal perspective than the remainder of the book because the law on rape has so many implications for constructions of both gender and crime. Moreover, the law also frames the discourses within which women's experience of rape is reconstructed so it is legal language that is both used and interrogated in this chapter. Further, rape is perhaps the most intimate and physical of gendered crime: it is about one body penetrating another. Rape does not require ejaculation – it is the act of taking another body outside of the purpose of reproduction, that very separation of sex from reproduction that is the antithesis of the family discourses discussed in Chapter 6. Rape's purpose in legal terms is not procreation, though that may well be a side effect. Yet rape in English law is not gender neutral; it requires penile penetration, hence a woman cannot rape, only a man, so it is *the* gendered crime. The 2003 review also defined consent as requiring *freedom and capacity* to choose, hence the arguments made here that men who buy sex might technically be raping, as prostituted women are significantly disempowered and rarely freely able to consent, and certainly not if the women are trafficked as is finally being addressed. Moreover, does 'no' mean 'yes' to a *reasonable and honest* man (by whose measure, and what this means is not defined), if a woman is drunk, confused and unable to act clearly *taking account all the circumstances*, which still includes women's dress, behaviour and lifestyle. The 2003 Act has done little to impact on the *hermeneutics of suspicion* (Denike 2000 in Kelly et al. 2006) directed at women's accounts of rape. *Hermeneutics of suspicion* is 'a method of interpretation which assumes that the literal or surface-level meaning of a text is an effort to conceal' (Ricoeur 1970: 33). The law on rape replaces women's view of themselves, both as sexed bodies and social femininities, with men's view of women, whilst men who are the offenders are not addressed as male sexed bodies and social masculinities but as criminal or not, in relation to the law's view of women. Effectively changing the law has achieved little in relation to most gendered crime because it doesn't challenge masculinity.

Masculinity

Efforts to impact on women's disadvantage in both crime and the criminal justice system have focused on everything but the problem of masculinity. Masculinity, not masculinities, because violence is the prerogative of a singular masculinity that is shared across races, classes, ages and creeds. Masculinity equates to all the inherent qualities associated with the male sexed body, undiluted by the other variables that offer a range of masculinities accordant with biologies, experiences and representations. Crime appears to serve masculinity twice, as a means of overall social and sexual control that legitimates the exercise of power through normalisation of gender, and a means by which normalised men control others – the different, deviant or dangerous who may or do challenge or threaten the legitimated norm, whether male or female. Both appropriations of crime depend on discourse from the authority of the law to the damning castigations of tabloid stereotypes.

Through discourses, language links the material conditions of the socio-cultural world to the psychological construction of the gendered subject and writes these on to the sexed body. It is, adapting Foucault (1977), a technology of *gendered* power. Its meanings shift and change over time and place, ultimately serving dominance but always in struggle and tension (Hall 1997) because humans 'act'. Meanings both tend to prefer dominance and are necessarily in arrears of the experiences they represent. So, much of our culture, and thus ourselves, remains informed by old models of gender and social organisation steeped in old dominances that are struggling now to keep their sense in a world with fewer boundaries, more communication and massive representation of others and difference in open and unregulated forums, all through the mechanisms of digitisation and cyber-space. Whilst long-oppressed groups find more and more spaces and means to assert themselves and resist dominance, language is steeped in tradition and conservatism, with the associated sexism, racism and nationalism that served old capital and patriarchy and underwrites the British state.

New capital, though, embraces new markets and consumers, so women are now urged to work, earn and buy whilst still depicted as earth mothers, adoring wives and homemakers. Meanwhile, mainstream heterosexual masculinity has little other than its old patriarchal identity base to equip it for this new world. Consequently, while the therapeutic industries burgeon to try and deal with the detritus of many of our disappointing families (compared to the ideal, 'real' families), much publicity and politics continues to try to shore that ideal up, reinforcing old stereotypes of gender and morality. It is perhaps unsurprising, therefore, that long-existent abuse against women and children is being exposed as women struggle to overcome the dissonance of the roles provided them, whilst men cling to their old roles – however destructive of themselves and others – fixed in their sexed bodies imbued with power and fear of loss and not knowing of anything else.

Conclusions

The cost of gendered violence is not just in harms and economic loss – private and public – but in knowledge, justice and human rights. All these costs are the price paid for the problems identified throughout this book, which are, in turn, mutually reinforcing: the diversionary mediations of violence, gender and justice; methodological and evidential inadequacies; lack of theoretical address of the masculinity /crime nexus; resourcing and research that does not deal with men; lack of critique of family myths and realities; assumptions that law can deliver justice and criminology's failure to deal with the masculinity at the heart of its subject.

Those lacks in epistemology and the ensuing practices have ensured that however much better women's and children's place in crime is understood, and however much better they are treated and cared for as victims, they remain victims. That is not justice. Justice is more than just a legal issue relating to due punishment; justice is a matter of human rights, of equity and of freedom from fear, oppression, denigration, negation and harm. Given the costs of violence for women and children across the world, unimaginable if war were added to the data on damage, the failure to engage with violence as gendered is unjust. Moreover, violence too is not just a legal issue but deeply symbolic – it violates things discursively through textual annihilation and abuse just as it does in reality.

This is gendered political work on a global scale for a more just world and it is work that cannot succeed without men – only men can stop violence because nearly all violence is committed by men. In 1990 Lynne Segal's last words from *Slow Motion: Changing Masculinities, Changing Men* were a call for justice and creativity to end gendered inequity:

> With women today permanently entrenched in the Western work-force, the absurdity of the traditional gendered divide between public and private is daily more apparent. Men could continue to strive to maintain their privileges and dominance in both spheres. But it is likely they will increasingly be battling all the way. More justly and more creatively, they could join women in fighting for an end to the exploitation of women at work and at home. If they do, of course, it will spell the end of masculinity as we have known it. (Segal 1990: 319)

The *condition of post-modernity* has made it difficult to take overviews. Academia has devolved down to biographies, focus groups and celebrations of differences recognised, parodies played out and decoupage re-presented. Post-modernism is the blur and blend resulting from challenges to the acceptance of single unifying truths deriving from the major social challenges in the latter part of the twentieth century, but has also become *ironically* an effective tool of hegemonic power by disabling criticism and knowledge to the point at which they become merely different points of view. This disguises, protects and nurtures hierarchies of power, global and local, that remain deeply divisive, exploitative and punitive. Capitalism has found lucrative market-places in the abuse of women, both in reality and representation, power which remains patriarchal, as is clear by the global evidence of gendered violence. Crime is a constituent of masculinity. Crime operationalises the power of the state to describe, protect and legitimate normal masculinities and gender roles and relations through law by discursively marking out others. Crime is also the illegitimate attempt to exercise power by 'others', normally men who pose the greatest threat to power, but sometimes women. In both instances, through law and crime, discursively and in practice, there is *violence* in the constitution of masculinity that will remain, so long as good men do nothing. Reconstruction towards *justice* must include both masculinity and femininity in order to change the social construction of *gender*.

BIBLIOGRAPHY

Adler, F. (1975) *Sisters in Crime: The Rise of the New Female Criminal*. New York: McGraw Hill.

Adler, Z. (1982) 'Rape – the intention of Parliament and the practice of the courts', *MLR*, 45: 664.

Adler, Z. (1987) *Rape on Trial*. London: Routledge and Kegan Paul.

Ahmed, K. (2002) 'Soham media "circus" forces legal scrutiny', *Observer*, 25 August. http://media.guardian.co.uk/politics/2002/aug/25/childprotection.presspublishing

Aichorn, A. (1955) *Wayward Youth* (trans. orig. 1925). New York: Meridian Books.

Allen, B. (1996) *Rape Warfare: Hidden Genocide in Bosnia-Herzegovina and Croatia*. Minnesota: University of Minnesota Press.

Allen, G. (2002) http://www.grahamallen.labour.co.uk/ViewPage.cfm?Page=4762

Allen, H. (1987) *Justice Unbalanced: Gender, Psychiatry and Judicial Decision*. Maidenhead: Open University Press.

Althusser, L. (1997) 'Marxism and humanism', in *For Marx*. London: Verso.

Amnesty International (2007) http://www.domestic-violence-norwich.org.uk/index.php?page=statistics

Anderson, M. (1983) 'How much has the family changed', *New Society*, 27 October.

Andreas, S. (2008) *Daily Telegraph*, 8 May. http://www.telegraph.co.uk/news/newstopics/josef_fritzl/1937916/Josef-Fritzl-andlsquoThe-Nazis-were-to-blameandrsquo-for-my-Austrian-incest-dungeon.html

Anna, T. (1988) 'Feminist responses to sexual abuse: the work of the Birmingham Rape Crisis Centre', in M. Maguire and J. Pointing (eds) *Victims of Crime: A New Deal?* Milton Keynes: Open University Press.

Ashworth, A. (2006) *Principles of Criminal Law*. Oxford: Oxford University Press.

Australian Bureau of Statistics (2005) *Personal Safety Survey*. Canberra: Australian Bureau of Statistics.

Bainham, A., Sclater, S. and Richards, M. (2002) *Body Lore and Laws*. Oxford: Hart Publishing.

Barak, G., Henry, S. and Milovanovic, D. (1997) 'Constitutive criminology: an overview of an emerging postmodernist school', in *Vol. 1. Introduction to Postmodern Criminology*. http://uwacadweb.uwyo.edu/RED_FEATHER/journal-pomocrim/vol-1-intro/001overview.html

BBC News (26 October 2001) 'Immigrants to take citizen classes'. http://news.bbc.co.uk/1/ hi/uk_politics/1620900.stm

BBC News (11 December 2001) 'Race "segregation" caused riots'. http://news.bbc.co.uk/1/hi/england/1702799.stm

BBC News (29 July 2002) 'Dando killer's appeal rejected' http://news.bbc.co.uk/1/hi/uk/2158386.stm

BBC News (9 October 2003) 'Sex law changes target paedophiles' http://news.bbc.co.uk/1/hi/uk/3178626.stm

BBC News (17 December 2003) 'Soham press release'. http://www.bbc.co.uk/pressoffice/pressreleases/stories/2003/12_december/17/realstory_soham.s.html

BBC News (22 June 2004a) 'At-a-glance: Soham report'. http://news.bbc.co.uk/1/hi/uk/3829125.stm

BBC News (22 June 2004b) 'Huntley case: Key mistakes made'. http://news.bbc.co.uk/1/hi/uk/3826355.stm

BBC News (24 February 2005) 'Maxine Carr wins identity secrecy'. http://news.bbc.co.uk/1/hi/uk/4295007.stm

BBC News (25 February 2005) 'Rape convictions hit record low'. http://news.bbc.co.uk/1/hi/uk/4296433.stm

BBC News (7 October 2005) '"No predicting" stalker murder'. http://news.bbc.co.uk/1/hi/england/london/4317458.stm

BBC News (9 October 2006) 'Cells plan to ease prisons crisis'. http://news.bbc.co.uk/2/hi/uk _news/6032515.stm

BBC News (12 October 2006) 'Tagged offenders went on to kill'. http://news.bbc.co.uk/2/hi/uk_news/politics/6038926.stm

BBC News (10 July 2007) 'End anti-marriage bias say Tories'. http://news.bbc.co.uk/1/hi/uk_politics/6288578.stm

BBC News (30 October 2007) 'Stop and search "race gap" grows'. http://news.bbc.co.uk/1/hi/uk/7069791.stm

BBC News (17 October 2005) Dorling Report. http://news.bbc.co.uk/1/shared/bs/hi/pdfs/17_10_05_murder_report.pdf

BCS surveys at http://www.homeoffice.gov.uk/rds/bcs-publications.html

BCS (2005/06) http://www.crimestatistics.org.uk/output/page63.asp

Beauman, N. (2007) *Guardian*, 5 April. http://blogs.guardian.co.uk/books/2007/04/men_dont_kill_women_manga_does.html

Becaria, C. (1764) *On Crimes and Punishments*. Indianapolis: Bobbs-Merrill.

Becker, H. (1963) *Outsiders*. New York: Free Press.

Benedict, H. (1992) *Virgin or Vamp: How the Press Covers Sex Crimes*. New York and Oxford: Oxford University Press.

Bentham, J. (1789; 1948) *An Introduction to the Principles of Morals of Legislation*. New York: Hafner.

Berger, J. (1973) *Ways of Seeing*. Penguin: Harmondsworth.

Bichard Inquiry (2004) http://www.bichardinquiry.org.uk/

Binney, V., Harkell, G. and Nixon, J. (1981) *Leaving Violent Men: A Study of Refuges and Housing for Battered Women*. Bristol: Women's Aid Federation of England.

Binney, V., Harkell G. and Nixon, J. (1985) 'Refuges and housing for battered women', in J. Pahl (ed.) *Private Violence and Public Policy*. London: Routledge and Kegan Paul.

Blair, I. (1985) *Investigating Rape*, London: Croom Helm.

Borkowski, M., Murch, M. and Walker, V. (1983) *Marital Violence: The Community Response*. London: Tavistock.

Bowker, L. (1982) 'Police services to battered women: bad or not so bad?', *Criminal Justice and Behaviour*, 9(4).

Bowlby, J. (1951) *Maternal Care and Mental Health*. Geneva: WHO.

Braithwaite, J. (1989) *Crime, Shame and Reintegration*. Cambridge: Cambridge University Press.

Bridgeman and Millns (1998) *Feminist Perspectives on Law*. London: Sweet and Maxwell.

Brooks-Gordon, B. and Gelsthorpe, L (2002) 'Hiring bodies: male clients and prostitution', in A. Bainham, S. Sclater and M. Richards (eds) *Body Lore and Laws*. Oxford: Hart. pp. 193–210.

Brown, B., Burman, M. and Jamieson, L. (1992) *Sexual History and Sexual Character Evidence in Scottish Sexual Offence Trials*. Edinburgh: Scottish Office Central Research Unit Papers.

Brown, M., Burman, L. and Jamieson, L. (1983) *Sex Crimes on Trial: The Use of Sexual History Evidence in Scottish Courts*. Edinburgh: Edinburgh University Press.

Brown, S. (2003) *Crime and Law in Media Culture*. Buckingham: Open University Press.

Brownmiller, S. (1975) *Against our Will*. Harmondsworth: Penguin.

Brownmiller, S. (2000) *In our Time: Memoir of a Revolution*. US: Delta.

Burn, G. (1985) *Somebody's Husband; Somebody's Son*. London: Viking.

Burt, C. (1925) *The Young Delinquent*. London: University of London.

Bush, T. and Hood-Williams, J. (1995) 'Domestic violence on a London housing estate', *Research Bulletin*, No 37. London: Home Office Research and Statistics Department.

Butler, J. (1990) *Gender Trouble: Feminism and the Subversion of Identity*. London: Routledge.

Butler, J. (1993) *Bodies that Matter: On the Discursive Limits of 'Sex'*. London: Routledge.

Buzzle.com (2003) http://www.buzzle.com/editorials/12-19-2003-48805.asp

Cain, M. (1989) 'Feminists transgress criminology', in M. Cain (ed.) *Growing up Good*. London: Sage.

Cain, M. (1990) 'Towards transgression: new directions in feminist criminology', *International Journal of Sociology of Law*, 18(1): 18.

Cambridge News (1 September 2006) http://www.cambridge-news.co.uk/news/ely/8

Cambridge News (18 September 2006) http://www.cambridge-news.co.uk/news/letters/

Campbell, B. (1988) *Unofficial Secrets*. London: Virago.

Campbell, B. (1991) 'Kings of the road', *Marxism Today*, December.

Campbell, B. (1993) *Goliath*. London: Methuen.

Campbell, R. and Martin, P.Y. (2001) 'Services for sexual assault survivors: the role of rape crisis centres', in C.M. Renzetti, J.L. Edleson and R. Kennedy Bergen (eds) *Sourcebook on Violence Against Women*. Thousand Oaks, CA: Sage.

Carlen, P. (1985) (ed) *Criminal Women: Autobiographical Accounts*. Cambridge: Polity Press.

Carlen, P. (1988) *Women Crime and Poverty*. Milton Keynes: Open University Press.

Carlen, P., Hicks, J., O'Dwyer, J., Christina, D. and Tchaikovsky, C. (1985) *Criminal Women*. Cambridge: Polity Press.

Carlen, P. and Worral, A. (1987) *Gender, Crime and Justice*. Milton Keynes: Open University Press.

Carter, C. (1998) 'When the "extraordinary" becomes ordinary: everyday news of sexual violence', in C. Carter, G. Branston and S. Allan (1998) *News, Gender and Power*. London: Routledge. pp. 219–33.

Carter, C. and Weaver, K. (2003) *Violence and the Media*. Buckingham: Open University Press.

Chambers, G. and Miller, A. (1983) *Investigating Sexual Assault*. Edinburgh: Scottish Office Central Research Unit.

Chambers, G. and Miller, A. (1986) *Prosecuting Sexual Assault*. Edinburgh: Scottish Office Central Research Unit.

Chibnall S. (1977) *Law and Order News*. London: Tavistock.

Chodorow, N. (1978) *The Reproduction of Mothering*. Berkeley: University of California Press.

Christian Institute (2001) http://www.christianinstitute.org.uk/html-publications/sexoffencessubmission.doc

Christmas, L. (1996) *Chaps of Both Sexes*. Devizes: BT Forum.

Cixous, H. (1989) 'Sorties: out and out: attacks/ways out/forays', in J. Moore and C. Belsey (eds) *The Feminist Reader*. London: Macmillan.

Clarke, A., and Moran-Ellis, J. and Sleney, J. (2002) *Attitudes to Date Rape And Relationship Rape: A Qualitative Study*. Sentencing Advisory Panel Research Report. http://www.sentencing-guidelines.gov.uk/docs/research.pdf

Clarke, J., Hall, S., Jefferson, T. and Roberts, B. (1993) 'Subcultures, cultures and class: a theoretical overview', in S. Hall and T. Jefferson (eds) *Resistance through Rituals: Youth Subcultures in Post-war Britain*. London: Routledge.

Clark, K. (1992) 'The linguistics of blame: representations of women in *The Sun's* reporting of crimes of sexual violence', in M. Toolan (ed.) *Language, Text and Context: Essays in Stylistics*. London: Routledge. pp. 208–24.

Clifton, J., Jacobs, J. and Tulloch, J. (1996) *Helping Women Survive Domestic Violence: A Report to the Sussex Domestic Violence Multi-Agency Consultative Group*. Brighton: University of Sussex.

Cloward, R.A. and Ohlin, L.E. (1961) *Delinquency and Opportunity: A Theory of Delinquent Gangs*. London: Routledge.

CNN (2007) http://edition.cnn.com/2007/WORLD/meast/05/18/iraq.honorkilling/index.html

Cohen, A.K. (1955) *Delinquent Boys*. New York: Free Press.

Cohen, N. (2001) 'Criminal crackers', *Guardian*, 8 July. http://www.guardian.co.uk/print/0%2C858%2C4218000-102273%2C00.html

Cohen, S. (1972) *Folk Devils and Moral Panics*. London: MacGibbon and Kee.

Cohen, S. and Young, J. (1973) *The Manufacture of the News: Deviance, Social Problems and the Mass Media*. Constable: London.

Coleman, C. and Moynihan, J. (1996) *Understanding Crime Data: Haunted by the Dark Figure*. Buckingham: Open University Press.

Coleman, K., Hird, C. and Povey, D. (eds) (2006) *Violent Crime Overview, Homicide and Gun Crime 2004/2005*, 2nd edn (Supplementary Volume to *Crime in England and Wales 2004/2005*). Home Office Statistical Bulletin 02/06. London: Home Office.

Collier, R. (1998) *Masculinities, Crime and Criminology*. London: Sage.

Connell, R.W. (1987) *Gender and Power*. Cambridge: Polity Press.

Connell, R.W. (1995) *Masculinities*. Cambridge: Polity Press.

Connell, R. and Messerschmidt, M. (2005) 'Hegemonic masculinity. rethinking the concept', *Gender and Society*, 19(6): 829–59.

Corbett, C. (1987) 'Victim Support services to victims of serious sexual assault', *Police Surgeon*, 32: 6–16.

Corbett, C. and Hobdell, K. (1988) 'Volunteer-based services to rape victims: some recent developments', in M. Maguire and J. Pointing (eds) *Victims of Crime: A New Deal?* Milton Keynes: Open University Press.

Cornish, D. and Clarke, R. (1986) *The Reasoning Criminal*. New York: Springer-Verlag.

Cowan, R. (2004) 'Home abusers "likely to commit other crimes"', *Guardian*, 20 March. http://www.quardian.co.uk/crime/article/0,2763,1174026,00.html

Cowan, S. (2007) 'Freedom and capacity to make a choice: a feminist analysis of consent in the criminal law', in V. Munro and C. Stychin (eds) *Sexuality and the Law: Feminist Engagements*. London: Cavendish.

Cowling, M. (2006) 'Postmodern policies: the erratic interventions of constitutive criminology', *Internet Journal of Criminology*. http://www.internetjournalofcriminology. com/Cowling%20-%20Postmodern%20Policies.pdf

Crime in England and Wales (2005) Report, http://www.homeoffice.gov.uk/rds/crimee w0405.html

Crime Reduction (2005) http://www.crimereduction.homeoffice.gov.uk/statistics/statistics 39.htm#1

Crime Reduction (2006–07) http://www.crimereduction.gov.uk/dv/dv01.htm

Criminal Law Revision Committees (CLRC) (1980) *Working Paper on Sexual Offences*. London: HMSO.

Croall, H. (1998) *Crime and Society in Britain*. London: Longman.

Cumberbatch, M. (1998) 'The Windrush years: the real story', *Africa, Centred Review*, Issue 2, June/July. University of Sheffield: DACE.

Daily Mail (7 April 2008) http://www.dailymail.co.uk/pages/live/articles/news/news.html? in_article_id=557566&in_page_id=1811&ito=1490

Daly, K. (1994) *Gender, Crime and Punishment*. New Haven: Yale University Press.

Davies, P. (1999) 'Women, crime and an informal economy: female offending and crime for gain' at www.britsoccrim.org/volume2/001.pdf

Davis, N. (1985) 'The re-education of police personnel in the investigation of sexual offences', *Police Surgeon*, 28: 8–14.

DeKeseredy, W.S. and Schwartz, M.D. (2001) 'Definitional issues', in C.M. Renzetti, J.L. Edleson and R. Kennedy Bergen (eds) *Sourcebook on Violence Against Women*. Thousand Oaks, CA: Sage.

Denike, M. (2000) 'Sexual violence and fundamental justice: on the failure of equality reforms to criminal proceedings', *Canadian Women's Studies*, 20:3, 151–9, quoted in L. Kelly, J. Temkin and S. Griffiths (2006) *Section 41: An Evaluation of New Legislation Limiting Sexual History Evidence in Rape Trials*. Home Office Online Report 20/06. London: Home Office.

Department of Health (1999) *Working Together to Safeguard Children*. London: HMSO.

Department of Health, Welsh Office, Scottish Office Department of Health, Department of Health and Social Services Northern Ireland (1998) *Why Mothers Die: Report on Confidential Enquiries into Maternal Deaths in the United Kingdom 1994–1996*. London: HMSO.

Derbyshire Police (2006) 2 October. www. derbyshire.police.uk/news/572.html.

Desai, S. and Saltzman, L.E. (2001) 'Measurement issues in studying violence against women', in C.M. Renzetti, J.L. Edleson and R. Kennedy Bergen (eds) *Sourcebook on Violence Against Women*. Thousand Oaks, CA: Sage.

Dobash, R.E. and Dobash, R.P. (1979) *Violence Against Wives*. New York: Free Press.

Dobash, R.E. and Dobash, R.P. (1980) *Violence Against Wives*. Shepton Mallett, Somerset: Open Books.

Dobash, R.E. and Dobash, R.P. (1984) 'The nature and antecedents of violent events', *British Journal of Criminology*, 24(3): 269–84.

Dobash, R.E. and Dobash, R.P. (1987) 'The response of the British and American women's movements to violence against women', in J. Hanmer and M. Maynard (eds) *Women, Violence and Social Control*. London: Macmillan Press.

Dobash, R.E. and Dobash, R.P. (1992) *Women, Violence and Social Change*. London: Routledge.

Dobash, R.E. and Dobash, R.P. (1995) 'Reflections on findings from the Violence Against Women Survey', *Canadian Journal of Criminology*, July: 457–84.

Dobash, R.E. and Dobash, R.P. (2004) 'Women's violence to men in intimate relationships, working on a puzzle', *British Journal of Criminology*, 44: 324–49.

Dobash, R.E., Dobash, R.P. and Cavanagh, K. (1985) 'The contact between battered women and social and medical agencies', in J. Pahl (ed.) *Private Violence and Public Policy*. London: Routledge and Kegan Paul.

Dobash, R.E., Dobash, R.P. and Noakes, L. (eds) (1995) *Gender and Crime*. Cardiff: Cardiff University Press.

Dobash, R.E., Dobash, R.P., Cavanagh K. and Lewis, R. (2002) *Research Bulletin, No 1: Focus on Male Offenders*, 2002:2, ISSN 1476–7457. Research Bulletins 1–3. http://www1.rhbnc.ac.uk/sociopolitical-science/vrp/Findings/rfdobash.PDF.

Dominy, N. and Radford, L. (1996) *Domestic Violence in Surrey: Developing an Effective Inter-Agency Response*. Surrey County Council and Roehampton Institute, London.

Douglas, N., Lilley, S.J., Kooper, L. and Diamond, A. (2004) *Safety and Justice: Sharing Personal Information in the Context of Domestic Violence – An Overview* (Home Office Development and Practice Report No. 30). London: Home Office.

Downes, D. (1966) *The Delinquent Solution*. London: Routledge and Kegan Paul.

Downes, D. and Rock, P. (1988) *Understanding Deviance: A Guide to the Sociology of Crime and Rule Breaking*. Oxford: Clarendon Press.

Drake, M. and Pilditch, D. (2007) 'Maddy: Russian is quizzed', *Daily Express*, 7 May. http://www.express.co.uk/posts/view/7230

Dustin, H. (2006) *Understanding your Duty: Report on the Gender Equality Duty and the Criminal Justice System*. London: Fawcett Society.

Dworkin, A. (1981) *Pornography: Men Possessing Women*. London: Women's Press.

Dyer R. (1997) *White*. London: Routledge.

Eastel, P. (1998) *Balancing the Scales – Rape, Law Reform and Australian Culture*. Sydney: Federation Press.

Economist (9 February 2004) 'http://www.economist.com/opinion/displayStory.cfm?story_id=3151258

Edge of the City, C4 (26 August 2004) http://news.bbc.co.uk/1/hi/entertainment/tv_and_radio/3602854.stm

Edwards, S.S.M. (1986a) 'The real risks of violence behind closed doors', *New Law Journal*, 136/628: 1191–3.

Edwards, S.S.M. (1986b) *The Police Response to Domestic Violence in London*. London: Central London Polytechnic.

Edwards, S.S.M. (1989) *Policing 'Domestic Violence': Women, the Law and the State*. London: Sage.

Edwards, S.S.M. (1996) *Sex and Gender in the Legal Process*. Oxford: Blackstone Press Ltd.

Edwards, S.S.M. and Halpern, A. (1991) 'Protection for the victim of domestic violence: time for radical revision?', *Journal of Social Welfare and Family Law*, 2.

Elias, N. (1978) *The Civilizing Process*. New York: Pantheon.

Else, L. (1994) 'Family values', *New Scientist*, 15 October.

ESRC (2002) *Taking Stock: What do we Know About Interpersonal Violence?* London: Royal Holloway University.

ESRC (2007) *Young Offenders, Policing and Prisons in the UK*. http://www.esrcsociety today.ac.uk/ESRCInfoCentre/facts/UK/index49.aspx?ComponentId=12690&SourceP ageId=18134

Faragher, T. (1985), 'The police response to violence against women in the home', in J. Pahl (ed.) *Private Violence and Public Policy*. London: Routledge and Kegan Paul.

Farrington, D. (2007) 'Childhood risk factors and risk-focused prevention', in M. Maguire, R. Morgan and R. Reiner (eds) *The Oxford Handbook of Criminology* (4th edn). Oxford: Oxford University Press. pp. 602–40.

Farrington, D. and Morris, A. (1983) 'Sex, sentencing and reconviction', *British Journal of Criminology*, 23(3).

Fawcett Society (2005) 'Are we there yet?' http://www.fawcettsociety.org.uk/index.asp?PageID=109

Featherstone, M. (1995) *Undoing Culture: Globalization, Postmodernism and Identity*. London: Sage Publications.

Feldman-Summers, S. and Norris, J. (1984) 'Differences between rape victims who report and those who do not report to a public agency', *Journal of Applied Social Psychology*, 14: 562–73.

Fernandez, E. (2006) 'Domestic violence called underreported. Police document few of the thousands of children put at risk, researchers say', *San Francisco Chronicle*, 7 September. http://www.sfgate.com/cgi-bin/article.cgi?f=/c/a/2006/09/07/BAGNFKS8RS32.DTL

Ferrante, A., Morgan, F., Indermaur, D. and Harding, R. (1996) *Measuring the Extent of Domestic Violence*. Western Australia: Hawkins Press.

Ferrell, J. and Sanders, C.R. (eds) (1997) *Cultural Criminology*. Boston: Northeastern University Press.

Fielding, N. (1994) 'Cop canteen culture', in T. Newburn and B. Stanko, *Just Boys Doing Business*. London: Routledge.

Finch, E. and Munro, V.E. (2003) 'Intoxicated consent and the boundaries of drug assisted rape', *Criminal Law Review* 773

Finch, E. and Munro, V.E. (2006) 'Breaking boundaries? Sexual consent in the jury room', *Legal Studies*, 26(3): 303–20.

Finney, A. (2006) 'Domestic violence, sexual assault and stalking', *Findings from the 2004/05 British Crime Survey*. Home Office Online Report 12/06, London.

Firth, A. (1975) 'Interrogation', *Police Review*, 28 November: 1507.

Foley, M. (1996) 'Who is in control?: Changing responses to women who have been raped and sexually abused', in M. Hester, L. Kelly and J. Radford (eds) *Women, Violence and Male Power*. Buckingham: Open University Press.

Foucault M. (1967) *Madness and Civilisation*. London: Random House.

Foucault, M. (1977) *Discipline and Punish*. Harmondsworth: Penguin.

Foucault, M. (1978, 1981) *The History of Sexuality, Vol. 1: An Introduction*. Harmondsworth: Penguin.

Fracher, J. and Kimmel, M. (1995) 'Hard issues and soft spots: counseling men about sexuality', in M. Kimmel and M. Messner (eds) *Men's Lives* (3rd edn). Boston: Allyn and Bacon. pp. 365–74.

Freeman, M. (1979) *Violence in the Home*. Farnborough: Saxon House.

Freud, S. (1905, 1953) 'Three essays on the theory of sexuality', in *Complete Psychological Works*. London: Hogarth.

Freud, S. (1925) *Some Psychical Consequences of the Anatomical Distinction Between the Sexes*, Standard Edition XIX.

Furstenburg, F. (1976) *Unplanned Parenthood: the Social Consequences of Teenage Childbearing*. New York: Free Press.

Fuss, D. (1991) 'Inside/out', in D. Fuss (ed.) *Inside/out*. New York: Routledge.

Gadd, D. and Jefferson, T. (2007) *Psycho-social Criminology*. London: Sage.

Gadd, D., Farrell, S., Lombard, N. and Dallimore, D. (2002) *Domestic Abuse Against Men In Scotland*. Edinburgh: Scottish Executive Central Research Unit.

Gadd, D., Farrell, S., Dallimore, D. and Lombard, N. (2003) 'Equal victims or the usual suspects? Making sense of domestic abuse against men', *International Review of Victimology*, 10: 96–116.

Galtung, J. and Ruge, M. (1965) 'Structuring and selecting news', in S. Cohen and J. Young, *The Manufacture of News: Deviance, Social Problems and the Mass Media* (1982 edn). London: Constable.

Gardner, J. and Shute, S. (2000) 'The wrongness of rape', in J. Horder (ed.) *Oxford Essays in Jurisprudence* (4th Series). Oxford and New York: Oxford University Press.

Garland, D. (2002) 'Of crimes and criminals', in M. Maguire, R. Morgan and R. Reiner, *The Oxford Handbook of Criminology* (3rd edn). Oxford: Oxford University Press. pp. 7–51.

Gelles, R.J. (1974) *The Violent Home: A Study of Physical Aggression Between Husbands and Wives*. Beverly Hills, CA: Sage.

Gelsthorpe, L. (2002) 'Feminism and criminology', in M. Maguire, R. Morgan and R. Reiner, *The Oxford Handbook of Criminology* (3rd edn). Oxford: Oxford University Press. pp. 112–43.

Gerrard, N. (2004) *Soham: A Story of our Times*. London: Short Books.

Gibbs, N. (1991) 'Cover stories behavior: when is it rape?' *Time*, 3 June. http://www.time.com/time/magazine/article/0,9171,973077-1,00.html

Giddens, A. (1992) *The Transformation of Intimacy: Sexuality, Love and Eroticism*. Cambridge: Polity Press.

Gillespie, T. (1994) 'Under pressure: rape crisis centres, multi-agency work and strategies for survival', in C. Lupton and T. Gillespie (eds) *Working with Violence*. Basingstoke: Macmillan.

Goodey, J. (1997) 'Boys don't cry', *British Journal of Criminology*, 37(3), Summer: 401–18. http://www.academicarmageddon.co.uk/library/cry.htm

Go-petition (22 June 2007) http://www.gopetition.co.uk/petitions/removal-of-maxine-carr-from-our-village.html.

Goring, C. (1913) *The English Convict: A Statistical Study*. London: HMSO.

Grace, S. (1995) *Policing Domestic Violence in the 1990s*, Home Office Research Study, No. 139. London: HMSO.

Grace, S., Lloyd, C. and Smith, L. (1992) *Rape: From Recording to Conviction*, Research and Planning Unit Paper 71. London: Home Office.

Grady, A. (2002) 'Female-on-male domestic violence: uncommon or ignored?', in C. Hoyle and R. Young (eds) *New Visions of Crime Victims*. Oxford: Hart Publishing. pp. 71–96.

Graham, R. (2004) 'Revisiting the O.J. circus, the media is guilty again', *Boston Globe*, 8 June. http://www.boston.com/ae/media/articles/2004/06/08/revisiting_the_oj_circus_the_media_is_guilty_again/

Gramsci, A. (1971) *Selections from the Prison Notebooks*. New York: International.

Gregory, J. and Lees, S. (1999) *Policing Sexual Assault*. London: Routledge.

Grosz, E. (1987) 'Feminist theory and the challenge to knowledge', *Women's Studies International Forum*, 10(5): 208–17.

Grubin D. (1998) *Sex Offending against Children: Understanding the Risk*. Police Research series, Paper 99. London: Home Office. http://www.homeoffice.gov.uk/rds/prgpdfs/fprs99.pdf

Guardian (3 July 2001) 'The murder of TV's golden girl'. http://www.guardian.co.uk/jilldando/story/0,7369,516098,00.html

Guardian (15 July 2002) http://media.guardian.co.uk/edinburghtvfestival/story/0,7523,530635,00.html

Gunter, B., Harrison, J. and Wykes, M. (2003) *Violence on Television: Distribution, Form, Context and Themes*. Hillsdale, NJ: Lawrence Erlbaum.

Gupta, R. (2003) 'A veil drawn over brutal crimes', *Guardian*, 3 October. http://www.guardian.co.uk/comment/story/0,3604,1054858,00.html

Hagan, J., Simpson, J. and Gillis, A. (1979) 'The sexual stratification of social control', *BJC* 30: 25–38.

Hague, G. and Malos, E. (1998) *Domestic Violence: Action for Change*. Cheltenham: New Clarion Press.

Hall, C. (1988) 'Rape: the politics of definition', *South African Law Journal*, 105, pp. 67.

Hall, R.E. (1985) *Ask Any Woman: A London Enquiry into Rape and Sexual Assault*. Bristol: Falling Wall Press.

Hall, S. (ed.) (1997) *Representations: Cultural Representations and Signifying Practices*. London: Sage.

Hall, S. and Jefferson, T. (eds) (1993) *Resistance through Rituals: Youth Subcultures in Post-war Britain*. London: Routledge.

Hall, S. and Vasager, J. (2003) 'Soham policeman cleared of child porn charges after computer evidence blunder', *Guardian*, 21 August. http://www.guardian.co.uk/uk_news/story/0,3604,1026099,00.html

Hall, S., Critcher, C., Jefferson, T. and Clarke, J. (eds) (1978) *Policing the Crisis: Mugging, the State, Law and Order*. Basingstoke: Macmillan.

Hanmer, J. (1989) 'Women and policing in Britain', in J. Hanmer, J. Radford and E.A. Stanko (eds) *Women, Policing and Male Violence: International Perspectives*. London: Routledge.

Hanmer, J. and Saunders, S. (1984) *Well Founded Fear*. London: Hutchinson.

Hanmer, J., Radford, J. and Stanko, E.A. (1989) *Women, Policing and Male Violence: International Perspectives*. London: Routledge.

Hansard (2007) http://www.parliament.the-stationary-office.co.uk/pa/cmhansrd/cm200607/debtext/70305-0014.htm

Haraway, D. (1990) 'A manifesto for cyborgs: science, technology, and socialist feminism in the 1980s', in L. Nicholson (ed.) (1990): *Feminism/Postmodernism*. London: Routledge: pp. 190–234.

Harding, S. (ed.) (1987) *Feminism and Methodology*. Bloomington: Indiana University Press.

Harris, J. and Grace, S. (1999) *A Question of Evidence? Investigating and Prosecuting Rape in the 1990s*. Home Office Research Study 196. London: Home Office.

Harris, P. (2001) *Observer*, 8 July. http://www.guardian.co.uk/politics/2001/jul/08/uk.race.

Harris, P., McVeigh, T. and Ferguson, E. (2002) 'The massive manhunt – and the nightmare of two families – was played out under the glare of relentless publicity', *Observer*, 18 August. http://observer.guardian.co.uk/focus/story/0,,776492,00.html

Havelock Ellis, H. [(1897) 2004] *Studies in the Psychology of Sex. Volume 2. Sexual Inversion* at http://www.gutenberg.org/etext/13611

Hawkins Darnell, F. (ed.) (2003) *Violent Crime: Assessing Race and Ethnic Differences*. Cambridge: Cambridge University Press.

Heidensohn, F. (1968) 'The deviance of women: a critique and an enquiry', *British Journal of Sociology*, 19: 160–75.

Heidensohn, F. (1985) *Women and Crime*. London: Macmillan.

Heidensohn, F. (1994) 'Gender and crime', in M. Maguire, R. Morgan and R. Reiner (eds) *The Oxford Handbook of Criminology*. Oxford: Clarendon Press.

Heidensohn, F. (2006) 'New perspectives and established views', in F. Heidensohn (ed.) *Gender and Justice*. Cullompton: Willan.

Heinonen, P. (2006) 'Changing perceptions: globalization, women and development', paper given at International Women's Congress Istanbul, 28–29 January.

Helm, T. (2007) 'Brown draws battle lines on family policy', *Daily Telegraph*, 9 March. http://www.telegraph.co.uk/news/main.jhtml?xml=/news/2007/03/08/nfamily08.xml

Henry, S. and Milovanovic, D. (1996) *Constitutive Criminology: Beyond Postmodernism*. London: Sage.

Hester, M. and Westmarland, N. (2005) *Tackling Domestic Violence: Effective Interventions and Approaches*, Home Office Research Study 290. London: Home Office.

Hester, M. and Westmarland, N. (2006) *Service Provision for Perpetrators of Domestic Violence*. Bristol: University of Bristol.

Hillyard, P., Pantazis, C., Tombs, S. and Gordon, D. (eds) (2004) *Beyond Criminology. Taking Harm Seriously*. London: Pluto Press. http://news.bbc.co.uk/1/shared/bsp/hi/pdfs/17_10_05_murder_report. pdf

Hitchcock, A. (dir.) (1945) *Spellbound*.

'Hitting home', *Panorama* http://www.bbc.co.uk/health/hh/

Holland, P. (1998) 'The politics of the smile: "Soft news" and the sexualisation of the popular press', in C. Carter, G. Branston and S. Allan (1998) *News, Gender and Power*. London: Routledge.

Hollway, W. (1989) *Subjectivity and Method in Psychology: Gender, Meaning and Science*. London: Sage.

Hollway, W. (2001) 'Gender difference and the production of subjectivity', in M. Wetherall, S. Taylor, S.J. Yates (eds) *Discourse, Theory and Practice*. London: Sage. pp. 272–83.

Holmes, M., Resnick, H.S., KilPatrick, D.G., Best, C.L., Moore, J.G. and Moreno, H. (1996) 'Rape-related pregnancy: estimates and descriptive characteristics from a national sample of women', *American Journal of Obstetrics and Gynecology*, 175(2): 320–5.

Holmstrom, L.L. and Burgess, A.W. (1980) 'Sexual behavior of assailants during reported rapes', *Archives of Sexual Behavior*, 9(5): 427–39.

Home Office (1998) *Speaking up for Justice. Report of the Interdepartmental Working Group on the Treatment of Vulnerable or Intimidated Witnesses in the Criminal Justice System*. London: Home Office.

Home Office (1998–99) http://www.homeoffice.gov.uk/crime-victims/reducing-crime/youth-crime/

Home Office (1999) *Information on the Criminal Justice System in England and Wales: Digest 4*. London: Home Office.

Home Office (2000a) *Setting the Boundaries: Reforming the Law on Sexual Offences*. London: Home Office.

Home Office (2000b) *Domestic Violence: Revised Circular to the Police*. London: Home Office.

Home Office (2002) *Protecting the Public – Strengthening Protection Against Sex Offenders and Reforming the Law on Sexual Offences*. London: Home Office.

Home Office (2002/03) 'Crime in England and Wales'. http://www.statistics.gov. uk/cci/nugget.asp?id=442

Home Office (2003) *Safety and Justice – the Government's Proposals on Domestic Violence*. Home Office Consultation Paper Cm 5847. London: Home Office.

Home Office (2004) http://www.homeoffice.gov.uk/documents/*Paying-the-Price-*RIA.pdf?view=Binary

Home Office (2005) *Domestic Violence: A National Report*. London: Home Office.

Home Office (2006) 'Domestic Violence'. http://www.homeoffice.gov.uk/crime-victims/reducing-crime/domestic-violence/

Home Office (2006–07) http://www.homeoffice.gov.uk/crime-victims/reducing-crime/sexual-offences/

Home Office, Women's Unit, Crown Prosecution Service, the Department for Education and Employment, the Department of the Environment, Transport and the Regions, the Department of Health, the Lord Chancellor's Department, the Department of Culture, Media and Sport (2000) *Multi-Agency Guidance for Addressing Domestic Violence*. London: Home Office.

Hood, R., Shute, S., Feilzer, M. and Wilcox, A. (2002) 'Sex offenders emerging from long-term imprisonment' in *BJC* 42: 371–94.

Hood-Williams, J. (2001) 'Gender, Masculinities and crime: from structures to psyches', *Theoretical Criminology*, 5(1): 37–60.

Hough, M. and Roberts, J.V. (2003) *Youth Crime and Youth Justice: Public Opinion in England and Wales*. Bristol: Policy Press.

Hoyle, C. (1998) *Negotiating Domestic Violence: Police, Criminal Justice and Victims*. Clarendon Studies in Criminology. Oxford: Oxford University Press.

Hoyle, C. and Sanders, A. (2000) 'Police response to domestic violence: from victim choice to victim empowerment?', *British Journal of Criminology*, 40: 14–36.

Husband, C. (1984) 'Social identity and race', in E3542 5-6, Open University Course.

ICM (2005) *Sexual Assault Research Summary Report*. http://www.amnesty.org.uk/uploads/documents/doc_16619.doc

Islington Borough Council (2008) http://www.islington.gov.uk/

Jansson, K., Coleman, K., Reed, E. and Kaiza, P. (2007) *Homicides, Firearm Offences and Intimate Violence 2005/06*, Supplementary Volume 1 to *Crime in England and Wales 2005/06*. Home Office Statistical Bulletin 02/07. London: Home Office.

Jefferson, T. (1992) 'Wheelin' and stealin', *Achilles Heel*, Summer.

Jefferson, T. (1994) 'Theorising masculine subjectivity', in T. Newburn and E. Stanko (eds) *Just Boys Doing Business: Men, Masculinities and Crime*. London: Routledge.

Jefferson, T. (2002) 'Subordinating hegemonic masculinity', *Theoretical Criminology*, 6(1): 63–88.

Jeffreys, S. (2008) *The Global Sex Trade: The Industrial Vagina*. London: Routledge.

Jewkes, Y. (2004) *Media and Crime*. London: Sage.

Jones, H. and Westmarland, N. (2004) 'Remembering the past but looking to the future', http://www.rapecrisis.org.uk/history.htm

Jones, S. (2006) *Criminology*. London: Butterworths.

JUSTICE Committee (1998) *Victims in Criminal Justice*. London: JUSTICE.

Justice for Women (2006) http://www.jfw.org.uk/casehistories.htm#Sara

Kaganas, F. (2001) 'Domestic homicide, gender and the expert', in A. Bainham, S. Sclater and M. Richards (eds) (2002) *Body Lore and Laws*. Oxford: Hart Publishing.

Keen, Carolyn (n.d.): *On the Cyborg Manifesto*. http://www.english.upenn.edu/~jenglish/Courses/keen2.html

Kelly, L. (1987) 'The continuum of sexual violence', in J. Hanmer and M. Maynard (eds) *Women, Violence and Social Control*. Basingstoke: Macmillan.

Kelly, L. (1988) *Surviving Sexual Violence*. Cambridge: Polity Press.

Kelly, L. and Regan, L. (2000) *Stopping Traffic: Exploring the Extent of, and Responses to, Trafficking in Women for Sexual Exploitation in the UK*. Police Research Series Paper 125. London: Home Office.

Kelly, L., Lovett, J. and Regan, L. (2005) *A Gap or a Chasm? Attrition in Reported Rape Cases*, Home Office Research Study No. 293. London: Home Office.

Kelly, L., Temkin, J. and Griffiths, S. (2006) *Section 41: An Evaluation of New Legislation Limiting Sexual History Evidence in Rape Trials*. Home Office Online Report 20/06. London: Home Office.

Kennedy, H. (1992) *Eve Was Framed*. London: Chatto and Windus.

Kidd-Hewitt, D. and Osborne, R. (eds) (1995) *Crime and the Media*. London: Pluto Press.

Kilday, Anne-Marie (2003) 'Just who was wearing the trousers in nineteenth century Britain', in *Social Deviance in England and in France (c. 1830–1900)*, Actes de Colloque Maison Française d'Oxford. http://www.mfo.ac.uk/Publications/actes1/kilday.htm

Koss, M.P., Dinero, T.E., Seibel, C. and Cox, S. (1988) 'Stranger and acquaintance rape: are there differences in the victim's experience?', *Psychology of Women Quarterly*, 12: 1–23.

Krafft-Ebbing, R. von [(1886) 1965] *Psycopathia Sexualis*. Chicago: University of Chicago Press.

Kristeva, J. (1980) *Desire in Language: A Semiotic Approach to Literature and Art*. Oxford: Blackwell.

Kristeva, J. (1989) 'Women's time', in C. Belsey and J. Moore (eds) (1989) *The Feminist Reader*. London: Macmillan. pp. 197–217.

Kundnani, A. (2006) 'Bradford riots', 26 April. http://www.irr.org.uk/2006/april/ak000030.html

Kupfersmid, J. (1995) 'Does the Oedipus complex exist?', *Psychotherapy*, (32) 535–547.

Lacan, J. (1976) *The Language of Self* (1953, trans. Anthony Willden). Baltimore: Johns Hopkins University Press.

Lacan, J. (1977) *Ecrits*. London: Tavistock.

Lacey, N. (1998) 'Unspeakable subjects, impossible rights: sexuality, integrity and criminal law', XI *Canadian Journal of Law and Jurisprudence*, 47: 62.

Lacey, N. (2001) 'Beset by boundaries: the Home Office review of sexual offences', *Criminal Law Review*, 3.

Langman, L. (2000) 'Identity, hegemony and the reproduction of domination', in Richard Altschuler (ed.) *Marx, Weber and Durkheim*. New York: Gordian Knot Press. pp. 218–35.

Langman, L. and Cangemi, K. (n.d.) 'Transgression as identity'. http://www.angelfire.com/or3/tss2/transid.html

Larrson, S. (2002) *National Analytical Study of Racial Violence and Crime*. Raxen Focal Point Study for Sweden EXPO Foundation. http://fra.europa.eu/fra/material/pub/RAXEN/4/RV/CS-RV-NR-SE.pdf

Law in a box (2008) http://www.lawinabox.net/lbnewswire08e.html

Law Commission (2000) *Consent in Sex Offences A Report to the Home Office Sex Offences Review*. London: Law Commission.

Lea, S.J., Lanvers, U. and Shaw, S. (2003) 'Attrition in rape cases. Developing a profile and identifying relevant factors', *British Journal of Criminology*, 43: 583–99.

Leapman, B. (20 January 2008) *Daily Telegraph*. http://www.telegraph.co.uk/news/main.jhtml?xml=/news/2008/01/20/nyouth120.xml

Lees, S. (1989) 'Naggers, whores and libbers: driving men to violence', paper presented at BSA, Plymouth.

Lees, S. (1995) 'Media reporting of rape: the British date rape controversy', in D. Kidd-Hewitt and R. Osborne (eds) (1995) *Crime and the Media*. London: Pluto Press.

Lees, S. (1997) *Carnal Knowledge: Rape on Trial*. Harmondsworth: Penguin.

Lees, S. (1999) 'The Accused', *Guardian*, 1 March.

Lees, S. (2002) *Carnal Knowledge: Rape on Trial*. London: Women's Press.

Lees, S. and Gregory, J. (1996) 'Attrition in rape and sexual assault cases in England and Wales', *British Journal of Criminology*, 36: 1–17.

Levi, M., Maguire, M. and Brookman, F. (2007) 'Violent Crime', in M. Maguire, R. Morgan and R. Reiner (eds) *The Oxford Handbook of Criminology* (4th edn). Oxford: Oxford University Press. pp. 687–732.

Lister, R. (ed.) (1996) *Charles Murray and the Under-class: The Developing Debate*. IEA Health and Welfare Unit No 33. http://www.civitas.org.uk/pdf/cw33.pdf

Local Government Act 1988 Section 28 http://www.opsi.gov.uk/acts/acts1988/ukpga_19880009_en_5

Lombroso, C. and Ferrero, W. (1895) *The Female Offender*. New York: Appleton.

London Rape Crisis Centre (1984) *Sexual Violence: The Reality for Women*. London: Women's Press.

London School of Hygiene and Tropical Medicine Report (2005) http://www.lshtm.ac.uk/news/2005/domesticviolence.html

Lovett, J., Regan, L. and Kelly, L. (2004) *Sexual Assault Referral Centres: Developing Good Practice and Maximising Potentials*. Home Office Research Study 285. London: Home Office.

Lukes, S. (1986) *Power*. London: Blackwell.

MacKinnon, C. (1987) *Feminism Unmodified: Discourses on Life and Law*. Boston, MA: Harvard University Press.

Maguire, M. (1996) *Street Crime*. Aldershot: Dartmouth.

Maguire, M. (1997) 'Crime statistics, patterns and trends', in M. Maguire, R. Morgan and R. Reiner (eds) *The Oxford Handbook of Criminology* (2nd edn). Oxford: Clarendon Press.

Maguire, M. (2002) 'Crime Statistics: the data explosion and its implications', in M. Maguire, R. Morgan and R. Reiner (eds) *The Oxford Handbook of Criminology* (3rd edn). Oxford: Clarendon Press.

Maguire, M., Morgan, R. and Reiner, R (eds) (2007) *The Oxford Handboook of Criminology* (4th edn). Oxford: Oxford University Press.

Mahria, N. (2008) *Just Representation: Press Reporting and the Reality of Rape*. London: Eaves Lilith Project.

Mama, A. (1996) *The Hidden Struggle: Statutory and Voluntary Sector Responses to Violence Against Black Women in the Home*. London: Whiting Birch.

Martin, D. (2007) 'Top Tory says date rape might just be a "disagreement" between lovers', *Daily Mail*, 17 December. http://www.dailymail.co.uk/pages/live/articles/news/news.html?in_article_id=503112&in_page_id=1770

Masher, D.L. and Anderson, D.L. (1986) 'Macho personality, sexual aggression and reactions to guided imagery of realistic rape', *Journal of Research and Personality*, 20: 77–89.

Maudsley, H. (1895) 'Criminal responsibility in relation to insanity', *Journal of Mental Science*, 41: 657.

Mawby, R. and Gill, M. (1987) *Crime Victims: Needs, Services, and the Voluntary Sector*. London: Tavistock.

Mayell, H. (2002) *National Geographic News*, 12 February. http://news.national geographic.com/news/2002/02/0212_020212_honorkilling.html

Maynard, M. (1985) 'The response of social workers to domestic violence', in J. Pahl (ed.) *Private Violence and Public Policy*. London: Routledge and Kegan Paul.

McColgan, A. (1996a) 'Common law and the relevance of sexual history evidence', *Oxford Journal of Legal Studies*, 16: 275.

McColgan, A. (1996b) *The Case for Taking the Date out of Rape*. London: Pandora.

McGibbon, A., Cooper, L. and Kelly, L. (1989) *What Support? An Exploratory Study of Council Policy and Practice, and Local Support Services in the Area of Domestic Violence within Hammersmith and Fulham*. London: Hammersmith and Fulham Council Community Police Committee Domestic Violence Project. Polytechnic of North London: Child Abuse Studies Unit.

McGuigan, J. (1993) *Cultural Populism*. London: Routledge.

McIntosh, M. (1988) 'Introduction to an issue: family secrets as public drama', *Feminist Review*, 28, January.

Mckie, L. (2005) *Families, Violence and Social Change*. Maidenhead: Open University Press.

Mcleod, E. (1982) *Women Working: Prostitution Now*. London: Croom Helm.

Mcveigh, K. (2002) 'Missing girls: two quizzed', *Scotsman*, 17 August. http://thescots man.scotsman.com/index.cfm?id=902862002

Merton, R.K. (1968) *Social Theory and Social Structure*. New York: Free Press.

Messerschmidt, J.W. (1993) *Masculinities and Crime: Critique and Reconceptualization of Theory*. Lanham, MD: Rowan and Littlefield Publishers, Inc.

Messerschmidt, J. (1997) *Crime as Structured Action: Gender, Race, Class and Crime in the Making*. Thousand Oaks, CA: Sage.

Messerschmidt, J.W. (2000) *Nine Lives: Adolescent Masculinities, the Body, and Violence*. Boulder, CO: Westview Press.

Metropolitan Police (2006) Bulletin 0000000549, 'Gang sentenced for trafficking women into the UK', 3 November, http://cms.met.police.uk/news/convictions/ gang_sentenced_for_trafficking_women_into_the_uk

Metropolitan Police (2007) 20 September, http://www.met.police.uk/foi/pdfs/how_ are_we_doing/corporate/mps_stop_and_search_borough_breakdown_report_april august_2007.pdf

Miller, F. (1890) 'From a speech to the National Liberal Club', http://members.lycos. co.uk/HastingsHistory/19/overview.htm

Milmo, C. (08 February 2008) 'Ipswich Murders: accused tell of troubled life', *Independent*.

Mirlees-Black, C. (1995) *Estimating the Extent of Domestic Violence: Findings from the 1992 British Crime Survey*. Research Bulletin No. 37. London: Home Office Research and Statistics Directorate.

Mirlees-Black, C. (1999) *Domestic Violence: Findings from a New British Crime Survey Self-Completion Questionnaire*. Home Office Research Study 191. London: Home Office.

Moi, T. (1989) 'Feminist, female, feminine', in J. Moore and C. Belsey (eds) *The Feminist Reader*. London: Macmillan.

Mooney, J. (1996) 'Researching domestic violence: the North London Domestic Violence Survey', in S. Lyon and L. Morris (eds) *Gender Relations in Public and Private: Changing Research Perspectives*. London: Macmillan.

Mooney, J. (1999) *The North London Domestic Violence Survey*. Centre for Criminology, Middlesex University.

Mooney, J. (2000) *Gender, Violence and the Social Order*. London: Macmillan.

Morley, R. and Mullender, A. (1992), 'Hype or hope? The importation of pro-arrest policies and batterers programmes from North America to Britain as key measures for preventing violence against women in the home', *International Journal of Law and the Family*, 6: 265–88.

Morley, R. and Mullender, A. (1994) *Preventing Domestic Violence to Women*. Police Research Group Crime Prevention Unit Series Paper 48. London: Home Office.

Mort, F. (1987) *Dangerous Sexualities: Medico-moral Politics in England since 1830*. London: Routledge.

Motz, A. (2001) *The Psychology of Female Violence: Crimes against the Body*. Hove: Brunner-Routledge.

Mullen, P.E., Pathe, M., Purcell, R. and Stuart, G.W. (1999) 'A study of stalkers', *American Journal of Psychiatry*, 156: 1244–9.

Mullender, A. (2000) *Reducing Domestic Violence … What Works? Meeting the Needs of Children*. Policing and Reducing Crime Briefing Note. London: Research, Development and Statistics Directorate.

Mullender, A. (2004) *Tackling Domestic Violence: Providing Support for Children who have Witnessed Domestic Violence*. Home Office Development and Practice Report No. 33. London: Home Office.

Mullender, A. and Morley, R. (eds) (1994) *Children Living with Domestic Violence: Putting Men's Abuse of Women on the Child Care Agenda*. London: Whiting Birch.

Murdoch, G. (1973) 'Political deviance: the press presentation of a mass militant demonstration', in S. Cohen and J. Young (eds) (1982) *The Manufacture of News: Deviance, Social Problems and the Mass Media*. London: Constable.

Murray, C. (1990) *The Emerging British Underclass*. London: IEA Health and Welfare Unit.

MVA (2000) *The 2000 Scottish Crime Survey: First Results*. Crime and Criminal Justice Research Finding No. Edinburgh: 51. Scottish Executive.

Myhill, A. and Allen, J. (2002) *Rape and Sexual Assault of Women: The Extent and Nature of the Problem*. Findings from the British Crime Survey. Home Office Research Study 237. London. http://www.homeoffice.gov.uk/rds/pdfs2/r159.pdf.

Naffine, N. (1994) 'Possession: erotic love in the law of rape', *Modern Law Review*, 10: 25.

National Children Homes (1994) *The Hidden Victims*. NCH Action for Children.

National Statistics UK (2006) http://www.statistics.gov.uk/cci/nugget.asp?id=442.

Ndangam, L. (2002) 'Child abuse in the media', PhD thesis, University of Sheffield.

Newburn, T. and Stanko, E. (eds) (1994) *Just Boys Doing Business? Men, Masculinities and Crime*. London: Routledge.

New South Wales Department for Women (1996) *Heroines of Fortitude: The Experiences of Women in Court as Victims of Sexual Assault*. Woolloomooloo, NSW: Department for Women.

Nicholas, S., Kershaw, C. and Walker, A. (eds) (2007) *Crime in England and Wales 2006/2007*. http://www.homeoffice.gov.uk/rds/crimeew0607.html

NIJ (2004) *Violence Against Women: Identifying the Risk Factors*. November US Dept of Justice.

NOMS (2006) *Prison Population & Accommodation Briefing for* – 13th October. http://www.hmprisonservice.gov.uk/assets/documents/1000225413102006_web_report.doc

Norwood East, W. (1927) *An Introduction of Forensic Psychiatry into the Criminal Courts*. London: J.A. Churchill.

NSPCC (2007) http://www.nspcc.org.uk/whatwedo/aboutthenspcc/keyfactsandfigures/keyfacts_wda33645.html

Obaid, T.A. (2008) *Launch of the Secretary-General's Campaign on Violence against Women* http://www.un.org/womenwatch/daw/csw/52sess.htm#themes

Oppendlander, N. (1982) 'Coping or copping out? Police service delivery in domestic disputes', *Criminology*, 20 (3–4): 449–65.

Ormerod, D. (2005) *Smith & Hogan, Criminal Law*. Oxford: Oxford University Press.

Osborne, R. and Kidd-Hewitt, D. (eds) (1996) *Crime and the Media*. London: Pluto Press.

Pagelow, M.D. (1981) *Women Battering: Victims and their Experiences*. Beverly Hills, CA: Sage.

Pahl, J. (1978) *A Refuge for Battered Women: A Study of the Role of Women's Centre*. London: HMSO.

Pahl, J. (1985) *Private Violence and Public Policy*. London: Routledge and Kegan Paul.

Painter, K. (1991) *Wife Rape, Marriage and the Law*. Manchester: UMP.

Painter, K. and Farrington, D. (1998) 'Marital violence in Great Britain and its relationship to marital and non-marital rape', *International Review of Victimology*, 5: 257–76.

Park, R. and Burgess, E. (1925) *The City*. Chicago: University of Chicago Press.

Parker, H. (1974) *View from the Boys*. Newton Abbott: David and Charles.

Parmar, A., Sampson, A. and Diamond, A. (2005a) *Tackling Domestic Violence: Providing Advocacy and Support to Survivors of Domestic Violence*. Home Office Development and Practice Report No. 34. London: Home Office.

Parmar, A., Sampson, A. and Diamond, A. (2005b) *Tackling Domestic Violence: Providing Advocacy and Support to Survivors of Domestic Violence from Black and Other Minority Ethnic Communities*. Home Office Development and Practice Report No. 35. London: Home Office.

Parsons, T. (1937) *The Structure of Social Action*. New York: McGraw Hill.

Paterson, G. (2006) 'Tackling domestic violence at work', 14 March, BBC News. http://news.bbc.co.uk/1/hi/uk/4581808.stm

Paterson, T. (2005) 'How many more women have to die before this society wakes up?', *Daily Telegraph*, 27 February. http://www.telegraph.co.uk/news/main.jhtml? xml=/news/2005/02/27/wturk27.xml

Paterson, T. (2008) *Independent*, 29 April. http://www.independent.co.uk/news/europe/josef-fritzl-the-man-who-haunts-austria-817212.html

Pearson, G. (1983) *Hooligan: A History of Respectable Fears*. London: Macmillan.

Percy, A. and Mayhew, P. (1997) 'Estimating sexual victimisation in a national crime survey: a new approach', *Studies on Crime and Crime Prevention*, 6: 125–50.

Phillips, C. and Bowling, B. (2002) 'Racism, ethnicity, crime and criminal justice', in M. Maguire, R. Morgan and R. Reiner (eds) *The Oxford Handbook of Criminology* (3rd edn). Oxford: Oxford University Press.

Phillips, O. (2006) 'Gender, justice and human rights in post-colonial Zimbabwe and South Africa', in F. Heidensohn (ed.) *Gender and Justice*. Cullompton: Willan. pp. 243–79.

Phoenix, J. (2006) 'Regulating prostitution: controlling women's lives', in F. Heidensohn (ed.) *Gender and Justice*. Cullompton: Willan.

Phoenix, J. and Oerton, S. (2005) *Illicit and Illegal Sex, Regulation and Social Control.* London: Willan.

Pinheiro, P.S. (2006) *A/61/Report of the Independent Expert for the United Nations.* General Assembly Resolution S9/261. http://www.violence study.org/IMG/pdf/GA report study VAC.pdf

Pizzey, E. (2001) cited in D. Gadd et al. (2002) *Domestic Abuse Against Men in Scotland.* Edinburgh: Scottish Executive Central Research Unit.

Pizzey, E. (1974) *Scream Quietly or the Neighbours Will Hear.* London: IF Books.

Pollak, O. (1950) *The Criminality of Women.* Philadelphia, PA: University of Pennsylvania Press.

POST (12/2003) No. 210. http://www.parliament.uk/documents/upload/postpn210.pdf

Presdee, M. (2000) *Criminology and the Carnival of Crime.* London: Routledge.

Propp, V. (1968) *Morphology of a Folk-Tale* (trans. L. Scott). Bloomington: Indiana University Press.

Protection from Harassment Act, http://194.128.65.3/acts/acts1997/97040–a.htm#2.

Radford, J. (1987) 'Policing male violence/policing women', in J. Hanmer and M. Maynard (eds) *Women, Violence and Social Control.* Basingstoke: Macmillan.

Radford, J., Friedberg, M. and Harne, L. (eds) (2000) *Women, Violence and Strategies for Action.* Buckingham: Open University Press.

Radford, J. and Russell, D.E.H. (1992) *Femicide: The Politics of Woman Killing.* New York: Twayne Publishers.

Raxen NFP (2005) *Racist Violence in 15 EU Member States.* EUMC.

Ray, L. (2005) 'Violent crime', in C. Hale, K. Hayward, A. Wahidin and E. Wincup, *Criminology.* Oxford: Oxford University Press.

Ray, L., Smith, D. and Wastell, L. (2003) 'Understanding racist violence', in E.A. Stanko (ed.) *The Meanings of Violence.* London: Routledge. pp. 112–19.

Ray, L. Smith, D. and Wastell, L. (2004) 'Shame, rage and racist violence', *British Journal of Criminology,* 44: 350–68.

Reeves Sanday, P. (1991; 2007) *Fraternity Gang Rape: Sex, Brotherhood and Privilege on Campus.* New York: New York University Press.

Refuge (2004) *Refuge Response to Government's Compensation Consultation Documentation,* April. London: Refuge.

Regan, L., Lovett, J., Kelly, L. (2004a) *Forensic nursing: an option for improving responses to reported rape and sexual assault.* Home Office Online Report No. 28/04. London: Home Office.

Regan, L., Lovett, J., Kelly, L. (2004b) *Forensic nursing: an option for improving responses to reported rape and sexual assault.* Home Office Development and Practice Report No. 31. London: Home Office.

Reiner, R. (1978) *The Blue Coated Worker.* Cambridge: Cambridge University Press.

Reiner, R. (1985) 'Cop culture', in *The Politics of the Police.* Brighton: Harvester. Chapter 3.

Reiner, R. (1992) *The Politics of the Police* (2nd edn). Hemel Hempstead: Wheatsheaf.

Reiner, R. (1997) 'Policing and the police', in M. Maguire, R. Morgan and R. Reiner (eds) *The Oxford Handbook of Criminology.* Oxford: Clarendon Press.

Reiss, A.J., Jr. (1971) *The Police and the Public.* New Haven: Yale University.

Ricoeur, P. (1970) *Freud and Philosophy: An Essay on Interpretation.* New Haven: Yale University Press.

Ripper website, http://www.yorkshireripper.co.uk/hyper/005.htm

Roberts, C. (1989) *Women and Rape.* New York: New York University Press.

Roberts, C.M. (1985) *Victimisation Through Rape: Public and Personal Responses*. Colchester: University of Essex.

Roberts, Y. (2007) 'What makes mothers kill?' *Observer*, 21 April. http://www.guardian.co.uk/society/2002/apr/21/childrensservices.observerfocus

Robinson, A. (2008) 'Women's battle has still not been won', *Guardian*, 18 April: 37.

Rome (2001), cited in D. Gadd et al. (2002) *Domestic Abuse Against Men in Scotland*. Edinburgh: Scottish Executive Central Research Unit.

Rosenberg, M.L. (2004) *The Public Health Approach to Ending Child Sexual Abuse*, 7 May, Royal College of Physicians, London. http://www.stopitnow.org.uk/Dr%20Rosenberg%20presentation.ppt

Rumney, P. (2001) 'The review of sexual offences and rape law reform: another false dawn?', *Modern Law Review*, 890.

Russell, D. (1982) *Rape in Marriage*. New York: Macmillan.

Saraga, E. (2001) 'Dangerous places: family as a site of crime', in J. Muncie and E. Mclaughlin (eds) *The Problem of Crime*. London: Sage. pp. 191–239.

Savran, D. (1996) 'The sadomasochist in the closet: white masculinity and the culture of victimization', *Differences: A Journal of Feminist Cultural Studies*, 8(2): 127–52.

Scarman, Lord Justice (1981) *The Brixton Disorders 10–12 April 1981*. Cmnd 8427. London: Home Office.

Scottish Government (2007) *Racist Incidents Recorded by the Police in Scotland, 2003/04 to 2005/06*. http://www.scotland.gov.uk/Publications/2007/03/26094831/0

Scottish Office (1998) *Women Offenders – A Safer Way*. http://www.archive.official-documents.co.uk/document/scotoff/women/chap6.htm

Scutt, J.A. (1980) *Rape Law Reform: A Collection of Papers*. Canberra: Australian Institute of Criminology.

Segal, L. (1990) *Slow Motion: Changing Masculinities, Changing Men*. London: Virago.

Segal, L. (1994) *Straight Sex: The Politics of Pleasure*. London: Virago.

Shaw, C. and Mackay, H. (1942) *Juvenile Delinquency and Urban Areas*. Chicago: University of Chicago Press.

Sheffield City Council (2003) http://www.sheffield.gov.uk/index.asp?pgid=13754

Shilling, C. (2003) *The Body and Social Theory*. London: Sage.

Silvestri, M. 'Gender and crime: a human rights perspective', in F. Heidensohn (ed.) *Gender and Justice*. Cullompton: Willan. pp. 222–42.

Skinner, T. and Taylor, H. (2005) *Providing counseling, support and information to survivors of rape: an evaluation of the Surviving Trauma After Rape (STAR) Young Person's project*. Home Office Online Research Report. 51/04. http://www.homeoffice.gov.uk/rds/onlinepubs1.html

Smart, C. (1976) *Women, Crime and Criminology*. London: Routledge.

Smart, C. (1990) 'Feminist approaches to criminology or postmodern woman meets atavistic man', in A. Morris and L. Gelsthorpe (eds) *Feminist Perspectives in Criminology*. Milton Keynes: Open University Press.

Smart, C. (1995) *Law, Crime and Sexuality*. London: Sage.

Smith, C., Rundle, S. and Hosking, R. (2002) *Police Service Strength 10/02 England and Wales, 31 March 2002*, 17 September, http://www.homeoffice.gov.uk/rds/pdfs2/hosb1002.pdf

Smith, D. (1997) 'Ethnic origins, crime and criminal justice', in M. Maguire, R. Morgan and R. Reiner (eds) *The Oxford Handbook of Criminology* (2nd edn). Oxford: Oxford University Press.

Smith, G. (1980) 'Rape' (paper presented to the Association of Police Surgeons' Symposium), *Police Surgeon*, 17: 46–56, quoted in Temkin (1996).

Smith, L.J.F. (1989) *Domestic Violence*. Home Office Research Study 107. London: HMSO.

Smith, M.H. (1922) *The Psychology of the Criminal*. London: Methuen.

Snare, A. (1983) 'Sexual violence against women', *Sexual Behaviour and Attitude and Their Implications for Criminal Law*, Report of 15th Criminological Research Conference, Council of Europe.

Social Trends 37 (2007) Office for National Statistics. Basingstoke: Palgrave Macmillan.

Solomos, J. (2003) *Race and Racism in Britain*. Basingstoke: Palgrave Macmillan.

Sorsby, A. and Shapland, J.M. (1995) *Responding to Victims of Domestic Violence*. Sheffield: University of Sheffield.

Sounes, H. (1996) *Fred and Rose*. London: Warner Books.

Southall Black Sisters (2008) http://www.southallblacksisters.org.uk/index.html

Southgate, P. (1986) *Police Public Encounters*. Home Office Research Study 77. London: Home Office.

Stanko, E.A. (1985) *Intimate Intrusions: Women's Experience of Men's Violence*. London: Routledge and Kegan Paul.

Stanko, E.A. (1989) 'Missing the mark? Policing battering', in J. Hanmer, J. Radford and E.A. Stanko (eds) *Women, Policing and Male Violence: International Perspectives*. London: Routledge.

Stanko, E.A. (1990) *Everyday Violence: How Women and Men Experience Physical Danger*. London: Pandora.

Stanko, E.A. (1995), 'Policing domestic violence', *Australian and New Zealand Journal of Criminology Special Supplementary Issue*.

Stanko, E.A. (2000) 'The Day to Count: A Snapshot of the Impact of Domestic Violence in the UK', *Criminal Justice*, 1: 2.

Stanko, E.A. (2003) *The Meanings of Violence*. London: Routledge.

Stanko, E.A., Crisp, D., Hale, C. and Lucraft, H. (1998) *Counting the Costs: Estimating the Impact of Domestic Violence in the London Borough of Hackney*. Swindon: Crime Concern.

Statistics Canada (1993) *Violence against Women – Survey Highlights and Questionaire Package*. Canada: Statistics Canada.

Steward, K. (2006) 'Gender considerations in remand and decision making', in F. Heidensohn (ed.) (2006) *Gender and Justice*. Cullompton: Willan.

Stewart-Robertson, T. (2008) *Scotsman*, 15 March. http://thescotsman.scotsman.com/latestnews/-Rescued-schoolgirl-put-into.3881786.jp

Stobbe, M. (2006) '37 Percent of U.S. births out of wedlock', *Guardian*, 22 November. http://www.guardian.co.uk/uslatest/story/0,,-6231215,00.html

Storr, A. (2001) *Freud: A Very Short Introduction*. Oxford: Oxford University Press.

Straus, M.A. and Gelles, R.J. (1986) 'Societal change and change in family violence from 1975 to 1985', *Journal of Marriage and the Family*, 48: 465–79.

Straus, M.A. (1980) 'Measuring interfamily conflict and violence: the conflict tactics scales', *Journal of Marriage and the Family*, 41: 75–88.

Straus, M.A. and Gelles, R.J. (1990) (eds) *Physical Violence in American Families*. New Brunswick, NJ: Transaction Publishers.

Study on Violence Against Children. United Nations. http://www.childrenareunbeatable.org.uk/pdfs/unreportoctober06.pdf

Sullivan, M. (2007) 'Algarve "haven" for paedophiles', *Sun*, 7 May. http://www.thesun.co.uk/article/0,,2005320001-2007210600,00.html

Summerskill, B. (2002) 'Moral vacuum leads black men to crime', *Guardian*, 17 February. http://www.guardian.co.uk/uk/2002/feb/17/race.socialsciences

Sun 18/12/2003 'From boy to beast', supplement.

Sutton, J. (1978) 'The growth of the British Movement for Battered Women', *Victimology*, 2(3–4): 576–84.

Taket, A. (2004) *Tackling Domestic Violence: The Role of Health Professionals*. Home Office Development and Practice Report No. 32. London: Home Office.

Taket, A., Beringer, A., Irvine, A. and Garfield, S. (2004) *Tackling Domestic Violence: Exploring the Health Service Contribution*. Home Office Online Report No. 52/04. London: Home Office.

Taylor, I. (1971) 'Soccer consciousness and soccer hooliganism', in S. Cohen, *Image of Deviance*. Harmondsworth: Penguin.

Taylor, I., Walton, P. and Young, J. (1973) *The New Criminology*. London: Routledge and Kegan Paul.

Temkin, J. (1984) 'Regulating sexual history evidence – the limits of discretionary legislation', 33 *ICLQ*, 942.

Temkin, J. (1987) *Rape and the Legal Process*. London: Sweet and Maxwell.

Temkin, J. (1993) 'Sexual history evidence – the ravishment of section 2', *Criminal Law Review*, 3.

Temkin, J. (1996) 'Doctors, rape and criminal justice', *Howard Journal*, 35(1): 1–20.

Temkin, J. (1997) 'Plus ça change: reporting rape in the 1990s', *British Journal of Criminology*, 37: 507–28.

Temkin, J. (1999) 'Reporting rape in London: a qualitative study', *Howard Journal of Criminal Justice*, 38: 17–41.

Temkin, J. (2000) 'Getting it right: sexual offences law reform', *New Law Journal*, 4 August: 1169.

Temkin, J. (2002) *Rape and the Legal Process* (2nd edn). Oxford Monographs on Criminal Law and Justice. Oxford: Oxford University Press.

Temkin, J. and Ashworth, A. (2004) 'The Sexual Offences Act 2003: rape, sexual assault and the problems of consent', *Criminal Law Review*, 328.

The Age 11/02/2005 http://www.theage.com.au/news/Breaking-News/Homeless-flee-domestic-violence-study/2005/02/11/1108061832504.html

Thomas, T. (2000) *Sex Crime: Sex Offending and Society*. Cullompton: Willan.

Thompson, E.P. (1970) *The Making of the English Working Class*. London: Penguin.

Thrasher, F.M. (1963) *The Gang*. Chicago: Phoenix Press.

Timeline (2007) *Reuters.co.uk*, 9 September. http://today.reuters.co.uk/news/

Timeline for the search (2002) http://www.guardian.co.uk/missing/story/0,,773472,00.html

Tjaden, P. and Thoennes, N. (2000) *Full Report of the Prevalence, Incidence, and Consequences of Intimate Partner Violence Against Women: Findings from the National Violence Against Women Survey*, US Dept. of Just., NCJ 183781. http://www.ojp.usdoj.gov/nij/pubs-sum/183781.htm

Tolson, A. (1978) *The Limits of Masculinity*. Tavistock: London.

Townsend, M. (2005) 'Sex with trafficked women is rape, says minister', *Observer*, 16 October. http://observer.guardian.co.uk/uk_news/story/0,6903,1593227,00.html

Travis, A. (2008) *Guardian* online, 17 April. http://www.guardian.co.uk/technology/2008/apr/17/internet.childprotection?gusrc=rss&feed=networkfront

Troup, J. (2002) 'Did fiend lure them: chatroom pervert fear', *Sun* 6 August.

Tuchman, G. (1978) 'The symbolic annihilation of women in the media', in S. Cohen and J.Young (1983) *The Manufacture of the News: Deviance, Social Problems and the Mass Media*. London: Constable.

Tunstall (1996) *Newspaper Power*. Oxford: Clarendon Press.

Turner, V. (1969) *The Ritual Process: Structure and Antistructure*. Chicago: Aldine Publishing Co.

UN (2008) *Human Trafficking: A Crime that Shames us All*. Vienna: UN Office on Drugs and Crime.

US Department of Justice (1996) *Victim Costs and Consequences: A New Look*. Virginians Aligned Against Sexual Assault, New York.

US Department of Justice (2007) http://www.ojp.usdoj.gov/bjs/homicide/gender.htm.

Van Zoonen, L. (1998) 'One of the girls: the changing gender of journalism', in C. Carter, G. Branston and S. Allan, *News, Gender and Power*. London: Routledge. pp. 33–47.

Victim Support (1996) *Women, Rape and the Criminal Justice System*. London: Victim Support.

Viner, K. (2004) 'Rape convictions', *Guardian*, 24 September. http://politics. guardian.co.uk/women/story/0,,1311939,00.html

Wainwright, M. (2001) 'Riot-torn city voices dismay at lawless idiots', *Guardian,* 10 July. http://www.guardian.co.uk/racism/Story/0,2763,519413,00.html#article_continue

Walby, S. (2004) *The Cost of Domestic Violence*, from research funded by the DTI Women and Equality Unit, London: DTI.

Walby, S. and Allen, J. (2004) *Domestic Violence, Sexual Assault and Stalking: Findings from the British Crime Survey*. Home Office Research Study 276. London: Home Office.

Walby, S. and Myhill, A. (2001) 'New survey methodologies in researching violence against women', *British Journal of Criminology*, 41: 502.

Walker, J. and McNicol, L. (1994) *Policing Domestic Violence: Protection, Prevention or Prudence*. Relate Centre for Family Studies, University of Newcastle upon Tyne.

Walklate, S. (1995) *Gender and Crime*. New Jersey: Prentice-Hall.

Walklate, S. (2001; 2004) *Gender Crime and Criminal Justice*. Cullompton: Willan.

Walklate, S. (2003) *Understanding Criminology*. Maidenhead: Open University Press.

Walsh, J. (2006) *The Hidden Costs of the DRB*. http://www.hrw.org/english/docs/ 2005/06/07/uganda11092.htm

Wang, C. and Holton, D. (2007) *Child Abuse and Neglect in the United States*, Prevent Child Abuse America, Chicago, Illinois. *The Pew Charitable Trusts*. http://www. preventchildabuse.org/about_us/media_releases/pcaa_pew_economic_impact_study_ final.pdf

Weedon, C. (1987) *Feminist Practice and Post-structuralist Theory*. Oxford: Blackwell. pp. 12–42.

Weedon, C. (1994) 'Feminism and the principles of post structuralism', in J. Storey (ed.) (1994) *Cultural Theory and Popular Culture*. Hemel Hempstead: Harvester Wheatsheaf.

Welsh, K. (2008) 'Partnership or palming off? Involvement in partnership initiatives on domestic violence', *Howard Journal of Criminal Justice*, 47(2): 107–226.

Welsh, K. (2008) 'Current policy on domestic violence: a move in the right direction or a step too far?', *Crime Prevention and Community Safety: An International Journal*, 10(4): 248–66.

Westmarland, N. (2004) *Rape Law Reform in England and Wales*. School for Policy Studies. Working Paper No. 7. Bristol: University of Bristol.

Wetherell, M. and Edley, N. (1999) 'Negotiating hegemonic masculinity: imaginary positions and psycho-discursive practices', *Feminism and Psychology*, 9(3): 335–56.

Whitehead, S.M. (1994) 'Theorizing masculine subjectivity', in T. Newburn and E.A. Stanko (eds) *Just Boys Doing Business? Men, Masculinities and Crime*. London: Routledge.

Whitehead, S.M. (1998) 'Hegemonic masculinity revisited', *Gender, Work, and Organization*, 6(1): 58–62.

Whitehead, S.M. (2002) *Men and Masculinities: Key Themes and New Directions*. Cambridge: Polity.

Wilczynski, A. (1995) 'Child killing by parents: social, legal and gender issues', in R.E. Dobash, R.P. Dobash and L. Noakes (eds) *Gender and Crime*. Cardiff: University of Wales Press.

Williams, L.S. (1984) 'The classic rape: when do victims report?', *Social Problems*, 31: 459–67.

Williamson, E. (2006) *Just the Domestic*? Safe – the domestic abuse quarterly, Issue 19, Autumn. Bristol: Women's Aid Federation of England.

Willis, P. (1978a) *Profane Culture*. Saxon House: London.

Willis, P. (1978b) *Learning to Labour: How Working Class Kids Get Working Class Jobs*. London: Saxon House.

Wilson, D. (2007) *Guardian*, 2 August. http://commentisfree.guardian.co.uk/david_wilson/2007/08/when_is_paedophilia_not_paedop.html

Wilson, P.R. (1978) *The Other Side of Rape*. St Lucia: University of Queensland Press.

Wollstonecraft, M. (1792) *A Vindication of the Rights of Woman*. http://www.bartleby.com/144/4.html

Women and Equality Unit (2004a) http://news.bbc.co.uk/1/hi/uk/4581808.stm

Women and Equality Unit (2004b) http://www.womenandequalityunit.gov.uk/domestic_violence/key_facts.htm

Women's National Commission (1985) *Violence Against Women: Report of an Adhoc Working Group*. London: Cabinet Office.

Women's Unit (1999) *Living Without Fear: An Integrated Approach to Tackling Violence Against Women*. London: HMSO.

Worrall, A. (2004) 'Twisted sisters, ladettes and the new penology: the social construction of violent girls', in C. Alder and A. Worrall (eds) *Girls' Violence*. Albany: SUNY Press.

Wright, R. (1984) 'A note on attrition of rape cases', *British Journal of Criminology*, 24: 399–400.

Wright, R. and West, D.J. (1981) 'Rape – a comparison of group offences and lone assaults', 21 Med Sci Law 25.

Wykes, M. (1995) 'Passion, marriage and murder', in R. Dobash and L. Noaks (eds) *Gender and Crime*. Cardiff: University of Wales Press.

Wykes, M. (1998) 'A family affair', in C. Carter, G. Branston and S. Allan, *News, Gender and Power*. London: Routledge. pp. 233–48.

Wykes, M. (2001) *News, Crime and Culture*. London: Pluto Press.

Wykes, M. (2002) 'Evil beast meets dangerous stranger: mediating masculinities in news about violent crime', paper presented at British Criminology Conference, Keele, July.

Wykes, M. (2003) '(De)-constructing the body: violence, image and self-identity', BCS Conference, Bangor, June (unpublished).

Wykes, M. (2007) 'Constructing crime: culture, stalking, celebrity and cyber', *Journal of Crime, Media, Culture*, August, 3(2): 158–74.

Wykes, M. and Gunter, B. (2005) *The Media and Body Image*. London: Sage.

Yates, N. (2005) *Beyond Evil: Inside the Twisted Mind of Ian Huntley*. John Blake.

Young, A. (1996) *Imagining Crime: Textual Outlaws and Criminal Conversations*. London: Sage.

Young, A. (1988) 'Wild women: the censure of the suffragette movement', *International Journal of the Sociology of the Law*, 16: 179–293.

Young, A. (1990) *Femininity in Dissent*. London: Routledge.

Young, A. and Rush, P. (1994) 'The law of victimage in urban realism: thinking through inscriptions of violence', in D. Nelken (ed.) *The Future of Criminology*. London: Sage. pp. 154–72.

Young, J. (1992) 'Ten points of realism', in J. Young and R. Matthews, *Rethinking Criminology: The Realist Debate*. London: Sage.

Young, M. (1991) *An Inside Job*. Oxford: Oxford University Press.

Young, W. (1983) *Rape Study*. Wellington, NZ: Dept. of Justice and Institute of Criminology at Victoria, University of Wellington.

Zedner, N. (1997) 'Victims', in M. Maguire, R. Morgan and R. Reiner (eds) *The Oxford Handbook of Criminology*. Oxford: Clarendon Press.

Zona, M.A., Palarea, R.E. and Lane, J.C. (1998), in J.R. Meloy (ed.) *The Psychology of Stalking: Clinical and Forensic Perspectives*. New York: Academic Press. pp. 85–112.

Zona, M.A., Sharma, K.K. and Lane, J.C. (1993) 'A comparative study of erotomanic and obsessional subjects in a forensic sample', *Journal of Forensic Sciences*, 38(4): 894–903.

INDEX

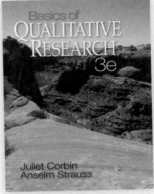

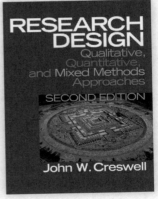

The Qualitative Research Kit

Edited by Uwe Flick

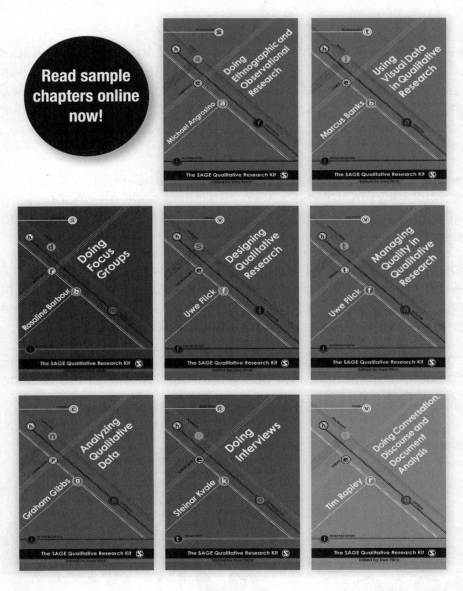

Read sample chapters online now!

Doing Ethnographic and Observational Research — Michael Angrosino

Using Visual Data in Qualitative Research — Marcus Banks

Doing Focus Groups — Rosaline Barbour

Designing Qualitative Research — Uwe Flick

Managing Quality in Qualitative Research — Uwe Flick

Analyzing Qualitative Data — Graham Gibbs

Doing Interviews — Steinar Kvale

Doing Conversation, Discourse and Document Analysis — Tim Rapley

The SAGE Qualitative Research Kit — Edited by Uwe Flick

www.sagepub.co.uk

Supporting researchers for more than forty years

Research methods have always been at the core of SAGE's publishing. Sara Miller McCune founded SAGE in 1965 and soon after, she published SAGE's first methods book, Public Policy Evaluation. A few years later, she launched the Quantitative Applications in the Social Sciences series – affectionately known as the "little green books".

Always at the forefront of developing and supporting new approaches in methods, SAGE published early groundbreaking texts and journals in the fields of qualitative methods and evaluation.

Today, more than forty years and two million little green books later, SAGE continues to push the boundaries with a growing list of more than 1,200 research methods books, journals, and reference works across the social, behavioral, and health sciences.

From qualitative, quantitative, mixed methods to evaluation, SAGE is the essential resource for academics and practitioners looking for the latest methods by leading scholars.

www.sagepublications.com